THE SCIENCE OF ACTING

What is good acting? How does one create believable characters? How can actors understand a character if they do not understand themselves?

In *The Science of Acting*, Sam Kogan uses his theories on the relationship between neuroscience, psychology and acting to answer these questions. Practical exercises provide a step-by-step guide to developing an actor's ability, culminating in Ten Steps to Creating a Character.

Kogan covers the following topics:

- Awareness
- Purposes
- Events
- Actions
- Imagination
- Free Body
- Tempo-rhythm
- Talent

He presents readers with a groundbreaking understanding of the subconscious and how it can be applied to their acting. The author's highly original perspective on Stanislavski's teaching gives readers a unique insight into their characters' minds.

Edited by his daughter Helen after his death, *The Science of Acting* is a study of the human mind and acting which no student or practitioner should be without.

Sam Kogan studied at the Moscow Institute of Theatre Arts (now the Russian Academy of Theatre Arts) under the tutelage of Professor Maria Knebel. He established *The Science of Acting*, a complete stand-alone technique.

Helen Kogan is the chair and former principal of the Academy of the Science of Acting and Directing, and has helped to shape her father's words and work for the publication of this book.

THE SCIENCE
OF ACTING

SAM KOGAN

edited by Helen Kogan

First published 2010 by Routledge
2 Park Square, Milton Park, Abingdon, Oxon OX14 4RN

Simultaneously published in the USA and Canada
by Routledge
270 Madison Avenue, New York, NY 10016

Reprinted 2010

Routledge is an imprint of the Taylor & Francis Group, an informa business

Typeset in Minion by
Keystroke, Tettenhall, Wolverhampton
Printed and bound in Great Britain by
TJ International Ltd, Padstow, Cornwall

British Library Cataloguing in Publication Data
A catalogue record for this book is available from the British Library

Library of Congress Cataloging-in-Publication Data
Kogan, Sam, 1946-2004.
The science of acting / Sam Kogan ; edited by Helen Kogan.
p. cm.
Includes bibliographical references and index.
1. Acting. I. Kogan, Helen, 1975– II. Title.
PN2061.K545 2009
792.02'8--dc22
2009002838

ISBN10: 0–415–48811–7 (hbk)
ISBN10: 0–415–48812–5 (pbk)
ISBN10: 0–203–87404–8 (ebk)

ISBN13: 978–0–415–48811–2 (hbk)
ISBN13: 978–0–415–48812–9 (pbk)
ISBN13: 978–0–203–87404–2 (ebk)

This book is dedicated to Sam Kogan 1946–2004

Whoever hesitates to utter that which he thinks the highest truth, lest it should be too much in advance of the time, may reassure himself by looking at his acts from an impersonal point of view . . . It is not for nothing that he has in him these sympathies with some principles and repugnance to others. He, with all his capacities, and aspirations, and beliefs, is not an accident but a product of the time. While he is a descendant of the past he is a parent of the future; and his thoughts are as children born to him, which he may not carelessly let die

Herbert Spencer, 1862[1]

And it is for you, the reader.

CONTENTS

ILLUSTRATIONS

FIGURES

TABLE

ABOUT THIS BOOK

The Science of Acting comes at the end of a celebrated line of Russian actors, directors, dramatists and pedagogues who shared a common goal of creating realistic theatre to enlighten their audiences.

Key players include Fyodor Volkov (1729–1763), considered the father of Russian theatre, the actor Mikhail Schepkin (1788–1863), Konstantin Stanislavski (1863–1938), Vladimir Nemirovich-Danchenko (1858–1943), Yevgeny Vakhtangov (1883–1922) and Michael Chekhov (1891–1955). Each of these men made great strides in their search for 'truth' – the creation of real, believable characters. No surprise that what determined how far their strides took them included the psychology, society and politics of their time.

Fleeing the Soviet Union in the 1970s eventually meant much more to Sam Kogan than to live in a land where he could choose where he worked unbiased by his ethnicity. The geographical and cultural distance he put between himself and the Soviet Union allowed him to develop his work and his thinking, free from the ideological constraints which would have stunted any such growth.

On top of the knowledge he inherited from his academic ancestors and other 'freer' thinkers, Sam exponentially developed clarity beyond that of his predecessors and (as has often been commented) 'beyond his time'.

Stanislavski, undoubtedly *the* major influence on Sam's work, has been described as 'turning audiences into eavesdroppers, peering through an invisible wall on to the lives of real people'.[1] Sam shared this ability; to create what he would often refer to as (with his due pride at having mastered this second language) the 'Peeping Tom' experience – watching others who did not know they were being watched. If anyone were to ask him why this was so enjoyable or even important, he would reply, 'We want to watch people who behave as though unobserved to find out how people live, so that we can better understand ourselves'.

The son of displaced parents, who was displaced himself a number of times both voluntarily and involuntarily before London became his home, Sam was aware how the passing down of stories was a fast disappearing tradition in a world of scattered families. He would say, 'Watching how people live ensures that self-understanding and growth could continue'.

By providing audiences with realism, it would show them a reality, a way of living that was different from what was in their heads. A passage in a book by his favourite psychologist 'thinker' sums this up:

> One of the most important things in life is to understand reality and to keep changing our images to correspond to it, for it is our images which determine our actions and feelings, and the more accurate they are the easier it will be for us to attain happiness and stay happy in an ever changing world.
>
> Eric Berne[2]

In other words, by seeing actors act believably, audiences can see how life is for others and compare this with how they think life is. The voyeur experience provides them the opportunity to ask questions of themselves, increase their self-awareness and in turn bring them one step closer to happiness.

This workbook is a new milestone in the evolution of understanding what good acting is and how to achieve it.

Among the pages you are about to read, you will see the weight of influence that Stanislavski was on the creation of *The Science of Acting*. If you are acquainted with the 'System' you will recognize a number of terms in the Contents of this book. When you reach those chapters you may, here and there, find familiar exercises or examples to explain that term – but more often you will find that *The Science of Acting* completely readdresses the subject, retaining only the label as a souvenir.

> Each thing not only 'is', it 'becomes'.
> 'Reality', to cite Whitehead, 'is a process and an integrative evolutionary process at that'.
>
> Ervin Laszlo[3]

Most profound is that this work stands out as progress beyond that which came before by way of filling in Stanislavski's knowledge gaps.

In particular and overridingly when it comes to Stanislavski's self-recognized limits to understanding that which is 'subconscious in origin',[4] 'Questions about the subconscious are not intellectually my business',[5] 'We shall wait for science to help us discover practical, legitimate approaches to another man's mind',[6] and 'Perhaps this will help us develop methods by which to search for subconscious, creative material not only in our environment but in people's inner lives.'[7] Here, Sam jumps in as the young enthusiastic protégé to lead the old master, as he asks the here-to unasked questions and eagerly sketches out the answers.

Where people have defined acting as 'reacting' or being 'all about emotions' or, as Stanislavski believed, 'feelings',[8] you will soon see that *The Science of Acting* goes to the roots of all these phenomena by classifying and explaining the origins, patterns, consequences and manifestations of thoughts, of which reactions, feeling, emotions and behaviour are all manifestations. It would then follow that if the actor can think the character's thoughts, these experiences will appear naturally – pun intentional.

> We are seeking for the simplest possible scheme of thought that will bind together the observed facts.
>
> Albert Einstein[9]

The progression from Stanislavski to *The Science of Acting* rests not only in the evolution of knowledge but also in its lucidity of delivery. Jean Benedetti perfectly summarizes general opinion in his introduction to *Stanislavski and the Actor* with: 'Konstantin Stanislavski is the most significant and most frequently quoted figure in the history of actor training. He is also the most consistently and widely misunderstood'.[10]

It is generally agreed that Stanislavski's style, even in Russian, not only is 'convoluted verbose and confusing',[11] but also 'there are passages which almost defy comprehension, let alone translation'.[12] Sam was of the very same opinion and often disassociated himself from Stanislavski's work for that reason. This work is a world away from any such cloudiness, either in content or narrative. In fact by the end of the Introduction, not only will you have your proof, but also you will understand why it was so crucial to this work that above all it was clearly understood.

> The Stanislavski system is the science of theatre art. As a science it does not stand still; being a science it has unlimited possibilities for experiment and discoveries.
>
> Sonia Moore[13]

Science is itself evolutionary. It not only 'is' but also is 'becoming' – the world went from being flat to being a sphere. With the Latin for science being 'knowledge', it is the job of a scientist or (shall we say here) 'knowledge-seeker' not only to establish new knowledge but also to constantly revisit established knowledge in the light of new findings. That is, in the light of often unexpected answers to previously unasked questions . . . progress. Given this and despite no formal science education, except for starting a biology degree in 2000, which it pained him not to have the time to complete, Sam was indeed a scientist.

As to the future and how this work will evolve, *The Science of Acting* is as Sam in his penultimate year described it, 'a complete work . . . a totality . . . they now have everything they need'. Therefore it is by way of refinement only, that I envision that as the fields of biology, psychology and neuroscience, and especially where all three meet to understand what creates and produces the consciousness of a person, there will simply be more scientific validation of *The Science of Acting*'s 'natural truth' for those who want it.

Sam uses the terms mind, brain and consciousness interchangeably as was acceptable at the time this body of work was created. I would guess however that in the decades to come, as the battle between the 'materialist' and 'non-materialist' thinkers comes to a close, and answers to whether consciousness is a 'function or a process?' and essentially 'Where is it?'[14] are found; then the precious clarity and honesty of this work will continue.

The earliest memory I have of my father talking to me about *The Science of Acting* is of being seven years old, sitting in a Chinese restaurant on Charing Cross Road on a rainy Saturday evening. The restaurant, its name now changed, still exists on the corner of a street that heads into China Town, diagonally opposite the landmark Aberdeen Steak House.

The waiter had just taken our order; my father had gone for beef brisket. I didn't know what brisket was, yet being used to Dad thinking through his decisions so thoroughly, with meals being no exception, the order went for two.

As the waiter headed for the steamy kitchen, my father took out a pen from his inside jacket pocket and then drew two dots on his paper napkin – it could have been, as it often was, on the paper tablecloth, meaning the diagram would be peeking out from under his plate for the duration of the meal – but on this occasion the diagram, which soon became a part of our eating-out ritual, was on a paper napkin. He would later ask for another to accompany his meal, and I would wonder what I should do with my diagrammed napkin.

Of the two dots, Dad labelled one A and the other B. He then asked me what I thought was the fastest way to get from one to the other. The waiter reappeared. He had forgotten to ask us which noodles we would like with our dish. Dad used the Cantonese word, but not very well. The waiter was confused. Dad tried to explain slowly, 'The flat, wide, white ones' showing the waiter the width of the noodle with his thumb and forefinger. Still confused. Dad turned over the napkin and drew a three-dimensional sketch of the end of one such noodle. Confusion turned into a smile and nod of comprehension and the waiter headed back into the steam.

Back to the A and B. I had had a little think. Either this was an easy question, in which case the answer had already come to me, or it was something completely out of the box, in which case I would never get it. I went for 'a straight line'. 'That's it!' he confirmed with a smile. Relief. Some of the out of box, or probably more accurately, out of my box, explanations went on for longer than my attention could hold. Having reversed the napkin he drew a curly line which, going from A, twisted back on itself before reaching B. 'Can you see if you go this way it will take much longer'.

And from here, our meals on my weekend visits were often in the same vein; napkins, tablecloths and diagrams for me and the waiters (only ever noodles for the waiters). The two dots developed into diagrams illustrating the journey towards happiness, to regular phone calls of him questioning whether ideas that had come up in his classes made sense to me, and once I had started my studies in neuroscience, if I thought they were scientifically valid.

My father, I'll go back to calling him Sam, was drafting the Introduction for this book as far back as the late 1980s on everything from mini pocket-sized notepads, to full-sized letter notepads (often with feint grids rather than lines – these reminded him of his school books). I even found his notorious scribbles on the back of an envelope with ideas for the book's opening paragraph. Once his drama school was established, to speed up the book writing process, he asked students to type up their class notes so that these could be used as early drafts for the subsequent chapters. These early efforts never took off, not only because the subject was growing so quickly that anything written through the early 1990s was rapidly becoming out of date, but also because he never had the time to focus on the project.

Finally, in 2003, to avoid the persistent nagging from myself and his thoughts, it was time to take the job in hand. Living in Nottingham, having just completed my PhD, I was taking some time to decide what to do next with my life. We came up with a plan. Rather than temping as a receptionist, I could 'do something worthwhile' (I'll come to his jokes) and start helping with The Book. And so video tapes of classes specifically recorded for The Book were sent to Nottingham and in my rented room, which overlooked one of the roughest neighbourhoods there, I played, stopped, started, rewound and replayed the tapes, transcribing the first draft of this manuscript – often to the sounds of screams and police sirens.

Six months after starting the project, with the transcribing almost complete, Sam's health began to rapidly deteriorate with the cause unknown. The Book project came to an abrupt halt. Tests and waiting and more tests and much more waiting pointed towards possible illnesses that we, together with his long-term partner Taisia, herself a pharmacist, had never heard of before. Another six months went by and Sam was diagnosed with a rare form of cancer. Again, another six months, and on 11 November 2004 he passed away.

That was a Thursday. The following Wednesday, a Russian Orthodox church in South Kensington was full of family, friends and students past and present, surrounded by still candlelight, the beautiful voices of the a cappella choir and an aura that exists only on such occasions. The people who came, the majority of whom had been taught by Sam at some point in their lives, came because he had touched their lives in a way unlike any other teacher and in most cases unlike any other person they knew. He taught with a self-sacrificial care for his students, wanting to change their lives by giving them not just a profession, but also an awareness of their potential.

Sam never considered his 12–16 hour days hard work, nor the years without a proper holiday a sacrifice. He simply believed in always doing his best and you would be rewarded accordingly. His work was his life and he loved what he did. His lifestyle of daily yoga, weekly steam baths, Sunday walks, minimal alcohol and a visible *joie de vivre* did however mean that his illness and death came as an incomprehensible shock to everyone who knew him.

No one noticed, he least of all, that his work had become his drug. The energy and vigour it gave him masked any concerns he or we needed to have. Looking back at video tapes of him teaching at a time when I knew his health was already on the decline, and when on the phone he was beginning to sound unusually tired and beaten, in class he was as ever on top form. These tapes show not the slightest discernible difference from the showman he had always been. Still he stood upright at the front of the class, authoritative, acute and cracking his jokes. Jokes were a major part of his teaching style, in fact his *being* style.

In class he would often help people see their thinking by making a joke of how they saw the world. At first yes, the person felt a little uncomfortable ('Hey! This is my life and I take it seriously!'), but by seeing the absurdity of their reality with humour, the tension was soon released. Meanwhile as the individual was processing this major 'life viewing' change, Sam would sit at his little table, silently holding in his hysteria at his own joke with tears of laughter brimming up, spilling over and rolling down his reddened cheeks. He would then take a handkerchief (which his mother told him he should always carry) from his trouser pocket and wipe the tears away. The handkerchief or pack of tissues would then remain on the table, waiting for his next joke.

From the start I knew I couldn't keep my hospital bedside promise of completing the book alone. Aside from being prompt for a number of plays during my teens, attending a couple of short workshops, and more recently being involved in the management of the Academy of the Science of Acting and Directing (ASAD), my understanding of *The Science of Acting* had always been theoretical or based on its application to life rather than to acting. Therefore to progress the manuscript a group of graduates from ASAD became invaluable in ensuring that the correct information with its practical application was communicated in the way that Sam would have communicated it. Despite my initial haste (From A to B! I've got to get from A to B!) I had to learn that some things take time, and the initial years after his passing needed passing themselves before The Book could get back on its path. And eventually, with help, it did.

The contributions, explanations, contacts, advice, text-checking, digging out of anecdotes, examples and key phrases or simply the dial-up help lines provided by David Bark-Jones, Katy Bartrop, Elizabeth Bowe, Philip Bulcock, Andrew Byron, Nick Cawdron (Introduction, and Chapters 1, 3, 4, 10), Alex Dower, Thomas Garvey (Chapters 7, 9, 11, 13, 14), Jennifer Mushumani, Paul Mushumani, Nick Piovanelli, William Ribo, Audrey Sheffield, Neil Sheffield, and Elanor Wallis-Scott have ensured that this book did not get stuck on that convoluted curly line going from A to B.

While attending one of his two-week workshops, I remember Sam standing at the blackboard of the precisely named 'L-shaped room', a piece of chalk between his thumb and forefinger, pausing, having just drawn a diagram. A student, realizing that we were talking about more than 'just acting', took us on a slight tangent from the topic being taught by asking, 'So what are we all here for . . . you know, humans on earth . . . living?' There were varied spontaneous answers from around the room and then Sam said, 'We all want to be remembered', and then as was customary, he raised his eyebrows and looked around the class: 'Don't we?'

Back then I wasn't sure if I agreed and writing this now, recognize that I don't. But for Sam, who took his last breath in the early hours of Remembrance Day 2004 and with the publication of this book, I think this will always be true.

With *The Science of Acting* Sam wanted to give his students the knowledge and confidence to know that they had a profession. This is now extended to you . . . as I hand you over to him.

PREFACE

The purpose of this book is to make the ways and means by which good acting is achieved crystal clear. It also explains why, while every actor wants to act well, so few do.

Descartes said, 'All the things which we very clearly and distinctly conceive are true'.[1] To which I add that if something is not clear and distinct, it is very likely to not be *truth*. In view of this I don't want to be known as the author of another book expressing yet another opinion on acting. I'd rather be the author of a book containing memorable, concrete knowledge. Knowledge based on the truth of how we live. This is why I have called both the book and what I teach, *The Science of Acting*.

I describe what I teach as a science because every time my students and graduates correctly use the ideas described in this book, they work. This means that as with any science it is accessible to everybody. It means that acting is a *certain* knowledge, which can be acquired and used by anybody who wants to do so. It does not however mean that anybody can be a good actor, nor does it mean that by acquiring the knowledge will all actors act the same.

To most if not all readers it might seem preposterous to put acting, an intuitive profession based on the finest of movements of the soul, onto a base of knowledge which gives the same results every time, to turn a profession chosen for its sensitivity and mobility of feeling into something mechanical and (how abominable!) into a conveyor-belt-like generator of characters!

I contest this argument. The need for *The Science of Acting* is precisely so that by using the knowledge of putting together whatever has to be put together, it can be done as efficiently as possible so that time is left to make it beautiful.

Actors like to use the dubious expression of 'exploring the character'. Dubious because the real meaning of this expression appears to me as the following analogy:

Set: A huge desert.

Action: A convoy of heavy trucks is struggling through the sands in search for oil. They stop, establish a camp, erect a rig and begin to drill.

A few days later, having found no oil, they dismantle the rig, decamp, load up their trucks and move off.

After a few days the same is repeated.

And after a few days the same is repeated.

The diggers have no knowledge as to where to search for the oil, so they search everywhere. They are not guided by a science that would give them knowledge – they have the same chance of finding oil as an actor has of creating a true character!

An important difference is that for the diggers, oil is the proof of the find, but who can ever know whether the result of the 'exploration' successfully located the character to be 'right' and 'alive', if no references can be made to the truth of knowledge. How many actors confidently think that they 'found the character'?

The phrase 'exploring the character' implies time can be wasted in creative research; we'll try this, and if it doesn't look right or feel right, well then we'll keep looking. What *The Science of Acting* demonstrates is that from the word 'Go' an actor knows what to do to create a character. No time is wasted (unless the script is so bad) on exploration; instead every step is made in the right direction.

Does this mean that once you have finished reading this book, you will know what to do to act better than you do now?

Yes.

Will you become a better actor?

Yes.

Will you become more talented?

Yes.

Will you be able to act really well?

No.

To act really well you will need to practise, most of the time on your own. This is more difficult than you think, particularly at the beginning, and this frustration will put your dedication to the test. Another stumbling block may be doubts as to whether you are using this knowledge correctly. Ideally you would need tuition and supervision from someone who is a licensed teacher from the Academy of the Science of Acting and Directing, but the chances of having such an opportunity may be remote.

So what do you do?

You think.

By thinking and searching for answers to the question, 'What is good acting?' I founded my school and developed my ideas. In conjunction with the thoughts contained in this book, your own thinking will enable you to find answers – and much more than just an understanding of the laws of good acting.

The term 'science of acting' was used by two actresses on opposite sides of the Atlantic at about the same time: Ellen Terry (1847–1928) in England,[2] and Minnie Madern Fiske (1865–1932) in the United States. In her book *Mrs. Fiske: Her Views on Actors, Acting, and the Problems of Production*, Fiske explains why there was a need for it:

> As soon as I suspect a fine effect is being achieved by accident I lose interest. I am not interested . . . in unskilled labor . . . Anyone may achieve on some rare occasion an outburst of genuine feeling, a gesture of imperishable beauty, a ringing accent of truth; but your scientific actor knows how he did it. He can repeat it again and again and again. He can be depended on.[3]

'The essence of acting is the conveyance of truth through the medium of the actor's mind and person. The science of acting deals with the perfecting of that medium.'[4]

Ongoing credit to Konstantin Stanislavski is a must, for his contributions to and systemization of theatrical knowledge. Without his books recording his lifetime's devoted search for such a system, this book would not be possible. Nor would it have been written if I had also not disagreed with most of his premises and conclusions.

Upon graduation from the Moscow Institute of Theatre Art I couldn't see that Stanislavski's system was unworkable without the man himself presiding over the rehearsal. As transcripts of his rehearsals clearly show, he made little, if any, use of his system's terminology. Yet it was only later that I came to the realization that some of his conclusions simply could not be applied to acting.

At the time I wrongly believed in his notion of the triumvirate of 'motive forces' – mind, will and emotion.[5] And I was not aware of the fundamental error in the comparison of a human being with four-legged animals in his chapter on physical tensions.[6] I did not understand then, that his idea of three circles of attention is unworkable,[7] though an impressive image and not without merit. Nor could I see that to say to an actor 'you must believe in what you are doing' is a self-defeating demand.[8]

It all began to dawn on me when researching some teaching material that I reread a book by one of Stanislavski's most devoted pupils, who worked with Stanislavski in the last months of his life.[9] This book said that Stanislavski often rejected his actors' preparation, though they thought that they had meticulously fulfilled all his demands.

This stuck in my mind.

If those actors, with their devotion, first-hand knowledge and access to the man himself, couldn't do it, who could?

It was then that my blindfold of adoration for the famous man began to slip and my fear of being wrong began to fade.

Are you also wearing a blindfold? Do you have a similar fear?

Throughout my studies Maria Knebel, a pupil of Stanislavski's and later a colleague of his, was my professor. I cannot thank her enough for her courage in insisting that I be admitted to the course against the wishes of people who had the final word on admissions – people who used criteria other than artistic to implement their 'final word'. To Maria I will also always be grateful for teaching me great care of and dedication to art.

Tender memories of Maria are never far from my visible thoughts; but she as so many people in the acting world nowadays felt the need for creativity to be cloaked in mysticism, as though clear thinking somehow lowers the status of art and artists.

The mysticism of art is a smokescreen.

I define art (to the aware mind) as 'Life selected and rearranged, designed to entertain' and have found that when mystified, art (therefore to the unaware mind) becomes a 'layer of consciousness which is used as a cover for Unfinished Thinking'.

Leonardo da Vinci's paintings did not get worse with his discoveries of the regularities in the process of painting, nor did human insight into his works of art diminish.

Looking back, my purpose to acquire a clearly defined workable knowledge during my five years of studying stage directing progressively became a small and irrelevant matter. My experiences while studying brought up other purposes which took precedent and which in turn brought a different problem into my life. The problem can best be described as the director's fear of producing a boring, unimpressive play.

When I finally confessed this fear to myself, I looked back only to realize that almost every show I had ever seen in the theatre was corroded to a greater or lesser degree by this fear, as were the plays I directed myself prior to the search for *The Science of Acting*. As a result of this fear I completely understood directors who say, 'I only direct plays that (a) touch me, (b) I feel deep affinity with, (c) I can relate to' etc. These words are the manifestation of that same fear.

I thus learned that there was a need to discover a system whereby one could direct any play from any country, period or style, without fear. One of the great men of the theatre, Yevgeny Vakhtangov, said, 'There is no art if an actor's tears do not reach the audience'.[10] That is to say, no matter how imaginative the director's thoughts are, if they are not reflected in the character's thinking they will not have any artistic impact on the audience and will merely be tricks. Therefore, without denying the importance of stage directing as the process of creating the totality and wholeness of artistic ideas, it must be said that good directing can be seen only through good acting.

As if by detour, my inner questions about directing had brought me to good acting, which in turn brought me to *The Science of Acting* – and you to this book. Herein you will find the knowledge to support you in your acting or directing profession and you will be introduced to many original insights into the workings of the consciousness which evolved simultaneously with this technique. To avoid any confusion or contention, I should state here that I define consciousness as 'an ever changing totality of thoughts and neurobiological processes that shape and are shaped by them'.

As an acting teacher and principal of ASAD, I have often been asked, 'Why is it important to understand the workings of the consciousness to become a good actor?' My answer, 'If you want to act well, consider this question – how will you be able to understand and portray the states of mind of different characters effectively if you do not understand the workings of your own mind?' Another common question is, 'Why would a workable theory of consciousness come out of a drama school and not a laboratory?' The answer is that scientists cannot create life situations in the artificial circumstances of a laboratory. In a theatre, we have to create different states of consciousness on a daily basis.

By explaining the workings of human nature I want to show you that by using the simple truths of nature as far as they are known, actors can express themselves to a much greater depth than ever before, because they are using the mechanisms that contribute to their own 'I'.

Because of this, throughout the book I will be posing questions for you to consider. I will be asking you to think about your life, your thoughts, and your motivations, just as I do in the classroom. You aren't in a classroom, so I won't be able to give you examples from your own life, but I will illustrate with examples from real class discussions and exercises, to show you how I work through ideas and problems. If you understand these then you will be able to find examples from your own life and apply the same process.

Before you proceed with the rest of this book, a couple of recommendations on how it should be used. This book is an acting manual and I'm sure you know what it's like when some machine you own is broken: you grab the manual, look up the key term in the index, flip to the page and hope to find your answers – 'but nothing makes sense!' That is why I suggest that the first time you read this book, you read the chapters consecutively. Once you have an understanding of its entirety, you can then go back to any of chapters as you need them.

You will find there is a lot of information contained in *The Science of Acting*. As I said, it's a manual. Deceptively however, this information reads very simply and you will be challenged to process, let alone apply, what you read as fast as you will read it. For that reason I recommend that on either your first or second read through that you read no more than a chapter a day, or every other day would be even better, so that you get the fullest benefit. When you are not reading you need to see if/how what you have read works in your life, if/how it fits in with what you already know to be true and as you get further in to the book, how what you are reading relates to previous chapters. This processing takes time and I recommend, so as you get the most from the good money you will have spent on this book, that you give yourself that time.

Following my Introduction, which explains why and how *The Science of Acting* evolved, Part One walks you through 'The Foundations'. If you consider it as a mechanic's toolbox in Part One, you, the mechanic, are becoming accustomed to each of your tools, you will pick each one up individually, get a feel for it and understand why, where and how it is used. Each of these tools will help you start to see how you think, and therefore how any character you want to create thinks. As you progress, you will understand *why* you think what you think.

Each chapter gradually builds on the previous – sometimes it may jump to a term you haven't heard of yet, but you'll be given enough knowledge to use at the stage you are at. Throughout Part One you will be reminded of the relevance of this knowledge, which may appear 'psychology heavy', to good acting. Note that you are being prepared for Part Two, 'Qualities of an Actor', and Part Three, 'Working on a Script'.

In Part Two you will see how The Foundations come together for actors in their work, where the different tools are used together to perform the required task of creating your character. As you progress you may come across acting terms that you may have heard and used before, but in a different light, with clarity and practical relevancy.

The Science of Acting culminates with Part Three, 'Working on a Script'. The finale is you the mechanic lifting the hood of the car as you would approach a new script, diagnosing the situation and using the Ten Steps as your guide to implementing your tools to do your job.

To create plausible and interesting characters and to communicate effectively with directors, actors need a common language or terminology with which they can discuss the unseen workings of the mind, so throughout this book, and collated in the Glossary, you will find definitions of all the terms used.

My intention is always to be clear and as far as possible use only provable examples. In the physical world this is very easy as we are all agreed on the rules and laws: the sun rises in the morning and sets in the evening, eyeglasses modify vision, birds fly, pens write, and so we use these points of references with confidence. However, although acting takes place in the physical world, it deals with the mental world, and for us to discuss and understand our subject we must agree on our points of reference. The more terminology and points of reference you acquire as you read this book, the clearer *The Science of Acting* and I hope your life will become.

I must add, I am human and reserve the right to make mistakes. I would encourage you to try out everything you read to ensure that you haven't inadvertently blindfolded *your*self along the way.

You are your own master – enjoy!

ACKNOWLEDGEMENTS

This book would not have been written but that my pregnant wife and I, both stateless refugees from the Soviet Union on the way from a short stay in Israel to a refugee camp somewhere in Europe, arrived on a two week visit to the theatre capital of the world, London.

The two weeks lasted three decades.

Comparing the fortunes of previous generations with my own, I know that if Britain with its particular type of democracy would not have become my home; if the British with their ideas of fairness or amusement often displacing common sense would not have become my people; and if English with its peacefully coexisting contradictory qualities of agility and rigidity would not have become my language, *The Science of Acting* would never have evolved. And my life would not have become what it has.

There is much in this book which has been said before by people wiser than me. I simply absorbed their knowledge and, together with a lifetime of observing people's patterns of thinking and more than twenty years of observing actors and acting students, did some thinking. I then made the bits fit.

This book would not be in your hands were it not for the books by Konstantin Stanislavski and Vladimir Nemirovich-Danchenko as it is based on their discoveries and mistakes – which are often of more value than truths.[1]

The Science of Acting would also have never evolved without the contribution of the millions of thoughts, experiences, insights, memories and jokes from the students and actors that I have had the pleasure to work with.

I thank you all.

Sam Kogan

INTRODUCTION

Where the world ceases to be the scene of our personal hopes and wishes, where we face it as free beings admiring, asking, and observing, there we enter the realm of Art and Science. If what is seen and experienced is portrayed in the language of logic, we are engaged in science. If it is communicated through forms whose connections are not accessible to the conscious mind but are recognized intuitively as meaningful, then we are engaged in art. Common to both is the loving devotion to that which transcends personal concerns and volition.

Albert Einstein (1879–1955), theoretical physicist[1]

My first experience in professional theatre went as follows:

My lines learned, I turned up to the rehearsal and came out on stage.
The director said, 'OK do this' and she showed me what to do.
I did what she did.
And then she told me it was no good.
I thought to myself, 'I know the lines, I know what she told me to do and I did exactly what she told me to do, but she says it is no good. I don't understand'.
And then she said, 'Do it again!'
I did it again, and she said, 'No, that's no good'.
'What is wrong?' I asked.
'Don't ask questions like this, I'll show you again'. So she showed me once again.
After seven tries she said, 'Sorry, I have to take you off the part.'

Standing on the stage of my local theatre in the Ukraine at the age of twenty, this moment triggered my search for *The Science of Acting*.

I had just finished five years at the College of Building Technology to reassure my parents that I had a proper profession. At the college, 'What is wrong?' was a reasonable question. If cement didn't bond correctly, we would ask this question, and the tutor's reply would enable us to make the necessary adjustments. That is what I believed learning a profession to be – acquiring the ability to answer such questions for oneself. When the director had said to me '. . . do this', she was telling me to 'do what I show you' – that is, to put aside my own understanding, and rely on her opinion of what was good and bad.

Since then, it has become clear to me that this has also been the experience of many others who have chosen the same career.

Throughout my years of study that followed, it was evident that this 'technique' pervaded the acting profession. Acting was subjective; sometimes good, sometimes bad; liked by this tutor, not by that one. I increasingly found that I was in a profession without firm points of reference which could be relied upon every time.

Wanting to answer that original question 'What is wrong?' in a way that would help the actor acquire a profession became my search for *The Science of Acting*.

> Student: I don't understand how it works
> Lee Strasberg: Darling, nothing here can be understood. You have to do it.[2]

The Four Paths

What follows is the story of how different experiences in my life led me to *The Science of Acting*. They are the Four Paths which led me to the contents of the remainder of this book. Not only does this give you the background to this work, but also by openly talking about myself from the start, I will be sharing my human experience to encourage you to see your life as a human experience, because this is after all, the subject of your profession.

Path One: The meaning of words

Soon after leaving university I got married and emigrated to England. In the 1970s English drama schools were hesitant to hire Jewish refugees fleeing the Cold War Soviet Union, so before I began teaching drama in London, I ran restaurants.

The first was a Russian bistro. My wife had been working there for two years as a waitress when she learned that the owners wanted to sell the business. Unable to find anyone to meet their asking price, they offered it to us as part of an agreed deal. The terms were still very high for recent immigrants. Nevertheless we accepted.

We now had our own business.

And colossal debt.

I agreed then with my wife that as soon as the debts were paid off, I would open my own theatre. But life doesn't always go according to plan and on the day we paid off the last of our debts, my wife and I split up. I then had to open another restaurant to ensure I had an income.

The next restaurant was Vietnamese.

I will come back to the restaurants.

Throughout my years as a restauranteur, reading about acting, going to plays and keeping my eye out for teaching jobs kept me going. Often the adverts would ask for somebody who knew Stanislavski and I would think, 'No one in this country can know Stanislavski better than me because I was taught by one of his own pupils' and I would apply. But no luck. This happened enough times for me to resign myself to the fact that the English drama industry was so steeped in tradition that any 'infiltration' would be difficult.

Years later, when my financial situation was more flexible, I saw *The Stage* running an advert from a new school recruiting students. Immediately I sent off a speculative letter and CV thinking, 'Being new this school hasn't established its traditions yet, perhaps there will be less concern over my "different" background'. A few days later a phone call asked me to come in for an interview. The next day I met with the principal and a week later I was invited in to teach my first class!

This was all that I had wanted to do. Immediately I went back to my books on Stanislavski to prepare for my first class.

Preparing for the first topic with Stanislavski's opening lesson in front of me, I noticed the word 'emotion' came up about ten times.

Emotions.

Emotions?

I realized I didn't know what it meant.

What will happen if a student asks me what the word emotion means?

I can't say emotion is feeling or feeling is emotion.

Having worked in restaurants, the service industry, I knew if you promise something, you have to deliver it. I had promised to teach acting and now had to deliver, but unable to explain the meaning of this word would mean I was a fraud. Keeping calm, it came to me that if Stanislavski uses the word so many times, there must be a definition in his work some-where. Burrowing through all eight of his volumes I had no luck. Then through all of my professor's books – still no definition!

But why didn't I know the meaning of the word after five years of study?

Memories took me back to the first time I heard the term used by a lecturer when I clearly wanted to ask what it meant, but my Ukrainian Jewish working-class thoughts of being inferior led me to look around the class and think, 'No one else is deterred by not knowing the meaning of this word – it's because they're intelligent. Given that they already think I'm backward, I'll keep quiet otherwise they will start laughing and think I shouldn't have been allowed into university'.

By keeping quiet, these thoughts of inferiority kept me feeling inferior.

Now preparing to teach my own class, all that could be done was hope that no one would ask me what the word meant and I will have survived.

I turned up to teach my first class. It was halfway through when, before considering the possible implication, the words 'Any questions so far?' tumbled out of my mouth.

You've guessed it.

Back came 'What is an emotion?'

It was a terrible moment. There I stood having used the word emotion ten times and now I was being asked to explain it. So I did what many tutors say when they don't know the answer, they say, 'It isn't really that important, let's carry on . . .' And that's all I said.

Leaving the class and feeling guilty, I knew this wasn't good enough and that they deserved an explanation.

I got into my car and drove straight to Foyles to buy the biggest book on psychology. At the time this cost almost £50, which was more than I had ever spent on a book, but needing my answer the price didn't deter me. After rushing back home I opened the chapter on emotions and read. I didn't understand anything.

And it seemed neither did the authors.

Reading the final sentence my heart sank – the words read something like, 'to this day we don't know what emotions are, it's still the subject of major psychological research'.

What next?

How could I teach acting if I couldn't get past this?

And here comes the relevance of my restaurants.

When my wife and I first took over the Russian restaurant, the menu was very simple. It was an A4 sheet with the names of dishes on one half of the sheet with a line leading to the corresponding price on the facing half. When customers arrived I would give them menus and go into the kitchen to help with cooking and cleaning. For lunch sittings, it was just me serving (to save money our extra waiter worked only the evening sittings). Casually returning to the dining area to see if the diners were ready, they would beckon me over and say, 'Excuse me, what is this?' pointing at one of the dishes on the menu.

And then, 'And how do you pronounce this?'

I would say it in Russian.

They then would ask, 'And what does this mean?' or 'How is this made?'

And I'd explain, answering question after question.

While this was going on, for what seemed like forever, I would see customers come in and sit down. They would wait a few minutes, then look at me, then stare, wanting service. Next, because they had been waiting for so long, they would stand up and walk out, with the money that I was supposed to be paying my debts with.

I had to do something.

The solution came.

I decided if I put clear descriptions of the dishes in the menu, this would save me time and earn me money.

And that's what I did.

For each dish on the menu, I thought back to the questions that the customers asked and ensured that they were all answered in the description. With the Russian restaurant this was relatively easy, having grown up with many of the dishes. When I came to repeat the process with the Vietnamese restaurant, it was more challenging. There was research to do. Where did the ingredients come from? What did they taste like? Were they fundamental to the dish? How large was the dish? What should accompany the dish?

This worked.

Not for this reason alone, but both restaurants went on to flourish and I retain fond memories of queues of people outside both restaurants waiting to be seated.

Now faced with my 'emotion' problem, I decided to use the same approach.

How did I define the dishes? By answering many questions.

How was I to understand what an emotion is? By answering many questions.

I started.

How many emotions are there? Is there a limited number of emotions? Are emotions ever the same? Was my anger on 1 September the same as my anger on 12 October? Is my joy of eating an ice-cream different to my joy of having a massage? Do emotions stop and start or do they continue? Do they have strengths?

The definition of the word 'emotion' can be found in the Glossary of this book, together with the definitions of all the terms that you will come across. (Emotion is the bio-physiological result of a thought.)

My experience with the word 'emotion' taught me that if I use a word, the meaning of which you don't understand, it leaves you with confusion which creates noise in your head which prevents you from thinking clearly.

In acting where thinking is your main tool – above all you need to be able to think clearly.

Path Two: What is good acting?

The second path also began very soon after I started teaching when given the job of directing a play.

Looking to how my students' expectations should be met, my thoughts took me to performance nights, where I thought the students would gain most benefit if they received notes after every performance. This led me to thinking that if I had to watch every performance and they acted badly in every performance, this would be unbearable. Night after night of boredom and frustration? What sort of life would that be?

The only solution was to ensure that they knew how to act well.

Fair enough. Good idea!

Act well . . .

But what did that mean?

What is good acting?

What was the type of acting that could be watched over and over again?

If I knew what this was, my students could be guided towards it.

Thinking back over the 'big names' I had seen in my life to see if there was something they did that my students could aspire to. I drew a blank.

There was no one.

Even after my five years of study, no one came to mind who could be watched every night.

Had I never seen good acting?

But didn't the fact that I knew what wasn't good acting, mean that somehow I knew what it was?

I let these thoughts cook for a while.

And one day the oven bell rang.

It was my first visit to the theatre at about age eleven.

Every month at school, selected pupils were given free tickets to a state production and that month those tickets were given to me.

Although I arranged to go with friends, they didn't turn up and so luckily (I'll come to why) my outing was solo.

I arrived at the theatre and found my seat. The auditorium was beautiful. The red velvet curtains, statues of half-naked ladies, gold-encrusted lighting, the audience's growing anticipation, and no one sitting either side of me. My friends not turning up was important because it meant that they weren't in my thoughts, and more importantly I wouldn't have to spend the performance thinking (with my thoughts of inferiority) 'What will I say afterwards when they ask me what I thought?' Free of this noise in my head I sat back to enjoy what I had come to see.

Everything went very dark.

The spotlight shone on the centre of the curtain.

My heart began to race, my eyes began to bulge, goose pimples popped up and I couldn't catch my breath. The curtains began to part and there was a man and a woman in a Russian kitchen; he was reading a newspaper, she was ironing, they were chatting and . . .

. . . and that's all I remember of the show.

Next I remember walking home having a thought that the play wasn't as good as I expected it to be.

What had I expected it to be?

And why had I been so excited?

What was it that I was expecting to see but hadn't?

You ask questions . . . you get answers.

The answers came to me in pictures from much earlier in my childhood.

From an age (somewhere between two and four years) where in the company of adults, they did what they often do when very young children are around, that is they talk and behave as if the child isn't there. They behave as though children can't judge or remember.

They behaved as though unobserved.

It was these that were the most fascinating moments of my life.

Me watching others live, wanting to find out how to live.

It was *this* that I was expecting from my first visit to the theatre. It was *this* enjoyment that I was looking for from all the great actors when searching for examples of good acting.

Good acting allowed the audience to be a voyeur, to see how other people lived and compare it to their own lives. Actors behaving as though unobserved is what the dramatic realists Denis Diderot, André Antoine and Stanislavski all referred to as the Fourth Wall.[3]

But why did so many 'great actors' not act well?

Because they acted as though they *were* being watched. Their thoughts were on what the audience thought of them rather than thinking the character's thoughts.

Have you noticed how after watching someone who doesn't know they are being watched, that once you are spotted, their behaviour changes and it is not as interesting?

The same thing.

What did this mean, to behave as though unobserved?

Turning to myself for the answer, what was it that I did on my own at home when nobody observed me?

First, I noticed mood swings. I could see I got happy, sad, angry or frightened with certain thoughts, but where these thoughts came from I didn't know.

And . . .

I noticed the habit of doing things that were detrimental to my well-being. I would start the day by saying that this would be my first chocolate-less day and two hours later I'd be buying a Mars Bar, which I would later punish myself for eating. And this would happen day after day.

There was more . . .

I had started to do the very things that I hated my parents doing. The example that struck me was that as a child at dinnertime my father would use his thumb to push the last morsels of his meal onto his fork. At the time it made me cringe. I hated seeing this. It made me think that the son of a man who did this could have no life.

Two months into my teaching, I noticed my thumb doing the same thing!

Any of these examples ring bells with you?

What all of these reflections showed me was that there was some thinking that I didn't see and couldn't control but which made me do certain things and affect my moods.

Perhaps this was the subconscious that Freud wrote about? But Freud always referred to the subconscious in very concrete pictures – mother, father, staircases, snakes in the grass etc. The thoughts I was recognizing seemed to be of a very different quality.

I had begun to recognize what I now term 'invisible' thinking.

The puzzle of invisible thinking stayed with me for quite some time. Until years later, in my own drama school, a student was doing an exercise in front of the class and part way through her performance something in her thinking changed which 'noticeably' affected her performance.

I started analysing the exercise. I asked her, 'Do you know when this happened you started thinking something different?' The student said, 'No, I don't think that's the case'. Thinking she was wrong, but not wanting to say more, I asked the rest of the class. 'Did you see this happen?' and one student said 'Yes' and then another agreed and then they all did. Could this have been an invisible thought that everyone else could see but the student couldn't? Looking back, I noticed the student cringed at the time I told her what the thought was. I recognized the cringe in myself from the moment I caught my thumb pushing some last morsels of food . . .

Then it occurred to me that the audience (in this case, myself and the other students) can see what other people think but when a person is acting, they can't see what they think because they aren't watching their thoughts. So how do you help people watch their thoughts? You buy a camera. From that lesson and still today, all classes at ASAD are videotaped to help students see their thinking and review their analyses, so when they want to know 'What's wrong?' aside from the tutor's opinion, they can see for themselves.

After years of watching many hundreds of students I had begun to realize there are many thoughts that we don't know we have, and that these thoughts have relationships between themselves. If I could understand the relationships between our thoughts and how they affect our everyday thinking and then understand the invisible thinking of characters in a play, well then, actors would be able to play characters behaving as though unobserved.

This is exactly what I went on to do.

Path Three: Right and Wrong

What does Right and Wrong mean?

It means we have points of reference to compare to, which help us decide whether something is right or wrong.

Bertrand Russell said education was 'learning to think for oneself under the guidance of a teacher'.[4] I would extend this definition to say that education is learning to think for oneself under the guidance of a tutor who provides points of reference, which in turn prompts the restructuring of consciousness based on continuous testing and cross referencing.

When I asked the director, 'What's wrong?', my experiences at the College of Building Technology led me to expect an answer which would be a point of reference.

My frustration at not receiving any point of reference left me feeling lost, insecure, helpless and frustrated with every subsequent repetition that she asked me to do.

But this is no way to live and is no basis for a profession. My education at the College of Building Technology was based on acquiring knowledge about the physical world, where I define knowledge as 'unfailingly tested information': quantities of cement, angles of beams, accuracy of measurements etc.

See for yourself.

Let go of this book – it will fall.

Go into your kitchen – there it is!

Put bread under the grill – it will toast.

Empty orange juice all over the floor – you will have a mess.

It's all reliable.

In the physical world points of reference are clear.

But the mental world, of which acting is a part, seems to have far fewer clear and definite laws . . . or knowledge.

How many times a day do you change your mind?

You argue with your partner in the morning because you were 'right' about something. That afternoon, you see it differently. Perhaps your partner had a point. You speak to a friend, talk about the argument: they tell you their thoughts. Now what?

You go to your favourite restaurant.

Your favourite waitress is in a bad mood.

She's not your favourite waitress any more.

How often have you been to see a film or a play that you heard was 'superb' and came away thinking, 'But that was complete rubbish'? Or read a book in a weekend that a friend 'just couldn't get in to'.

Opinions . . .

Opinions are incredibly unreliable points of reference.

And yet so much of the film and theatre industry is based on opinions, leaving actors lost, insecure, helpless and frustrated.

This is because they have no points of reference.

They go from one role to another, ricocheting between opinions, never knowing what is right and what is wrong. Over time this strengthens a pervading belief that, 'Life is a waste'.

Back to my sentence, 'The mental world, of which acting is a part, seems to have far fewer clear and definite laws'.

Seems to.

Thankfully this is not the case.

The notion that there is no right or wrong, no black and white but merely different shades of grey has become a secure cloak which hides mass confusion and unhappiness.

As will become apparent, much of *The Science of Acting* is about finding points of reference in the mental world, and seeing how they affect our consciousness. There are right and wrong thoughts, just as there is right and wrong acting. To some people, this is unpalatable, even dictatorial, but bear with me.

For more than twenty years of teaching acting and directing, watching people's thinking and reflecting on my own, I have found that there are natural points of reference for our thinking, cultivated over 3.5 billion years of evolution. These are innate in all of us as human beings and if we have swayed from them, every one of us is capable of returning to them. I have termed them the Natural Frame of Reference (and will cover them in Chapter 5), and every thought or action we think can be, and is, measured up against it.

It is precisely because as a species, we share these common thoughts and their patterns that acting becomes a science subject.

It is because there is a tangible natural 'truth of a living organism . . . as the laws of a living, natural organism demand' that acting can be subject to objective analysis that my instinct to ask 'What's wrong?' was right.[5]

Path Four: No idols

The fourth path came out of the belief that I was a part of the school of Stanislavski, that he was my God, so to speak, and that I had to follow his word to earn my bread and butter.

As you now know, at the start of my teaching career more and more issues were surfacing that bothered me. Two years after starting to teach, these mounting doubts took me to Paris for a conference on Stanislavski where I met two colleagues of my professor (Maria Knebl – who by then had passed away). Walking around Paris with one of them while the other ran a workshop, I asked a question that I should have asked during my studies: 'How would you define the system of Stanislavski?' She replied, 'The system of Stanislavski is very simple: we all have one point of departure but we all finish up in different locations'.

I thought about this.

It appeared that she meant we start with the same knowledge, but when we start applying the knowledge to our individual productions the results are all different.

Fine. This made sense.

The following day, having lunch with the second professor while the first one ran a workshop, I asked the same question. He replied, 'It's very simple, we all have different points of departure but we will all finish up in the same place.'

I interpreted this to mean we all have our own individual personalities but once applied to the system of Stanislavski we all do the same work.

What?!!

But these were contradictory statements.

How solid could 'The System' be if its own teachers did not have a unified opinion of it?

These replies together with my mounting doubts made me realize that because of my blind adoration of the man throughout my studies and beyond, I hadn't asked enough questions or the right questions.

From that day I decided no longer to bow towards his statue but to say, 'Thank you dear Stanislavski' and moved him from the altar he had been on for so long . . .

to a shelf.

The fourth path to *The Science of Acting* was to acknowledge that there are no Gods and just because somebody says something, whether he be Stanislavski or Sam Kogan, Plato or Pluto, everything has to be questioned by the individual.

Back to Einstein's words at the start of this Introduction, 'where we face it [the world] as free beings admiring, asking, and observing, there we enter the realm of Art and Science'.[6] This book admires with fascination the human experience, for that is what actors portray. To do this, it is full of questions based on, and to encourage observation of the human experience. You will read what it is I asked to reach the conclusions I made and will also find much asked of you – to encourage you, as a 'free being', to look for your answers.

Which may very well be different from mine.

Education

The Purpose of this book is to teach you how to act well. For your expectations at this end of the book to be met by the time you reach the other end of the book, here are a few words on education.

Let us look at a learning process.

Say you decide you want to study architecture.

You go to college and you are taught architecture. Over the years of your course you learn about design, structure, foundations, elevation, materials, you do the drawings, you write the explanations and you do this for many different assignments. Six years later you graduate. You walk down the street and notice that you see buildings very differently from how you saw them six and a half years ago. Now you look up and your brain automatically divides up sections, knows how deep the foundations are, what materials were used and why particular elements are placed where they are.

What happened to you? What does this mean?

It means that during the years of studying architecture, some restructuring of your perception of the world took place.

You are reading this book because you want to learn how to act. Which means creating consciousnesses and thinking the thoughts of those consciousnesses. To do this takes agility of mind. But most of us have a rigid consciousness, which causes us to make the same mistakes, get into the same relationships, succumb to the same moods, feel guilty when we don't want to feel guilty or frightened for no reason. These unwanted thoughts, while seeming visible, are always based on invisible thinking.

Figure I.1 illustrates the structure of a rigid consciousness. It is pretty much stuck this way, the four little rollers allow minor day-to-day shifts to accommodate different experiences, but otherwise it is set, getting in the way of us being able to think the thoughts we want to think, therefore live the lives we want and in terms of this book think the thoughts of the characters we want to play.

Figure I.2 represents where *The Science of Acting* intends to take you. By increasing your Awareness of your invisible thinking, the unwanted thoughts and their patterns, and helping you finish them off (Chapter 8), then that rigidity will fall away. With an agile mind your consciousness will allow you voluntarily to reposition the rollers to think the thoughts you want to think, enabling you to act any part, in any script, in any style, with any director.

Figure I.1 The actor's rigid consciousness

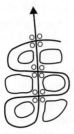

Figure I.2 The actor's agile consciousness thinking the character's thoughts

To become a 'good actor'.

Bertolt Brecht: Why did you become an actor?
Charles Laughton: Because people don't know what they are like . . . and
    I think I can show them.[7]

Let's begin.

PART ONE

The Foundations

ONE

COMPLEXES

The destiny of every human being is dictated by what goes on inside
his skull when he is confronted with what goes on outside his skull.
Eric Berne (1910–1970), psychiatrist and
creator of Transactional Analysis[1]

In this chapter we are going to start looking at the very basic processes
that take place inside our skulls when we are faced with what is going on
outside them.[2]

Look at the word on the following line, neatly typed on the page,
outside your skull:

Ear.

. . .

. . .

What happened inside your skull, when you read these letters?

You probably had a picture or an impression of an ear in your mind's
eye.

Perhaps it was your ear? Perhaps it was your partner's ear?

Or perhaps it was just a general impression of an ear.

Maybe with an earring attached?

If I ask you to imagine a 'stick of chalk', what comes to mind?

A new stick? Or is it half worn down?

Is it white or coloured?

What other thoughts come up? A teacher? A blackboard?

Now, 'Russia'.

Cossacks?

Snow?

Vodka?

Notice I give you one thought, it activates others.

This means that in our heads thoughts are stuck to each other in Complexes.

In fact there is no such thing as a loose thought; they are all attached to other thoughts as Complexes.

Let's take a closer look at what's happening:

Orange.

. . .

. . .

What came in then?

Did you see the fruit? A fruit bowl?

Could you imagine the texture? The smell? The taste?

Whatever came up for you was part of your Complex with 'orange', where orange was the main thought and all the associated thoughts are affinities.

AFFINITIES:

- Pictures and impressions that evolve as a result of thinking in active Imagination the entity under consideration
- Every activated thought in a Complex other than the main one

---

You will notice throughout this book that every term we use has to be defined so that all parties can be confident that we know what the other means and there's no confusion.

Each definition also has to be workable. There is no point in having definitions that don't help us to do our job. These terms are our tools and for them to be effective, they need to be fit for Purpose.

So then what is a Complex?

Freud's use of the term was defined as 'any cluster of impulses, emotions, thoughts etc.'[3] This works nicely.

Let's make it even clearer and shape the 'cluster' into a circle, so that we now have a circle of thoughts.

And then let's drop in the 'orange' example and see how that looks – see Figure 1.1.

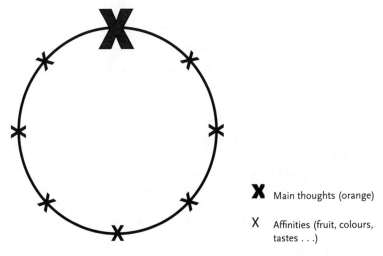

X Main thoughts (orange)

X Affinities (fruit, colours, tastes . . .)

Figure 1.1 A circle of thoughts

As a circle of thoughts, rather than a cluster, it is much easier to see how like a tambourine, when one side (main thought) is shaken, the rest of the jingles (incidentally these are called 'zils', the attached affinities) also sound.

We can now refine Freud's definition:

> COMPLEX: A circle of thoughts where when one is activated, then so are the others to different degrees

Imagine one morning I am buying a croissant on the way to work. Croissant is part of my 'breakfast' Complex, which is part of my 'meals' Complex, which is part of my 'food' Complex, which is part of my 'nutrition' Complex, which is part of my 'health' Complex, which is part of my 'well-being' Complex, and so on. Notice every Complex is part of a slightly bigger Complex which is part of a slightly bigger Complex, and so on, until we arrive at a super Complex of Complexes, where all the Complexes get united and which we will call, for the purpose of this topic, consciousness.

So why is it important for an actor to understand Complexes and how they work?

You may now start to see:

CHARACTER: A collection of thoughts (experiences), and results of their interactions

---

- some of the processes in the formation of their own (character's) consciousness
- creating a character is in a way creating Complexes
- whatever the character says or does is a result of their Complexes being activated
- Complexes can tell us many things about the character's past.

Have a think about it.

Then let's see how one of our earliest Complexes got formed.

Formation of Complexes

When I was born I did what all babies do when they are babies, I got used to thoughts about the face, shape, smell, smile and feel of what would eventually be labelled 'Mummy'. These simple thoughts form the Complex, 'Mummy'. I start calling my Mummy 'Mummy' before I can write.

Not surprisingly the first time I see the letter M, it means nothing to me until my mother starts making the sound 'mmm', 'mmm'. Then she writes, a, and makes the sound 'aah', 'aah'. Next she puts the two sounds together to make 'Maah'. After a few afternoons of my mum drawing pictures and making funny sounds, I notice that each time I see the picture, Ma, I hear the sound 'Maah' and when I hear the sound 'Maah' I see the picture, Ma. I have now formed my simplest picture-sound Complex. From now on everything I know about my mum comes and sticks to the label 'Ma'.

Soon I realized that my friend's mothers look like my mother and when there is more than one mother, or my Aunt Betty and her friend Norah come to the house, together they are 'Women'. So now my Complex gets larger with my 'Ma' now being part of the Complex 'Women' and vice versa.

As you may be starting to notice, creating Complexes is learning. The more we learn, the more thoughts are attached to these Complexes and these Complexes themselves become a part of other Complexes. With the formation of these and many other Complexes comes the formation of (one aspect of) my consciousness.

This book is all about creating the Complexes you need to be a good actor and to dismantle the Complexes you may have which will hinder you becoming a good actor. The key to this, as with all learning, is Frequent Repetitive Thinking. I will be coming back to this many times throughout this book. For now simply consider again the 'Ma' Complex. This is probably one of the strongest Complexes most people have because it is has been thought the most frequently and repetitively. Compare this to a weak Complex. This is a Complex which can be interrupted at any time. After your first driving lesson your Complex was still weak. Instead of automatically knowing what to do next, your 'driving a car' Complex may have been interrupted by pushing down the wrong pedal or knocking the windscreen wipers on by mistake.

My purpose with this book is for you to gain strong acting Complexes. That is why many topics will be touched on a number of times, in various ways, to recap or to take you to the next step, in order for your acting Complexes to get larger and stronger with every chapter, if not every page.

Well-known Complexes

Complexes that are part of our everyday language include 'inferiority' Complex or 'superiority' Complex and Freud's 'Oedipus' Complex. How do these work?

In the case of 'inferiority Complex', this means that every time I think about people (or a certain type of people), I automatically think that I am inferior to them. Likewise with a 'superiority Complex', whenever I think of other people (or some of them), I automatically think I am superior. When I say 'automatically', I mean that my thoughts in response to these other people is not consciously controllable – the attached thoughts are immediately thought by themselves. The whole tambourine is sounding – all the zils are jingling, to various degrees.

In this same way, the Oedipus Complex of a man wanting to kill his father and belong with his mother refers to a consciously uncontrollable Complex.

Another well-known Complex was documented by Ivan Pavlov in the 1890s while he was studying dogs' digestive mechanisms. Pavlov would ring a bell just before feeding a pair of dogs. Then one day Pavlov just rang the bell and observed: the dogs started to salivate and look for food. The dogs had formed a Complex between the bell ringing and being fed.

Even more interesting are the results of physiologist Benjamin Libet's recordings of electrical brain activity. He demonstrated that when humans did simple things like moving their hand, a massive surge in brain activity took place *before* the person had consciously decided to do it. Suggesting that brain activity, that isn't part of our conscious thinking, is involved in our decision making; that subconscious activity precedes and determines conscious decisions; that our choices are indeed unconsciously controlled.

How Complexes work and affect our lives is a fascinating insight into why people live the way they do. The next exercise will help you understand the implications of Complexes in our lives and why it is important for the actor to recognize this.

Jesus and Judas

Let us look at how we would approach a simple story where we would like to create the character of Judas, to see how and why Complexes need to be understood. This is one possible interpretation of the story. Your interpretation of the facts may be different and would produce a different story. The difference between each and every person's consciousnesses ensures that a conveyor-belt-like production of interpretations and therefore characters can never happen.

What facts can we start with?
- Judas betrayed Jesus to Pontius Pilate
- Jesus was arrested
- Judas was given thirty pieces of silver
- Jesus was crucified
- Judas hanged himself

First, it has to be pointed out that Judas was not given thirty pieces of silver to then betray Jesus. It was not given to him as an incentive. Instead the money was given to him afterwards, more like a reward.
Then why did he do it, if not for an incentive?

Whatever Judas' reason, it must have been part of a very strong Complex, because he was unable to interrupt it. It was so strong that he was unable to stop and see what the repercussions of his actions would be. If he had been able to do this he would have thought, 'What's the point in betraying Jesus if I am going to kill myself afterwards'.

But he did kill himself. So a Complex had been triggered that he could not consciously control.

Let's see if we can use what we know and can find out about Judas to find out what this 'invisible' Complex could have been.

There is evidence that Judas was of small stature and also that he was the treasurer of the disciples.

What does being a treasurer mean?

It means that he was better than anybody else at counting and looking after money. We also know that he was a tax collector before joining the disciples.

So what can we derive from what we know?

How does this lead us to the final betrayal of Jesus and Judas then hanging himself?

If Judas was of small stature, it is very likely that he was a small boy compared to his peers. Being small and possibly considered inferior could mean that he was picked on, in other words bullied. And people who are bullied aren't just bullied once; it is usually a regular occurrence, at least for a certain period.

So assuming with the facts that we have, that this is happening to Judas frequently, there will have come a point when he goes home to his mother in tears. He is in tears not only because he is picked on, but also he is too small to take revenge for the abuse that he is being subjected to.

Crying in anger and despair he tells her what has been happening. Judas' mother listens and comforts him and then she may have said something like, 'Don't worry about those nasty boys, your mother is here now and I'll cook you something nice – your favourite dish – and while I'm cooking, you do your homework so that you can get good grades'.

Immediately Judas feels safe and secure being at home with his caring mother. He goes to the table, pulls out his homework and with his head now clear of the abuse, he has time to think about what to do. And what do you think someone who is being bullied thinks about when they are in a place of safety and security?

Taking revenge on the bullies!

Doing his homework thinking, 'When I grow up I'm going to take revenge', Judas looks up and sees his mother cooking his favourite dish and she is looking over to check on him. He carries on with his home-work, now thinking not only about taking revenge on the bullies, but also that when he grows up he will 'have a life that mother will be proud of' because she was the only person who made him feel secure, when other people made him feel inferior.

So from these Events, Judas has formed two Complexes, one of taking revenge on any bully who makes him feel inferior and another, to become special and his mother's pride so that she knows her care didn't go unnoticed.

Then Judas grows up. We know that Judas grows up to be a tax collector. You can probably see how tax collectors could be viewed as taking revenge on others. In this profession Judas would feel very comfortable knowing that he is in a position of power to take money away from people's incomes and at the same time earn a wage his mother is proud of.

The two Complexes working nicely, Judas is content.

His life now fits the generalized thinking that was formed all those years ago.

Next Judas hears that there is some man called Jesus going around who is very special and everybody admires him. It's important for Judas that his mother is proud of him, so he thinks that if he becomes one of Jesus' disciples then he'll also achieve some fame and that would make his mother even more proud – fitting all the more comfortably with generalized thinking.

And so Judas joins Jesus, he gets noticed and he feels special.

What has happened to the Complex, 'I want to take revenge' while this is happening? For now, the 'I want my mother to be proud of me' is very strong and that is enough for him. For now.

Then things start to change.

Judas starts to see Jesus differently.

More and more it seems to Judas that Jesus is in a superior position to him and is starting to run Judas' life by telling him what to do.

Judas starts to see Jesus as a bully and with this the 'I want to take revenge on bullies' Complex gets activated. After all these years of frequently and repetitively thinking this thought, it is so strong that he cannot see it – let alone control it.

The result is that, without being aware of these thoughts, Judas then betrays Jesus.

The perfect revenge because he knows that this means Jesus will be sentenced to death.

And so in the Garden of Gethsemane Jesus is arrested and later crucified.

What happens next?

We know that Judas hangs himself.

Why?

Guilt.

The amount of suffering was too much for Judas to bear.

But why did Judas feel guilty?

Because he realized that his actions towards Jesus were not justified. It was out of context. Jesus did not bully him in the playground. Jesus had done nothing wrong.

All those years of thinking that taking revenge would make him feel better was relevant only within the context of the bullies in the playground. He thought revenge one day would make him feel better, now he is overcome with unbearable guilt.

All that had happened with Jesus is that a strong Complex had been activated. Not only this, but because his Complex of making his mother proud is also very strong, his betrayal of Jesus means now there is no way he can ever make his mother proud.

So, why does Judas hang himself?

There was no other choice.

To reiterate, this interpretation was made on some very basic facts with the main Purpose of helping you to see how Complexes work – not to rewrite history.

OK, so if you were now to play Judas as we have just designed him in this story, you would have to have all these Complexes in your head, formed within the circumstances of Judas' life, *not* your own. His playground, *not* yours. His favourite dish, *not* yours.

To do that this would mean doing the following:

First, researching his past in more detail – this would refine the logic and also the pictures of how the Complexes were formed. For example:

- Judas' father was Simon Iscariot: the name Iscariot means 'man with dagger' or Sicariot, a member of the party of Sicarii, coming from the Greek word 'assassin'. How would having this name his entire life have affected the formation of Judas' Complexes?
- Judas was a Zealot and a Judean. This had political and socio-economic implications. What were these? How would they have affected the formation of Judas' Complexes? Being the only disciple who was not a Galilean meant he was different. How would this affect his thinking when he was with the others, given that he was bullied as a child for being different?

Second, imagining details from Judas' past that you do not know, to design the circumstances in which the Complexes were formed. For example:

- What did his school playground look like?
- How is Judas bullied? What do the bullies look like?

- What is Judas' favourite dish likely to be?
- What is the layout of his house, ensuring that he can see his mother in the kitchen while doing his homework?

Once you have designed this thinking, you then have to lose yourself in these thoughts.

Have you started to notice from the Jesus and Judas story that we all have thoughts that we can't see but are running our lives? And that this applies to every character that we play?

Therefore if we can understand our own thinking, this will help us understand our characters'?

. . .

. . .

Great.

Then you are ready for the next chapter.

TWO

AWARENESS

We don't see things as they are; we see them as we are.
Anaïs Nin (1903–1977), author[1]

'Mirror self-recognition, coyness and verbal self-labelling which emerge between 15–24 months of age are considered by psychologists the first steps in the development of Awareness'.[2]

So at a certain age we know that we exist. That's good.

But what does Awareness mean for adults?

Often-used definitions are 'being in the here and now' or 'being in the moment'.

There are many more, some more precise than others, but when I was initially looking for a definition that actors could use, nothing I came across was suitable.

I knew I needed to find one that would help actors become aware of their thoughts, the patterns of their thoughts and to see how the same processes worked in their characters.

My students and actors needed to be able to see their own thinking.

And there I had it:

> AWARENESS: The ability to see one's own thinking

Chapter 1 on Complexes may have already helped you become more aware, that is see more of your thinking.

Now to nudge that along.

Take a look at these questions:

- Can you see thoughts?
- All of them?
- Are there thoughts you can see today that you couldn't see yesterday?
- Do you think being able to see these thoughts will make a difference to how you will behave in the future?

You already know we all have visible thoughts like, 'I'm late' or 'That was delicious' or just simple images of things or places like 'book', 'carpet' or 'Helsinki'.

What about thoughts that are not in your head at the moment, but are still in your mind somewhere?

For instance, think about your kitchen.

. . .

. . .

What happened?

It became a visible thought. You saw a picture of it in your mind.

But where was it before?

Where was 'kitchen' before you read the word?

Wherever it was you couldn't see it. It was invisible.

And then when you read the word it very easily went from being invisible to being visible.

Did you notice that?

The Model of Awareness in Figure 2.1 will help as we continue this discussion.

In this model, the Chamber of Visible Thinking (CVT for short) at the top of the box is as the name suggests the area where visible thoughts reside. Many call this the mind's eye.

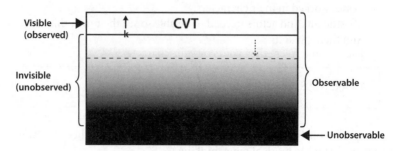

Figure 2.1 The Model of Awareness

Below the CVT are the thoughts that you cannot see, your invisible thoughts, divided into those that are observable and unobservable.

When you read the word 'kitchen', the thought went from the invisible section to the CVT. The reason that 'k' in the diagram, representing kitchen, is on the line is because 'kitchen' is very close to your visible thinking, it was very easy to pull into the CVT. Other thoughts and memories will be further down into the shaded area of the box – these are thoughts that are harder to see and that is why the box is shaded according to visibility.

Think about the following:

- What you wore on your first day of school
- What you had for lunch last Thursday
- The date of your aunt's birthday

A little tougher than thinking about your kitchen?

These thoughts are described as unobserved but observable. They are there and with a little time, or if something were to prompt your memory, you would be able to see them.

The solid black bottom layer is a chamber that represents our unobservable thoughts. Again as the name suggests, they can never be seen (although they can still be influenced). These are the thoughts that manage the internal workings of your body like your heart rate and sleep cycles.

All your visible and invisible thoughts are unique in detail to you. Likewise, your character will have his or her own unique visible and invisible thoughts, very different from yours. Cleopatra for example, would not have a picture of your kitchen in her head, nor would hers be so close to her CVT.

Start thinking about your visible and invisible thoughts and how they are unique to you and therefore when you are playing your character, how their thoughts and pictures are unique to them. Look back on any previous acting exercises or performances and see which thoughts you had at the time. Were they yours or your characters?

The more you do these little exercises, the more you will be pulling down the line between your visible and invisible thinking. You will be seeing more of your invisible thoughts and you will increase the size of your CVT.

By increasing the size of your CVT you will be increasing your Awareness.

This is the Purpose of *The Science of Acting*.

It is not for the CVT to take up the whole model but for it to increase in size by about 200 per cent.

It's also not necessary for it to remain this size, but for you to know that you can pull down that line at any time and have a look at what you really think – or to have a look at the invisible thoughts which created the visible thoughts you have.

Why is this so important?

As you get further into this book you will see that most of what you do, say and think is dictated by your invisible thoughts. Once you see these thoughts and how they affect your life, you will be able to apply that knowledge when creating believable characters.

Why do we have visible and invisible thoughts?

Good question.

Would you really like to be able to see all of your thoughts?

No way! There are too many.

The brain needs a filter on what we can see that is useful for our every-day functioning and holds back on what would get in the way.

Can you imagine waking up in the morning to all the thoughts from your past, all your dreams for the future and your thoughts in response to every present stimulus – your alarm clock, your blanket, the ceiling, all the physical changes that you need to go through to stand up? And that's without thinking about the rehearsal you have to be at in two hours.

Even if you stayed in bed all day (unable to sleep because of all of the thoughts) it would be agonizing.

So there is a filter for us to be able to function.

Importantly there are also many thoughts that are stuck in the invisible section because at some point in our lives we decided we didn't want to see them and for some reason we thought if we saw these thoughts, we wouldn't be able to function. Perhaps the first time we first experienced them they generated so much fear or shame that we didn't want to see them again.

So your consciousness made these thoughts invisible to you and shrunk the size of your CVT so that it holds just enough thoughts for you to be accepted as normal by yourself and others, at the same time keeping out unwanted thoughts. But those invisible unwanted thoughts are still there and just as with Judas, they are very powerfully running your life. They keep you stuck in rigid patterns of behaviour, which means rigid patterns of thinking.

Rigid thinking means that your brain isn't agile enough to think your character's thoughts and so you can't act well.

Fortunately for those of you who want to become good actors, this is a reversible process. Chapter 8 on Finishing-off Thinking is dedicated to helping you to look at the original thoughts that caused your CVT to shrink, help you understand that everybody has these kinds of thoughts, see them for what they are – just thoughts (yes, that's all!) – and show you how to finish them off so they no longer play an influential role in your consciousness.

No, don't jump to that chapter now!

Everything that you read between now and then are stepping stones that you need to take.

Like this next example.

The boy and the Mars Bar

A five-year-old boy called Johnny goes out of his front door to play with his friends. He finds them sitting on the wall outside, each eating a Mars Bar. He looks at them and they look at him, and the little boy's first thought is that he is inferior to his friends because he doesn't have a Mars Bar. Johnny thinks, 'For me to belong with my friends I have to have a Mars Bar'.

Johnny goes back into his house and finds his mother in the kitchen. He asks her, 'Mummy, can I have fifty pence to buy a Mars Bar?' His mother says, 'OK', takes out fifty pence from her purse and puts it on the table. As he reaches over to pick up the money his mother says, 'But remember Johnny, if you keep eating Mars Bars at the rate you have been, you will get rotten teeth like Uncle David.' When the boy hears this, he has a visible thought, 'Mummy doesn't like me'.

The logic for this thought in Johnny's head (and we are talking about little Johnny here, not all little boys, because every little boy will have his own thoughts) is that, if she liked me, she would want me to be happy, and she should know that if I had a Mars Bar I could belong with my friends.

But she doesn't. Instead she disapproves and is making me think about my teeth going rotten like Uncle David's.

'Mummy doesn't like me' is the visible thought Johnny is left with.

Mushrooms

What follows is an analysis of the thought, 'Mummy doesn't like me'.

At this point I should mention that everything we do in our daily lives has a Purpose (to be covered in detail in Chapter 4). So as soon as I have a thought, I must also have a Purpose. And with each thought I don't just have one Purpose; I have a Short-, Medium- and Long-term Purpose.

In *The Science of Acting*, when we analyse thoughts we take the visible thought and put it in the middle of a model called a Mushroom (Figure 2.2), so called because the model looks a little bit like a mushroom. The visible thought goes in as the stalk of the Mushroom and the Short-, Medium- and Long-term Purposes are all in the cap on top.

All of the Purposes are 'wants', changes that Johnny wants to achieve in the different time frames.

Let's start with this.

(You will receive more detail in Chapter 4 on Purposes and Chapter 6 on Mindprint; for now this exercise will give you a taster by introducing and defining some terms and walking you through the logic.)

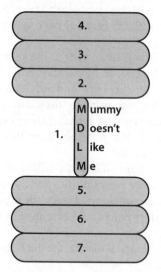

Figure 2.2 An empty Mushroom for the visible thought, 'Mummy doesn't like me'

1 Johnny's visible thought

Mummy doesn't like me.

2 Short-term Purpose – What he wants to achieve immediately after having this thought

After thinking 'Mummy doesn't like me', Johnny's thoughts are likely to immediately go to 'But I want to be liked', which would make this his Short-term Purpose, 'I want to be liked'.

3 Medium-term Purpose (from now on to be termed Objective) – What he wants to achieve in the circumstances

For Johnny, this would mean that when he leaves the room he would like to have a particular thought. It is likely that he wants to leave the room and know that his mother is not too upset with him and that he is still a part of her life. He wants to still belong with her. Therefore his Objective would be, 'I want to belong'.

4 Long-term Purpose – What he wants to achieve in the Long-term future

Johnny with his thought 'Mummy doesn't like me' at five years of age knows he needs his mother to look after him for many more years for him to be safe and secure. So his Long-term Purpose could be, 'I want to be loved' or 'I want to be cared for'.

Let's go with the latter.

As I will come to in Chapter 4, Long-term Purposes are written in terms of 'Happiness is . . .' So here, 'Happiness is always being cared for'.

We have covered the Purposes (1–4) – Johnny's wants.

For Johnny to have wants, he must know what he doesn't want or have.

And the basis for this is what he does have. So what does he have?!

He has his past.

Johnny has all of his past in his head. And all that past has generalized itself in certain thoughts.

Remember the interpretation of Judas' generalized important thoughts from his past?

From the Events and thoughts in his past, Johnny has generalized thoughts about himself, people, life and many more, but for this exercise we just look at these three.

We then attach these additional invisible thoughts to the original visible thought, placing them underneath the stalk as the roots.

5 People Event – What he thinks people are

From his past Johnny has a generalized thought about what he thinks people are.

On this occasion his main thoughts about people could be directed towards the other boys who made him feel he would belong only if he had a Mars Bar, or he may think about his mother. Let's say he is thinking more about his mother. In his mind he saw what happened as him going to his mother, asking for money, her giving him the money but also telling him off. She didn't care about him enough to know that he needed to have the Mars Bar so he could belong with the other boys. This would lead to him having the People Event and here women in particular, 'Women don't care'.

6 Life Event – What he thinks life is

Given our discussion so far can you see what Johnny probably now thinks about life is 'Life is unfair'? He can't belong unless he has a Mars Bar and when he wants his mother to care enough for him to unconditionally give him the money, she tells him off.

So for Johnny, his Life Event is 'Life's unfair'.

7 Self Event – What he thinks about himself

Johnny's mother has just warned him about his teeth rotting which gave him the thought that 'Mummy doesn't like me'. By this Johnny also realizes that he has upset her by asking her for her hard earned money to rot his teeth. He feels shit about himself, giving him the Self Event, 'I am shit'.

Once we have done our analysis we can fill in the Mushroom as in Figure 2.3.

Taking this Mushroom and transforming it into a capsule (the numbers corresponding to those in the Mushroom), Figure 2.4 illustrates how the capsule then drops into the Model of Awareness. Note how the visible thought is in the CVT and all the other thoughts are in the invisible, unobserved section.

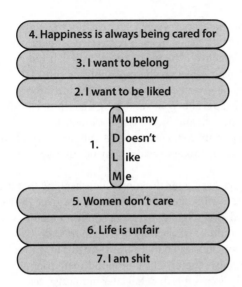

Figure 2.3 Johnny's Mushroom for the visible thought, 'Mummy doesn't like me'

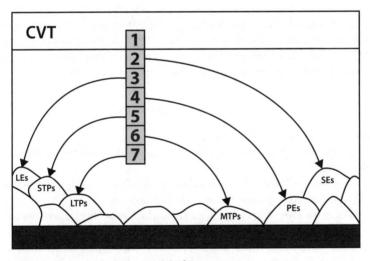

Figure 2.4 The capsule in the Model of Awareness

Figure 2.4 also demonstrates that when I have each of these invisible thoughts they precipitate into heaps of each respective thought, which have been precipitating here over the years, every time that individual thought was thought. This means that the more Johnny thinks 'Life is shit' or 'I want to belong' or any other thought from the Mushroom, the stronger that respective heap will become and the greater influence that thought will have on his present and future visible thoughts.

This is why it is so important to increase your Awareness, so that you can see more of your invisible thoughts which may be running your life more than 'you' are.

These invisible thoughts keep your thinking rigid, meaning that if as an actor you have the Life Event, 'Life is shit', when you are given the role in a fairy tale of a revered king reigning over a magnificent empire with the Life Event, 'Life is beautiful' – this would be very hard to do.

The Judas and Jesus story illustrated that some thoughts in your mind are pretty much continuously there? Like childhood memories: everybody has these, and I will discuss this in detail later in the chapter.

For now this means that we are routinely thinking certain situations over and over. Every situation, crudely speaking, is made up of about a hundred Mushrooms. And if you are frequently running these situations through your mind, you have to agree that you are continuously creating Mushrooms which become capsules, which then precipitate into their respective heaps. This also means that if you think about a certain Mushroom more than any other, the elements of that Mushroom will have a much larger impact on your thoughts and therefore your life.

The Model of Awareness and creating a character

So what's the relevancy to acting?

When we create a character we are creating the invisible thinking of the character.

As you have learned from this chapter, invisible thinking is located in the unobserved section of the Model of Awareness.

But at the start of the process we *know* which thoughts we are creating; they are visible. We sat down with the script, we have done our research, and discussed with the cast and director any outstanding information we needed to design that character. Then we *visibly* design the thoughts for that character. Therefore the capsule of the *character's* thoughts you will have created will be in the *actor's* CVT (a). See Figure 2.5.

Then with time as you remember the lines and remember what to think as you deliver each of your lines, the capsule will shift to where it is

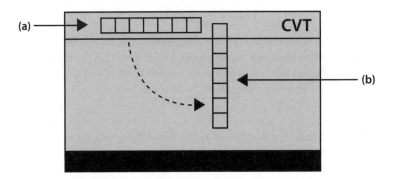

Figure 2.5 Programming the capsule

in our consciousness with only the visible thought in the CVT and the other thoughts in the unobserved section (b).

The result?

You have created a character by programming your character's thoughts.

What is key to moving the capsule from (a) visible to (b) invisible is Frequent Repetitive Thinking. With Frequent Repetitive Thinking the Complex of thinking the visible thought and this triggering the invisible thoughts will get stronger.

Think of tying your shoelaces for the first time. It was probably very awkward to manage the laces with your fingers, looping the laces without losing your hold on the lace, knowing what the next step was, what had you just done to get you where you are . . .?

It was a slooooww process and each movement was visible. But after repeating the series of movements over and over (frequently and repetitively), you soon needed only a flash of the visible thought of, 'I need to tie my shoelaces', you bend over and before you know it, they are tied and you may not even remember doing it – especially not going through each of the individual steps.

Similarly the initial process of programming a character is slooooww and at the start is very visible. But with Frequent Repetitive Thinking, thinking the character's visible thought will automatically trigger the attached invisible thoughts.

Emerging Awareness

The bedrock of psychotherapy is the influence of Events in our early lives on our thoughts and behaviour as adults. But it isn't just the Event having happened that's important – it's rethinking the visible and invisible thoughts that were generated from these Events that becomes so important.

Why?

Just as Anaïs Nin pointed out, the tendency grows to stop seeing 'things as they are [but] as we are'.[3]

For better or for worse.

(Or neutral.)

I'll explain in terms of *The Science of Acting*.

From the moment we are born, through to say the age of ten or even fifteen, lots of Events happen to us. Randomly yet periodically, throughout this time Events and our thoughts about them get captured in our heads as photographs or short films – memories.

These become imprinted in our minds.

Chronologically, I may have a memory of an important Event, say my second birthday, then perhaps an almost unimportant one of staring at the swirls in the carpet a few months later, then my next memory comes from an Event three years after that of playing with a worm in the garden with the sun on my back, then a few months or a few years after that another Event gets stuck as a memory.

EMERGING AWARENESS: The totality of first perceived and most remembered episodes from one's life

---

What's interesting is that although many of these memories seem very insignificant, they are probably some the most important influences on our lives.

Look at little Johnny.

Let's say that what happened that day with his friends and his Mummy was one such memory that stuck. Looking back today with adult 'John', it may seem completely unimportant. If we asked him to tell us about it he may say:

I remember wanting to hang out with my friends and they were all eating Mars Bars and because I felt left out, I asked my Mum for some money to buy a Mars Bar. Although she gave me the money, she made me think about what the chocolate would do to my teeth, because my uncle has such bad teeth.

The memory seems very unimportant and perhaps a little funny, and the invisible thinking is still invisible. But the invisible thoughts that accompany that memory have precipitated into heaps at the bottom of the Model of Awareness making those Complexes stronger each time he recalls the Event.

On this occasion we asked him about the memory, yet every time John goes to choose a chocolate bar on his lunch break, or when all his friends have a new car or a new gadget and he doesn't, the visible thought and all the attached invisible thoughts get activated.

Note also, we designed Johnny's invisible thinking just to do our Mushroom exercise. If John were real, he may also have an imprinted memory a year after that Event of sitting on Uncle David's knee staring at his teeth, thinking, 'I'm never going to have teeth like that'. Replaying these memories over and over means John grows up with important thoughts about having clean and perfect teeth. He may decide to be a dentist. He may make sure he watches his children brush their teeth every night to save them from future dental horrors.

Why I am talking about this is because Emerging Awarenesses affect the way we live for the rest of our lives and will dictate how we will behave in certain situations. Even the captured memory of staring at swirls on a carpet could influence our thoughts, leading to important thoughts like, 'Life is fascinating' or 'Happiness is being left in peace'.

Hence, another way of increasing your Awareness is to start looking at your Emerging Awarenesses and see how they are affecting your life today. Some will be very mundane simple influences, such as why you spend more on toothpaste than your partner, or why you like to wonder around carpet shops. Others may have greater effect, for example you feel waves of insecurity when you feel you can't belong with your friends. Some will have left you with very positive thoughts, some neutral and some not conducive to thinking the thoughts you want to think

Here are some examples from my life for you to see how this works.

Example

My first Emerging Awareness occurred in my village in the Ukraine just before I was twelve months old. I was in the garden where there was a small fence with little posts about six feet apart. The posts were connected by two small whitewashed wooden beams. The fence was not to protect anybody from anything, it was merely to mark out the edges of the garden. I remember that about fifteen feet from where I was standing, there were three wooden steps, also whitewashed, with a little handrail leading to the house. I don't remember the house, but I do remember there was a kitchen and my mother was in the kitchen cooking. I couldn't see her face. All I remember is her skirt and legs, and knowing that she is there, cooking and thinking about me.

The next thing I remember is that suddenly there is a goose in the garden with me. The goose is slightly taller than me and is facing away but with one eye looking at me.

The goose is looking at me and I am looking at it, thinking . . .

The first thought which gave me some Awareness is that the goose is going to tap me on my head with its hard beak and that this would hurt. I then realized that in fact the goose doesn't want to tap me. Instead it is watching me to see whether I am going to do something to it, while I am watching it to see whether it is going to do something to me.

I then understood that if I wasn't aggressive then the goose wouldn't be either. That is all I remember.

One of the main thoughts I picked up from this Emerging Awareness was not to be afraid. I understood that just because I began to feel fear, it did not necessarily mean that there was a real threat, the goose did not actually want to attack me.

A little later in life I was involved in a car accident, where I was trapped in my vehicle. I knew at the time that I was injured but couldn't get out of the car and recognized the seriousness of the situation. I nevertheless clearly remember not being afraid. My consciousness had learned from my earlier Emerging Awareness with the goose how to behave in situations where fear was present. I didn't have to decide about whether to be afraid or not, unawarely my thinking patterns had done this for me.

This is how Emerging Awareness influences our thoughts and behaviour.

Notice from my example and see from your own how Sense Data plays an important role in our memories. Perfumes, fabrics, weather conditions, flavours and so on – these all are Complexed with the Event. This is why it's also important that when you create your character's thoughts, be they the character's memories or pictures from their current life, that Sense Data is also there as this is an integral and beautiful part of how we live. Why else have all these senses?

> SENSE DATA: The information received through the five senses: hearing, sight, taste, touch and smell

Another example

My second emerging awareness was six or so months after the goose Event.

My mother didn't work full-time so she would come to the nursery at lunchtime to serve food or tidy up. I remember one lunchtime my mother was there watching over the children while the nurses had a break and when it came to serving lunch, it was her job to give out desserts.

The dessert that day was a small bar of chocolate. I remember thinking while my mother was giving out the chocolates that she loves me and she's going to give me two. Standing in a line with the other children, I kept thinking, 'Now she is going to give me two and I am going to be very proud that I got two', but at the same time I remember having the thought, 'If she gives me two I will have to explain the unfairness to the others' (and God forbid someone is left without a chocolate). This would make me feel uncomfortable and probably I would suffer knowing the unfairness of this.

My mother gave me only one chocolate.

Later I understood that she couldn't give me more because she was given only a certain number of chocolates. Even though I walked away with my chocolate, visibly being disappointed that she didn't show her love to me in front of everybody by giving me two, invisibly I was happy because I knew she had been honest which allowed me to have peace of mind.

Looking back, this Event was very important to my thoughts as an adult because I realized that the peace of mind that became a Complex with honesty outweighed any suffering that would accompany dishonesty – whatever the temporary pay-off.

Have these examples started to trigger memories for you?

Looking at Emerging Awarenesses is an important and enjoyable process. You start to make visible more of the invisible thinking that is rigidly running your life. You become more aware of the patterns of thinking that are running your life. Your rigid consciousness will start to loosen, your CVT will increase and holding your character's thoughts will become easier and easier.

In short, the more aware you become, the more you will perfect your Acting Technique.

ACTING TECHNIQUE: Aware use of usually unaware thinking processes

---

THREE

EVENTS

I am more and more convinced that our happiness or unhappiness depends far more on the way we meet the events of life, than on the nature of those events themselves.

Wilhelm von Humboldt (1767–1835), philosopher and linguist[1]

How are you feeling right now?
  Good mood?
  Bad mood?
  . . .
  . . .
  Do you know why?
  Do you know which Event may have affected your mood?

  The weather outside?
  Meeting your bank manager two days ago?
  Reading this book?
  Your cat having just knocked your coffee onto your new carpet?
  Going on holiday tomorrow?

Do you ever remember coming home, walking into the room where your Mum and Dad were sitting, and thinking they're different to how they usually are, like something has happened.

  Well, they probably recently had an Event.

  There isn't a moment in our lives that we do not live under the influence of an Event or Events, whether past or future.

  As you have seen, even as you read these words you recall a happening in the past or anticipate one happening in the future, and this is influencing your mood.

> You walk on stage, and the director stops you and asks, 'Where are you coming from?'
> 'The kitchen,' you answer.
> 'And where are you going?'
> 'The bedroom.'

These answers would be satisfactory from a student in their first term, but any further into an acting course and it should be stated that we do not live between places. We (people and characters, either in life or in scripts) live between Events.

If you have just had your breakfast in the kitchen, where your slice of bread burned under the grill, you would be coming from the kitchen or as a more accurate reflection of how we live: from the 'breakfast' Event or even the 'burned toast' Event.

If you are going to the bedroom because the phone rings, or to change your clothes, you are going into the bedroom or as a more accurate reflection of how we live: to the 'phone ringing' Event or just 'change clothes' Event.

Can you see how important Events are?

In order to understand how Events directly affect our thinking and therefore the characters we play, we need to know how they work so that we can act them well.

First of all, however, we need a definition that we can work with so that we know exactly what we are talking about.

What is an Event?

Eric Berne, the creator of Transactional Analysis, discussed Events extensively, explaining that our emotions are tightly locked into Events.[2]

This gave me my starting point; it explained why Events affected my mood.

Referring to my well-researched definition of 'emotions' (see Introduction), 'the bio-physiological result of a thought', this had to mean that *thoughts* that are tightly locked into Events, as they are ultimately at the root of all emotions.

I could see how this worked. I noticed how I had thoughts tightly 'locked into' Events. More specifically what I noticed is that there was an *intensity* to the thoughts I had about Events, compared to other thoughts going through my mind.

I noticed that Events intensified my thinking.

EVENT: Anything which intensifies our thinking

Look over the examples above and see if you notice the same.

What do you think? Does it work?

Somewhat?

I was certainly much closer than where I started but not quite there yet.

Then I got it! An Event *is* the intensified thinking itself.

How about that?

. . .

. . .

Still digesting it?

By intensified, I mean that there is an increase in the frequency of thoughts in my mind.

For instance, 'drinking a cup of coffee': is that an Event?

No.

The Event is what you think about while you drink the coffee.

The intensified thinking itself.

Drinking the coffee is what happens – it is *a happening*. If the coffee is of particularly fine quality, or if you are very tired and need the coffee to stay awake, or if you accidentally put salt instead of sugar in the coffee, then 'drinking coffee' might be your Event. But you could be thinking about anything while you drink the coffee. If you are thinking about the new sweater you bought that morning as you drink the coffee, then 'new sweater' would be the Event.

You are at home, sitting reading a newspaper with your legs stretched out in front of you. It's a warm sunny day and the warmth has filled the room. Your cat strolls past, running the length of her body along one of your feet as she walks to her favourite spot on days like this. Suddenly a brick crashes through the window; the cat screeches and disappears out of the room. Meanwhile the brick circles your head and flies back out of the window. Thoughts that may be running through your head are: What happened? Did that really happen? Where did the brick come from? How did it get to my window? The shattered glass. How's the cat? Am I cut?

These are a lot of thoughts. And importantly they take a lot of effort to process.

The answers to your questions don't come up for a while because you don't often think this number of these particular thoughts.

You don't often have this Event.

The bigger the Event, the greater the intensity of thinking. The greater the intensity of thinking, the greater the energy or capacity required to process the greater number of thoughts.

Now let's say that your father is a magician and you have grown up with lots of weird and wonderful goings on in your home. For the last two months Dad has been practising his flying brick routine at about the same time every day. Today, as usual, a brick flies in through the window – which you have learned to keep open – circles your head and then flies out again. In this case the flying brick wouldn't be an Event, it would be a circumstance. Circumstances are happenings which are mundane, had on a regular basis and which are associated with very low intensity thoughts like brushing teeth or shaving. We use minimum thinking to carry out these tasks.

You see it's not the flying brick that's the Event, it's the thinking about the brick that is.

EVENT: Intensified thinking itself

Again, intensity of thinking isn't necessarily faster thinking, but the use of a greater amount of effort we put in to processing our thoughts.

Compare how many thoughts were triggered, that needed processing, the moment the brick came crashing through as opposed to how many you may have had when the cat walked by your feet.

To summarize so far:
- We know we're having an Event because we think about it more
- Therefore an Event is not something in the physical world
- Something that takes place in the physical world, e.g. a brick flying through the window, is a Happening
- The Event is the intensified thinking about the Happening

So we can define a Happening as:

HAPPENING: A change in the physical world

The Event Graph

With our definitions we can move on to the Event Graph in Figure 3.1 to help us understand Events a little more.

In this graph time is on the x-axis (the units of which are unnecessary for this example) and intensity of thinking on the y-axis. Anything that is an Event has a high intensity of thinking and something that is just circumstance has a low intensity of thinking. The cut-off point for what is a circumstance and what is an Event is different for everyone. Some people have many more Events in their day than others, for example a mother with three young children has more Events in an average day than a retired man whose hobbies are reading and fishing. So in Figure 3.1 the line is placed arbitrarily.

If we look at 'brushing teeth' (BT) illustrated by the dark bar, you can see that at time = 0, your day will have just begun: you have opened your eyes, you are feeling snug in your bed and aren't thinking about your teeth. A little time passes, you swing your feet out from under the blanket and you begin to head towards the bathroom, which, because it's part of the 'brushing teeth' Complex, starts to bring in 'brushing teeth' thoughts in increasing numbers: visualizing your bathroom, seeing your reflection in the mirror, your toothbrush, how much toothpaste you have left, a sense of its taste etc.

You are now at time = 1, in front of your reflection in the mirror brushing your teeth over the sink.

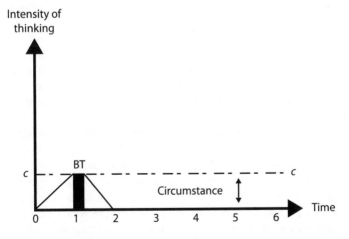

Figure 3.1 The 'brushing teeth' Event

At this point your intensity of thinking about teeth brushing is at its peak; you are thinking the most thoughts about it.

As you spit out your final rinse, your thinking about teeth brushing will start to decrease, and will continue to decrease until eventually at time = 2, you have no more thoughts at all about brushing teeth.

Notice that the BT bar is below the Line of Circumstance, meaning it is not an Event, it is a Circumstance.

CIRCUMSTANCE: A mundane happening

This means that brushing teeth on this average day did not involve any intensified thinking. However, if according to the script you are brushing your teeth the day after an ex-Nazi sadistically performed an extraction without anaesthetic, your intensity of thinking might well be above the Line of Circumstance.

And this would be an Event.

Events and the actor's life

Anticipation

OK, so that was a mundane happening on an average day.

Let's see how Events work in an actor's life.

An audition is a very important time for every actor: it's an Event.

See Figure 3.2.

One day at time = 0, a letter arrives inviting you to an audition in two weeks' time. From the moment you read the letter, your thinking about the audition will gradually become more and more intensified, reaching its peak just before entering the door to the audition room (if we magnify this line we would see that it is in reality jagged because the thoughts about your audition are interrupted with other Events that happen over the two weeks, e.g. how you did in an exercise at school, burning your breakfast one morning, your cat dying when a brick landed on her etc. To keep this simple however, I'll keep it as a straight line).

This upwardly diagonal line is a period where you increasingly start to imagine how the Event will take place; what your audition piece might be, what the room might look like, who could be there, what you will wear. You are thinking in imaginary pictures of how you imagine the Event will take place; this straight line is the Anticipation period of the Event.

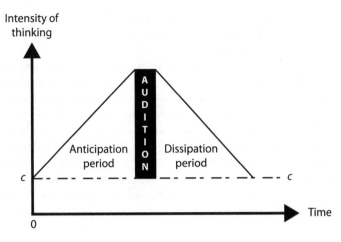

Figure 3.2 The 'Audition' Event

> ANTICIPATION: Increasing intensity of thinking in imaginary pictures and impressions

The Event takes place.
    And then the Event is over.

Dissipation

Before walking into the room, you didn't know what the room was going to look like, how many people would be attending or what they would be wearing.
    After the Event you know.
    What has changed is that from now on the thinking regarding the Event consists of *real* as opposed to *imaginary* pictures.
    This is the Dissipation period.

> DISSIPATION: Decreasing intensity of thinking in real but interpreted pictures and impressions

And did you notice the end of the definition?

'. . . but *interpreted* pictures and impressions.

What do I mean by interpreted?

Interpreted because what you think occurred might not actually be what really happened. For example, when you finished your audition piece, a woman on the panel smiled at you. Which you took to mean that she liked you and perhaps that you had done a good job. But in fact, she might have been covering up her despair because you were the tenth audition she had seen that day, the director can't make his mind up about what he wants, she hasn't had lunch, and there are still four more auditions to go.

Think about some Events in your life and see how you interpreted the Event during the Dissipation period.

Foreburn and Afterburn

Foreburn

Simply by reading what you have so far, you are becoming more aware of what were previously unaware processes and your Events Complex is growing as more thoughts about Events are getting attached to more thoughts about Events.

With this knowledge, can you see that when people are unaware of what their brain is doing before and after an Event, not only is the Anticipation taking place in imaginary pictures but also the rest is left to chance?

Which comes with a degree of fear, because

ANTICIPATION = INSPIRATION + FEAR

Fear isn't conducive to any experience, especially acting, so what can you do to alleviate the fear?

FEAR: The anticipation of failure or suffering (to varying degrees)

Knowing what you now do, rather than leaving the outcome of an Event to chance, you can instead prepare how you want the Event to take place, so that your life after the Event can be better than it was before the Event.

This is a Foreburn – aware thinking before the Event, that is you are not just expecting the Event to occur, you are preparing for it to happen the way you want it to happen.

FOREBURN: Aware Anticipation

Back to the audition example.

If you were to Foreburn that Event you would take some quiet time to imagine arriving at the venue, calm and prepared. You imagine the questions you may be asked and how you would respond. You also consider that a question may be asked that you don't know the answer to; you imagine staying calm and what you would reply. Not only do you bring in pictures of how you imagine the Event is most likely to be, but also you consider the state of mind that would be most conducive to the Event. So that if anything happens that is not as you planned (because there is only so much that you can be prepared for) you have the appropriate state of mind to deal with it and move on.

If something does come up that you could not have prepared for (e.g. you accidentally elbow the casting director as you enter the room or the director's phone starts ringing in the middle of your piece), you Foreburn Going Limp (for now consider this 'relaxing on a thought') and progressing as required.

By Foreburning, you take the Fear out of Anticipation, leaving space for Inspiration.

INSPIRATION = ANTICIPATION – FEAR

Afterburn

If there is a Foreburn, then there must be an Afterburn, that is aware rethinking after the Event that has passed.

AFTERBURN: Aware Dissipation

This involves analysing the Event after it has happened to find out what was your thinking during the Event. Did it go the way you wanted? If yes, why? No? Why not? What would you do the same or differently at your next audition?

Let's imagine you were held up in traffic and arrived late. The anger you felt towards yourself got unleashed on the receptionist. Your thinking sped up and was racing when you went in to your audition. When you Afterburn the Event, you may analyse the route you took and how public transport may have been. You notice when your anger was triggered and how you could have avoided it and how the rest of the Event would have followed if you had kept calm throughout.

Afterburning is not an opportunity to berate oneself or to feel guilty for any wrongdoings. Often something can have gone so well you want to recognize that and make sure you do it next time. Afterburns are a way of learning from past experiences to improve future experiences. What you learn from Afterburning this audition will help you Foreburn your next audition.

Unexpected Events and beautiful acting

- A plate, slipping from your hands and crashing on the floor
- Drinking a gin and tonic, expecting a vodka and lemonade
- Bumping into an ex on your honeymoon
- Cracking an egg and a chick coming out

An Unexpected Event has no Anticipation and no Foreburn – see Figure 3.3. You didn't know it was going to happen and so could not have had any thoughts about it.

So how can you act it, without 'pretending' that you didn't know it was going to happen? To act an Unexpected Event, we anticipate a different Event is going to take place.

You find this 'different Event' from within the context of the script and programme and design the corresponding state of mind (the types of thoughts) with Anticipation and Sense Data.
Then very slowly you think through all the thoughts.

With Frequent Repetitive Thinking, you slowly build a Complex containing all the designed thoughts of this 'different Event', which can then be used at normal speed in your performance.
Let's look at coming home from work to a surprise party – an Event that you aren't expecting.

During your rehearsal period (with the cast or in your own time), you

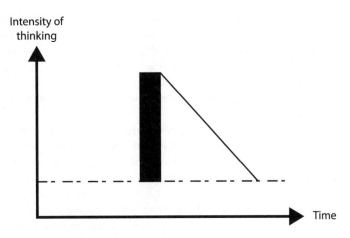

Figure 3.3 An Unexpected Event

programme coming home, expecting to put the key in the external door, pushing down on the cool handle (it's the middle of November) and then reaching for the light switch to the right of the interior wall. You then Anticipate going into the kitchen, opening the fridge door, seeing the light and feeling the light gust of cool air from its interior while you look for the ham that you want to make a sandwich with, before sitting down and watching television.

This is what you anticipate.

Note the use of Sense Data. Remember when we discussed Emerging Awareness how powerful the use of Sense Data is. It helps thoughts stick.

You come to act this scene.

You put the key in the door and push down on the cool handle, open the door and turn on the light switch to the right of the interior wall, just about to take your step towards the kitchen already thinking about the fridge and the ham, when forty people suddenly shout 'SURPRISE!!'

That's when you have an Unexpected Event. It was truly Unexpected, because you expected another. Just as happens in real life.

UNEXPECTED EVENT:

• An Event without Anticipation or Foreburn
• An Event that happens where another Event was expected

Because I see this so rarely done well, with most actors 'pretending' that they don't know what is going to happen next, here's another example. Your character is at home, comfortably sitting on the sofa reading the newspaper. It was a tough day at work and he is waiting for his wife to come home. Suddenly bullets shoot through the lock on the front door (in the corridor) and a gunman dressed head-to-toe in black storms into the lounge and shoots him.

This Event is unexpected, meaning your character was expecting something else. This 'something else' needs to be designed and programmed so that you are losing yourself in *those* designed thoughts while comfortably relaxing on the sofa.

Considering the context of the script, the expected Event we could design is that tomorrow your character and his wife are going to her best friend's birthday party. As the actor you would design the expected Event of the following evening. You could consider for example the time that you would need to leave work, the journey there (who would be driving?), who else is likely to be there, what drink you take along, how long you will stay, which that may depend on who is driving?

This is the initial design, the more you run through it, the more Sense Data you bring in: the clock at work indicating it's time to leave, what you will be wearing, the smell of your wife's perfume (hopefully the one you bought her for Christmas – can you smell it?), the route you will take (avoiding the town centre as it will be packed on a Friday night), the people that will be there (hopefully Mr and Mrs X, but please God, not Mr and Mrs Y), the food and drink (the juicy roast ham that she does so well).

During the rehearsal period the direction from which you are shot will have been decided and how that will influence where you fall etc. Given a few rehearsals, what you physically do with your body will be set to happen automatically. To then ensure that the gunman's entrance is truly unexpected, you just have to keep thinking your thoughts about tomorrow night's expected Event.

Figure 3.4 illustrates the long Anticipation of 'the party' Event, which doesn't happen, interrupted by the Unexpected Event of 'being shot' with its sharp Dissipation (I don't suffer long thankfully).

Try out this process with the simple examples at the start of this subsection – where in most cases the expected Event is given. Remember the use of Sense Data!

When Unexpected Events are acted well, you know you are watching good acting. When they are not, it's time to look for the Exit sign.

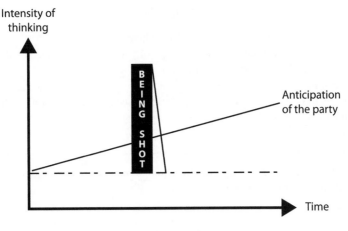

Figure 3.4 The Unexpected Event of 'Being shot'

Accumulated Events

Accumulated Events are slowly created over long periods of time.

They derive from invisible unimportant Events accumulating over many days, weeks, months or even years, eventually creating an Event themselves.

For example, I lend my 'friend' Bob 20 pounds and he doesn't give it back to me on the day he said he would. The day comes and goes and I get a small, negative, resentful thought about him. Then I see Bob two weeks later and I ask him for the money but he doesn't have it on him, and so I get another small negative thought about him, which I unawarely add to the previous one. Many months involving numerous occasions of Bob 'not having change', 'leaving his wallet at home', having 'to rush off' and I will have unknowingly developed an Event of 'People don't care' or 'I am being used' or 'Bob is a bastard'.

Accumulated Events have no Anticipation or Dissipation; they are permanently in your head and may be activated at any time, depending on the stimulus.

> ACCUMULATED EVENTS: An Event that was unnoticeably created from a series of unimportant thoughts, over a much longer period of time than a sudden Event

Mindquakes

Mindquakes are massive Events, of very high intensity.

During a Mindquake most, if not all, of your thinking capacity will be taken up with processing a thought.

Examples of Mindquakes would be winning the lottery, experiencing the death of a close relative, giving birth or seeing a thought for the first time like, 'I've wasted my life'.

> MINDQUAKE: A thought which requires much more thinking effort than most other thoughts

Events and Unfinished Thinking

Remember Unexpected Events are Events without Anticipation.

Can we have Events without Dissipation?

No.

What can happen instead is that the Event can go on for a very long time.

Say you are involved in a road traffic accident. You may still be thinking about it with the same intensity at the time that you were hit, through your time in the ambulance and while being rushed through the corridors of the hospital.

But eventually, even after days of shock, this 'road traffic accident' Event will have Dissipation.

However, as you increase your Awareness and start to notice more of your thoughts and their origins, you will see that there are many Events that you have never stopped thinking about. Although the Line of Dissipation started, it never reached the Line of Circumstance. Here we come to Unfinished Thinking. To illustrate this, take a look at Figure 3.5, where you can see three unfinished thoughts.

Often an Event will have taken place in our early childhood which as children we didn't understand or which caused us fear. Without the skill, experience or guidance to Afterburn these big Events, they are completely dissipated and we never stopped thinking about them. It then becomes a strong Complex to have the thought in our heads all the time like constant background noise. So much so that we don't notice it or how it is affecting our lives.

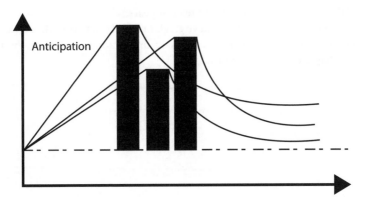

Figure 3.5 Unfinished Thinking

With this background noise you cannot think clearly and if you cannot think clearly you cannot act well.

To rectify this we have to bring these thoughts down in to the Line of Circumstance so that these are no longer Events. This is done by awarely thinking these thoughts through, by Afterburning the Event. When we look back at the Event to analyse what happened, what we thought, what the other people involved thought, the implications, what we would have changed and so on, the Dissipation can be brought down to the Line of Circumstance and the thoughts get finished off, illustrated in Figure 3.6 by the broken lines.

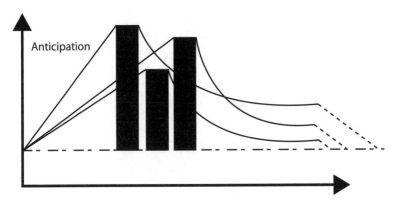

Figure 3.6 Finishing-off Thoughts

With this, the background noise disappears.

The noise switched off, you have greater mental capacity to think what you want to think – a skill that is especially important if you need to think your character's thoughts: to act well.

FOUR

PURPOSES

Everything that happens onstage must occur for some reason or other. When you sit there, you must also sit for a reason and not merely to show yourself off to the audience. But this is not easy, and you have to learn how to do it.
Konstantin Stanislavski (1863–1938), actor and director[1]

The idea or concept of the Purpose is not a new one. Ever since Stanislavski discussed the importance of the 'objective' in his books, the idea of a 'want' or a 'desire' or of 'motivation' has become increasingly significant in an actor's process. Regardless of what name it is given or how it is defined, the Purpose has become the cornerstone of almost every modern acting technique.

It is human nature as almost anyone will tell you, to want something more or something better, something different or more comfortable, tastier or healthier, faster or more admirable. From the moment we are born (in fact, even as a fetus) until the moment we die, we are always in the process of attempting to get something that we want.

The Purpose is the engine of evolution. It is how we evolved from amoeba to fish, from fish to amphibians, from amphibians to land mammals, to apes, to cavemen and ultimately to modern humans. We always wanted something more or better – or what we perceived to be so.

It is hardly surprising that this idea found its way into acting technique. To create life, or an interpretation of it on stage or for screen, we must first understand how we live.

And how we live is driven by our Purposes.

Ask yourself a few simple questions (you should be getting used to this by now).

Why do you put milk in your coffee? Why do you get upset when someone ignores you? Why do you vote Left, Right, Centre or Green? Why are you wearing that shirt?

The answer?

Because you want to.

Whether you want to be loved or hated, rejected or respected, abused or admired; everything you say, do or think – you do it because you want to, because you have a Purpose to say it or do it or think it.

Let's say two men are walking to work along the same street. They both see a blind man wanting to cross the road. One man looks at his watch and decides he hasn't got time to waste: if he's going to get that promotion at work he'd better not be late. The other man takes the blind man's arm and helps him to the other side. What is the difference between these two men? Is one of them good and one of them bad? Is one of them stupid and one of them smart?

No.

They just have different Purposes.

People's Purposes are what make them different from each other. Whether an actor is asked to play a housewife or a serial killer, the approach is the same – find the character's Purposes. As Yevgeny Vakhtangov, the Russian director once said, 'There are no evil, angry or aggressive people, only unhappy people in pursuit of their happiness'.[2]

So, what is a Purpose?

A Purpose is a want. It is a change you want to achieve.

Why?

Because you think this change will make you happy. Perhaps you chose to wear that shirt because you think people will admire you in it. You think if people admire you, you will be happy.

The closer you are to achieving your Purposes, the happier you are. The further you are (or the further you think you are) from achieving your Purposes, the unhappier you are. As you choose your words, gestures, actions and thoughts you are choosing your paths to happiness, or to what you think will make you happy. You are choosing the path of your life.

PURPOSE: What I want to achieve in the future, that is (far) beyond the circumstances or well after the circumstances have changed because I think it will make me happy
  Or simply,
  What I think will make me happy

Where,

> HAPPINESS: Achieving Purposes

So how many of these paths to happiness – these Purposes – are there? You would think they'd be infinite.

You would think we would all have our own unique Purposes and that we would all think differently because we have different personalities.

But this is not the case.

At the fundamental level we all think very similar thoughts, there are just infinite permutations and combinations of these thoughts, which is what makes us different.

Take one of the most common Purposes, 'I want to be loved'. We all want to be loved. If you and I were to describe how we want to be loved and the physical and mental sensations this Purpose gives us, the descriptions would probably be very similar. Sure, the specific thoughts would be different, your Purpose includes mental pictures of people and places that I don't know, but the generalized impression would be the same. 'I want to be loved' is just one of many generalized Purposes that you think will make you happy. We *all* have the capacity to 'want to be the winner', 'to want to be special', to 'want to feel secure', to 'want to take revenge', to 'want to be rejected' and so on.

And how many Purposes are there?

Altogether I have identified and defined one hundred and thirty different Purposes and these can be found in Appendix 1. I would recommend that you become more and more acquainted with the different Purposes and their unique definitions. With time you will be able to recognize when you are using a particular Purpose, why you are using it, what the obstacles are, the pay-offs are and how the Purpose manifests mentally and physically in your life. The more you do this the more you will understand how Purposes work and the easier it will be to choose the most suitable Purposes for your character. As you read scripts, watch films or plays start noticing the characters' Purposes. Are the Purposes within context? If so, could this in part be what is adding to your enjoyment? And if not, is it causing some noise in your head which is detracting from your enjoyment?

(Here I should point out that the definitions of Purposes and any other thoughts that you have and will encounter in this book have been amended and refined many times, and that the definitions reflect the finest descriptions of generalized thoughts that emerged from over twenty years of teaching acting.)

The formation of Purposes: Mind Erosions

What follows is a metaphor to give you an idea of how Purposes are formed within the mind and how they work. The metaphor can be applied to any of the types of thoughts that are discussed throughout this book, but for now, let's look at it simply in terms of the Purpose. Take a look at Figure 4.1.

Imagine that the man is walking towards you across a field. If he walks across the field three or four times a month he will leave no impression on the field at all. But if he walks across the field regularly a path eventually begins to form: see Figure 4.2. As the path forms it becomes easier to walk on the path than on any other part of the field. He gets used to his path and begins to feel comfortable walking there.

Imagine that the field is your consciousness and the path is a Purpose. You are the man (apologies if you are female). The more you use the same Purpose, the easier it becomes to walk that same path – that is to have that same Purpose. You get used to this Purpose and it begins to feel 'normal'.

Now look at Figures 4.3 and 4.4. If you repeatedly walk on the same path, it will eventually become a ditch. The deeper the ditch gets, the harder it is to climb out of it. It's the same with a Purpose. The more you use it, the more natural it feels and the harder it is to choose a different one.

Figure 4.1 Man walking across field

Figure 4.2 Path beginning to form

Figure 4.3 A Purpose beginning to feel normal

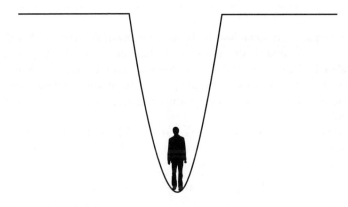

Figure 4.4 In the ditch

Eventually the ditch becomes so deep that it is almost impossible to climb out, it is almost impossible to choose another Purpose in a given situation.

At an earlier stage, as in Figure 4.2 when your head is above ground level you could still see the rest of the field, thereby the other Purposes that were available for you to use. There it was easier to jump out of the ditch and choose another path. However, the deeper the ditch, the harder it becomes.

We call these ditches Mind Erosions. A Mind Erosion is a thought we have used frequently and repeatedly. In the same way that the field is eroded over time to create a path, we create erosions in our mind by using the same thoughts again and again. This is how our personalities are formed; by Frequent Repetitive Thinking, it is how our Purposes, our Mind Erosions are created.

MIND EROSION:

- Unaware thinking, not preceded by orientating process
- Unaware use of formed patterns of thoughts of various qualities, their sequence and desirable processes
- Patterns of thinking followed irrespective of visible circumstances

---

To repeat, this metaphor can be used for any of the types of thoughts that are discussed in this book, as it illustrates how all thoughts are created. Perhaps now or later today you may want to have a think about how this metaphor works with Complexes, Mushrooms, and the capsule in the Model of Awareness precipitating into heaps of previously thought thoughts.

As you are about to see, this is also a useful tool for every aspect of acting.

The seven qualities of a Purpose

In order to understand how Purposes work and to be able to recognize them in our own lives and in the lives of the characters we create, we must know the fundamental qualities that all Purposes share.

1 A Purpose is a want

As we have already learned, a Purpose is a want and is always stated as such, for example, 'I want to be cared for', 'I want to be admired', 'I want to be hated'. It is something that you think is attainable (as opposed to a dream which is not). Purposes aren't dreams. If you think something is unattainable or if you can have no effect over its outcome, then you can't want it, it can't be a Purpose. There is a remote possibility that you might win the lottery if you buy a ticket every week, but you have no control over it and therefore it is a dream not a Purpose.

It must be emphasized that Purposes are always expressed in positive statements, such as, 'I want . . .', 'I want to . . .', or 'I want to be . . .'. They are never expressed in negative statements, such as, 'I don't want . . .'. This is because at any given moment there may be many things that you don't want, yet there is usually a single thing that you want more than anything else.

There are some other words to avoid when stating a Purpose, most importantly, 'try'. You never say, 'I want to try to . . .' because by doing so you are already anticipating failure; you are acknowledging that you might not be able to achieve whatever it is that you want. The words motivation and intention are also unhelpful as the statements: 'I intend to . . .' or 'My motivation is to . . .' are unclear and often confusing. Purposes are simple and clear: 'I want to . . .'.

2 Every Purpose is a change I want to achieve

Quite simply, you can't have a Purpose to sit down if you are already sitting down.

3 All Purposes are perfect, ideal and unique within the circumstances

In other words, whatever you want to achieve, you always have a perfect, ideal or unique version of it in your mind. If a teacher has the Purpose, 'I want to be respected' by her class, she will have an image in her mind of her students respecting her in exactly the way that she wants. Of course life is not perfect, ideal or unique, and the teacher will never achieve her Purpose just as she imagined it. Even if her students respect her greatly, it will never be quite the way that she pictured it. That is not to say that we never achieve happiness, but the result always differs from the original Purpose.

During my Russian summers as a teenager I, together with friends, would often go out for a whole day and pick strawberries. We would always notice how, for up to four hours after returning from the strawberry field, a vivid image of a strawberry would regularly pop into our minds. The image was always one of a perfect strawberry, large, dark red and ripe. We would joke that we hadn't actually picked any strawberries that were as ideal as this image during the day. It was still there though as our Purpose.

The perfect strawberry had been in our mind's eye as the one we had wanted to find; it was the mental image of our Purpose. We had used the Purpose so often during the day that our brain was still attempting to use it, even when it was seemingly illogical to do so. In other words, we had created a Mind Erosion.

I remember that every time I picked a strawberry I had felt a slight feeling of regret when I saw that it was not as ideal as the one in my Imagination. The regret didn't last long and passed almost instantly as I moved on to look for the next one.

This is a perfect example of how Purposes work in our lives. We always have a perfect, ideal and unique image of our Purpose in our mind and we experience regret that we don't achieve it (no matter how marginal it is), this regret spurs us on to the next Purpose and the next and the next, and so on. Purposes push (or pull) us through life. It is how we evolved to become modern man.

This is also a good example of how an actor creates Purposes for a character using Frequent Repetitive Thinking. After repeatedly and voluntarily using the character's Purposes during the rehearsal process (as we strawberry pickers did during our strawberry picking day), the Purposes involuntarily return to the mind of the actor later, during performances (as it did for us in the evening after our strawberry picking day).

4 All Purposes come in pictures and/or impressions

This refers to the form that Purposes take in our minds. In the example of the strawberry pickers above, I referred to a 'mental image' of a perfect strawberry. The perfect strawberry was the picture of the Purpose that we wanted to achieve. You will have already noticed that I refer to these mental images as pictures.

Sometimes though you don't have a clear picture of your Purpose in your mind, or you don't notice it. Instead you simply have an impression of what you want to achieve. An impression has the following definition.

IMPRESSION: A totality of mental and physical sensations

Where,

SENSATION: Perceivable deviation from the unnoticeable norm

Let's say, for instance, that you are telling a joke to a group of your friends and your Purpose is, 'I want to be admired'. The definition of the Purpose, 'I want to be admired', is 'I want others to want to become part of my life at the expense of theirs. I want them to envy me and think of me as being a little mysterious'. This is how you want people to think about you when you want to be admired.

Let's have a look at how this works. You are telling a joke to your friends. It's possible that while you are telling the joke, you don't have a clear picture in your mind of what you want to achieve – them admiring and envying you – but you have an impression of it. You also have an impression of how this will make you feel. That impression is your Purpose.

In fact if you were to break an impression down into very short units of time, you would see that it is made up of hundreds of tiny pictures. The reason that we don't see the pictures any more is because we have used the Purpose so frequently and repetitively it has become a deep Mind Erosion. The more frequently we use a Purpose, the more the pictures shrink. Eventually we hardly notice them at all.

Back to learning to tie your shoelaces. The first time, it seemed incredibly complicated and required a great deal of dexterity. It probably took ten minutes, if you managed it at all. For each movement of the lace you had a clear picture in your mind of where it needed to go – a clear Purpose. The more you practised though, the quicker you became. The pictures of what you wanted to achieve, with each individual movement, became smaller and smaller. Today you probably take three or four seconds to tie each shoe and you don't notice any pictures at all. You hardly think about it. Perhaps a momentary impression, with the Purpose, 'I want to have peace of mind that my laces are firmly tied'. The pictures are still there, they are just tiny.

It is the same process when we learn to drive a car, ride a bike, make a cup of coffee and so on. The pictures of our Purposes shrink with frequent repetitive use so as to make room for fresh pictures. This is what gives us the capacity to learn.

5 All Purposes come with Sense Data

Having mentioned 'Sense Data' before, it's time for more detail. Sense Data is the information that we receive via the five senses: sight, smell, sound, touch and taste. An obvious example of this would be if you want a cup of coffee. Your Purpose might be, 'I want to be special to myself' or perhaps, 'I want to lose myself'. Either way the Purpose will come not only with a picture of a steaming cup of coffee coming towards your lips, but also with the feeling of the hot cup in your hand, the smell of freshly ground coffee, the taste as the coffee hits your tongue and the feeling of the caffeine in your body. If you haven't had a cup of coffee in a while and you are looking forward to it, these pictures and impressions may be very clear to you. If this will be your third cup today, they might come merely as vague, generalized impressions.

For the actor Sense Data is very important. The more Sense Data you add to the Purposes of your character, the clearer those Purposes become to the audience and the more detailed the play becomes. The more Sense Data that actors create, the more they are allowing themselves to live within the context of the character's life.

It is important to note that it is not necessary to replicate a character's experiences to be able to create them with Sense Data. If you are playing a character who drinks two bottles of vodka a day, you don't need to drink two bottles of vodka a day during rehearsals. As long as you have experienced the effects of alcohol at least once in your life, and you know the taste of vodka, your Imagination can do the rest. Similarly if you are going to play the role of a marathon runner, you don't need to run entire marathons in preparation.

6 All Purposes come with impressions of the actions (mental as well as physical) that need to be carried out to achieve the Purpose

In short you always have an impression of what you are going to have to do and think to achieve a Purpose. If you are hungry and have a Purpose to go into the kitchen and prepare some food, you have an impression of all of the physical actions involved: every step you will need to take to reach the kitchen, the opening of the refrigerator door, turning on the cooker, boiling water etc. You may not see clear pictures of all of these physical actions because you have done these things many times before and the pictures may have shrunk, but you will have mental impressions.

Likewise, if you are selling your apartment and you want to get the best possible price for it, you will know that you are going to have to stand your ground when people make you low offers. The Action, 'I stand my ground' is a mental Action (as I will come to in Chapter 7) not a physical one, but you will have an impression of using it whenever you think about selling your apartment.

7 All Purposes come with obstacles

We all encounter both physical and mental obstacles. If your Purpose is simply to walk to the door on the other side of the room, but there is a table between you and the door, then the table is a physical obstacle that you have to overcome to reach the door. Obviously, you just walk around it. A lot of the time, however, the obstacles are in our minds. Sometimes the obstacle to your Purpose may actually be another

Purpose, contradictory to the first. Imagine a teacher who has a Purpose, 'I want to do my best'. He has an impression of doing everything within reason to ensure that his students receive a good education and he has pictures of his students enjoying their work. Next, imagine that the teacher also has a Purpose, 'I want to be liked'. There are times when he has to discipline his students in order to do his best as a teacher, but he is reluctant to do so because he wants to be liked by them. In this situation the contradictory Purposes are obstacles to one another.

OBSTACLE: Something that needs my effort to overcome it, so that I can achieve my Purpose

---

The 'cinema screen' metaphor

Imagine you've gone to the cinema to watch a film. You have chosen a seat in a comfortable position where you have a clear view of the whole screen. Just before the film begins, three tall people sit right in front of you. You decide to move, but funnily enough wherever you choose to sit, three tall people sit in front of you. You finally decide to stay put.

In this metaphor the screen is your Purpose: you want to see the entire screen. The heads and shoulders of the three tall people are the obstacles to your Purpose.

What you do and how you think in this situation will determine whether or not you achieve your Purpose and ultimately how happy you are. If you get increasingly frustrated by the people in front of you and remain constantly aware of their presence you will enjoy little of the film. Your Attention will have remained on your obstacle rather than on your Purpose. Alternatively you could make the best of the situation and watch whatever part of the screen is within your view. You will still be able to follow the film and enjoy it. Your Attention will have remained on achieving your Purpose rather than on the obstacles.

In the first case, if you watch the obstacles instead of the Purpose, you will find that the heads and shoulders of the tall people seem to get bigger and bigger the more you think about them, as in Figure 4.5. In fact you might get so frustrated that the obstacles are all you think about and ultimately you think that your Purpose to watch the film cannot be achieved. In this case you might even leave the cinema, angry and despondent, before the film is finished.

Figure 4.5 Obstacles at the cinema

In the second case, you will find that as you become more and more engrossed in the story that is unfolding on the screen, the heads and shoulders of the tall people seem to shrink and become less and less of an obstacle. Your slightly impaired view will seem insignificant and you will enjoy the film.

The important point made by this metaphor is that obstacles are only what we perceive them to be. We choose whether or not we want to watch the obstacles instead of the Purpose.

If we take the metaphor further we could say that when we are watching obstacles, it is as if we are wearing a pair of glasses with the heads and shoulders of the tall people drawn on them to obscure our vision like in Figure 4.6.

Figure 4.6 The obstacle glasses

If you don't want to watch the obstacles, then take off the glasses!

In life we perceive many obstacles to be real. To reach the door on the other side of the room, you have to walk around the table. This is a simple example and we are presented with much bigger obstacles all the time. It is how you go about overcoming them that determines your state of mind.

In the first example in the cinema, you leave thinking, 'Life is unfair', 'People are inconsiderate bastards', 'I am unlucky' and so on. Revelling in these thoughts will make you unhappy. In the second example, you simply watch the film with minor discomfort and then carry on with your life.

Taking the point further, it can be said that happiness is the absence of anticipated obstacles. When we are in a good mood it is because we are watching Purposes and when we are in a bad mood it is because we are watching obstacles.

For an actor understanding how obstacles work is very important. The easiest way to determine your character's Purpose is to identify the obstacles that they face, or think they face. It also allows an actor to *hold Purposes* rather than *act results*.

What do I mean?

If a character is angry in a scene, this is a result. It is the result of the character encountering obstacles to his or her Purpose. If an actor reads the scene and sees that the character is angry and then simply *acts anger*, the audience (whether they are aware of it or not) have slightly less understanding of the play as a whole, and their enjoyment of it will be fractionally less. If an actor holds the Purpose of the character when he or she comes on stage and allows the obstacle to naturally create anger, the play will make more sense and the audience's experience will be more fulfilling.

Different types of Purposes

Now that you know the qualities that all Purposes share, let's look at the different types of Purposes. Purposes can be divided into five different categories to help you understand and identify them.

1 Altruistic and Egotistic Purposes

Despite what the two words altruistic and egotistic imply, these categories are not necessarily good and bad, or positive and negative. They simply refer to how we want to achieve different Purposes.

Egotistic Purposes are, to put it simply, thoughts you want to achieve in other people's heads, for example the Purposes, 'I want to be admired', 'I want to be respected', 'I want to belong', 'I want people to suffer'. These Purposes all require a change in other people's thoughts to be achieved. The problem with Egotistic Purposes is that you can never know exactly how much of the Purpose you have achieved; only the other person can know that. That is why Egotistic Purposes always leave you with uncertainty.

Altruistic Purposes are thoughts I want to achieve in my own head. Consider them as unselfish or selfless in that they do not require other people to change *their* thoughts for your Purposes to be achieved. For example, 'I want to be healthy', 'I want to lose myself', 'I want to enjoy my time', 'I want to fail'. Altruistic Purposes are not necessarily better or worse than Egotistic Purposes, but at least you have an impression of how close you are to achieving them.

If actors who have Egotistic Purposes while on stage or in front of the camera such as, 'I want to be respected' (by the audience), they will live with the insecurity of never knowing exactly what the audience thinks of them. If they are enjoying themselves, holding the Purposes of the character while on stage, they will at least have an idea of how close they have come to succeeding.

2 Complementary and Contradictory Purposes

Complementary and Contradictory Purposes are what two people have with regards to one another at any time. When two people have Complementary Purposes, it is possible that they both might achieve them; with Contradictory Purposes it is not.

If two people are having a conversation and one has the Purpose, 'I want to take revenge' and the other has the Purpose, 'I want to suffer', then they have Complementary Purposes.

If two people are having a conversation and one has the Purpose, 'I want to be superior' and the other has the same Purpose, then they have Contradictory Purposes. Obviously when people have Contradictory Purposes there will always be conflict.

3 Short-, Medium- and Long-term Purposes

We briefly looked at this category when we created a Mushroom for Johnny and his Mars Bar Event. Now for more detail.

As an actor, Short-, Medium- and Long-term Purposes are the most important categories of Purposes to understand. It should become almost second nature for you to determine your Short-, Medium- and Long-term Purposes, both in life and on stage.

Although the terms short, medium and long refer to the length of time over which we want to achieve a Purpose, the main difference between the three is the quality of the pictures and impressions that constitute the Purposes, not the time span.

- **Short-term Purposes** come in crisp, clear, quick, flashing, uninterruptible pictures and impressions, usually in a short space of time. For example, if you want to pick up a pen you have quick, clear pictures of the pen in your hand and a flashing impression of its weight and texture.
- **Medium-term Purposes** (usually referred to as Objectives) come in easily perceivable, clear, stable impressions and pictures that can be frequently overlaid or interrupted by Short-term Purposes.
- **Long-term Purposes** come in blurred impressions and, less often, pictures. When the blur is analysed it will be found that it is made up of more concrete and clear pictures.

Imagine you are in your kitchen and you want to go to your living room to make a phone call to your bank manager. Your Medium-term Purpose (from now on I will call this your Objective) comes in the form of an easily perceivable picture and/or impression of you sitting on the sofa talking on the phone. To get there you have many shorter-term Purposes such as, 'I want to walk to the door', 'I want to turn the handle', 'I want to open the door', 'I want to walk down the corridor', 'I want to cross the living room' and so on. In fact, we can divide a situation in to any number of Purposes – each step is a Short-term Purpose in itself. Your Long-term Purpose might be, 'I want to have peace of mind' (that my financial affairs are in order) and would come in a more blurred impression.

The truth is that in life we often see very few of these pictures, because we do not break down the process of thoughts. We simply 'live'. In the example above, you might have a blurred impression of wanting peace of mind and a few pictures of making the phone call, but the rest would hardly register. If you were to act this scene on stage, however, you would prepare by slowly working through all of the individual Purposes during the rehearsal process, so that when it came to the performance you would be able to simply 'live' on stage as we do in life.

It is important to remember that all Short-term Purposes start out as Objectives which start out as Long-term Purposes. For example, when you were lying in your cot as a baby and someone switched off the light, you couldn't even dream of being able to do that yourself. After a while, however, as you watched people do it more and more often, it became a foggy Long-term Purpose. Then when you started to walk it became more like an Objective, something you had fairly clear pictures of achieving. One day when your mother picked you up so you could switch the light off yourself, it became a clear Objective. Eventually when you could reach the switch yourself it became a Short-term Purpose. Now, the pictures flash so quickly you don't even notice them.

Long-term Purposes are usually the Purposes that we are the least aware of because they are so blurred. But this does not mean that they are the least important, far from it. In fact, Long-term Purposes are usually an indication of happiness – in two ways. First, they are what we think will ultimately make us happy. In the example above, all of the Short-term Purposes and Objectives were ultimately serving the long-term desire, to have peace of mind. This is what we thought would make us happy. For this reason, when we say or write a Long-term Purpose we always start it with, 'Happiness is always . . .' instead of, 'I want to . . .'. In the example above, the Long-term Purpose is, 'Happiness is always having peace of mind'.

Second, the more Long-term Purposes you have and are aware of, the happier you are. Have you ever heard someone say, 'I got so wrapped up in the detail I didn't sit back and look at the bigger picture . . .' or 'I have been so bogged down in the day-to-day things that I never thought about what I really wanted . . .?' This means that their Attention was always on the Short-term Purposes and Objectives. They never considered what they thought would make them happy in the longer term.

Fluidity of Purposes

People often ask, 'So when does one Purpose finish and the next one start?' The answer is that there is no precise moment. As you get closer to achieving a Purpose, it begins to fade out, and the next one begins to fade in. Or, in simpler terms, the fewer obstacles between me and my Purpose the less of the Purpose is left.

Take the example of wanting to go into the living room to call the bank manager. You are standing in the kitchen, but your Purpose is to be in the living room. For you to achieve your Purpose you have to go to the door, open the door, walk up the corridor and open the door to the living room. Each of these stages is a Purpose. You will notice as you get to the kitchen door that your Purpose of 'opening the door' gets weaker and weaker and is steadily being replaced by the Purpose of 'walking down the corridor'.

Then the closer you get to the living room the Purpose, 'I want to get to the living room', gets weaker and weaker. What is happening each time is that there are fewer and fewer obstacles to you achieving each Purpose. As you learned earlier in the chapter, all Purposes come with obstacles. When there are no obstacles left, there is no Purpose.

Fluidity of Purposes is important for an actor. Let's say you are on stage and you know it is nearly the interval. You know that you are going to exit stage left, go to your dressing room and have a cup of tea. Instead of starting to think about the cup of tea while you are on stage, you should be holding the Purposes that the character wants to achieve over the next five or ten minutes, even though you know that nothing is going to take place. After all, the character doesn't know that there is going to be an interval.

The Super-Purpose and Unity of Purposes in a script

The Super-Purpose is the Purpose that we use the most, over any given period. In life it is not so important to be aware of our Super-Purpose as it may change from week to week or year to year, although it will probably always come down to a select few. When creating a character, however, it is extremely important.

By determining the Purpose that a character uses most often over the duration of the play, you have determined what the character wants to achieve most during that period. The character may use many different Purposes in a host of diverse situations in the course of a play that may span a hundred years, but the Super-Purpose will maintain the unity in the character's state of mind throughout the play.

In Figure 4.7 the straight line represents the time span of a character's life. Each curve represents a Purpose. The longest curve, arching from the beginning of the life to the end, is the Super-Purpose. The smaller curves on the timeline represent Objectives and Long-term Purposes in scenes throughout the script. Under the timeline you can see where one point in the script has been magnified, and then a point in that period has been magnified, and so on down to very short units of time.

The point illustrated in Figure 4.7 is that each Purpose must correspond with all of the others. The Short-term Purposes must correspond with the Objectives, the Objectives with the Long-term Purposes and so on up to, most importantly, the Super-Purpose. By correspond, I don't mean the Purposes should be the same. They will be as diverse as the script dictates, but it must make sense that this character in the context of this script, has all of these Purposes. The Super-Purpose gives the

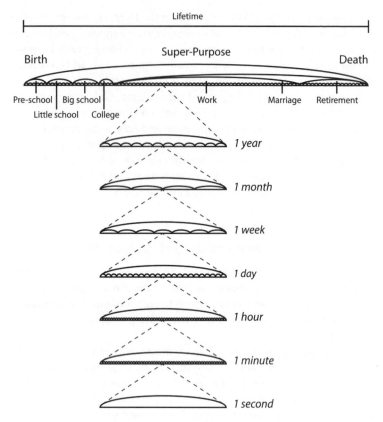

Figure 4.7 Unity of Purposes

character unity of Purpose and that in turn makes the play a totality. That is why Unity of Purposes is as important for an actor as it is for a director. In an ideal world both parties would work the analysis out together.

Conflict

The word conflict crops up a great deal in the world of acting, but its meaning is rarely clarified. In fact, I once came across a definition of the theatre as being 'a space where confrontations take place'. This makes me think that if whoever said this was a director, then his or her plays probably contain a lot of anger, loud voices, sharp movements, tension and so on.

Have you ever noticed that whenever a play seems to drag for a moment or two, theatre practitioners are often very keen to create some conflict on stage to keep it exciting, often to the detriment of the play. So, if it is apparently so important in the dramatic arts, what is conflict?

As established we do everything in life to achieve our Purposes and as you learned earlier in this chapter, all of our Purposes are unique. Then it is understandable that we are always in conflict with everything and everybody we come into contact with. We are never in complete harmony with anyone else because our Purposes always differ from one another, no matter how marginally.

Of course the majority of this conflict is not antagonistic. Even Romeo and Juliet, when they come together and kiss for the first time, will have had some conflict. Perhaps what Romeo wanted in his future family was four children and Juliet wants only three. It is negligible, but it is still there. Their Purposes being unique must be slightly different.

Take a look at your family and friends, the people you love the most. Don't you think that if they were all just slightly different life would be so much easier and all of those little conflicts would disappear?

Why is this important? Because it shows us that conflict does not have to be manufactured on stage. If conflict is a result of our uniqueness of Purposes, then all we have to be concerned with are the characters' Purposes. If the characters have clear Purposes, conflict will naturally arise.

Now let's have a look at how our Purposes came to be so different from everyone else's.

FIVE

THE FORMATION OF CONSCIOUSNESS

The worst of what is called good society is . . . that it does not allow of our being that which we naturally are; it compels us, for the sake of harmony, to shrivel up, or even alter our shape all together.
. . .
This demands an act of severe self denial; we have to forfeit three-fourths of ourselves in order to become like other people.

Arthur Schopenhauer (1788–1860), philosopher[1]

How much say did you have in the Formation of your Consciousness?
Have a little think.
. . .
. . .
And how much say do you think you have in the reFormation of your Consciousness?
Now there's a thought.
. . .
. . .
The more aware you are of how your consciousness works and how it got to be the way it is, then the more say you will have.

There are probably millions of books on the many arms of psychology which discuss the theories and proven hypotheses on how we came to be who we are. In this chapter I am going to take you through some concepts which I think are the most important influences on the lifelong Formation of Consciousness – see Figure 5.1. Of these general classifications (as the Purpose of this book does not require the detail), some have been recognized and verified by mainstream psychology and some I believe have yet to be.

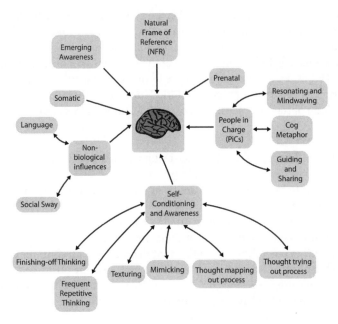

Figure 5.1 Major influences in the Formation of Consciousness

Regardless, the Purpose of this chapter is to help you identify the origins of many of your Mind Erosions so that you can understand your patterns of thinking and have a greater Awareness. This will take you closer to having an agile mind and enable you to think your character's thoughts with greater ease as well as understanding the possible influences on the Formation of your character's Consciousness.

The Natural Frame of Reference (NFR)

When we are born we have the innate Purpose 'to survive'.

How do we know this?

We breathe.

This is the sign of a Purpose. We are doing something to achieve a need.

We breathe so that we can survive and we cry so that our mother will know when to feed us.

Again, so that we can survive.

Nobody taught us to cry or to breathe or to open our eyes. Nobody taught us to listen or to touch. We do these things innately. As well as 'wanting to survive', there are other Purposes that we were born with. These Purposes are the primary needs that we have in common with all animals and are the most important influence on the Formation of Consciousness. In the Introduction at the start of this book, I referred to the NFR as being points of reference in the mental world. Their importance will become clear as you notice how often these Purposes and watching obstacles to these Purposes are featured in this book and your life.

1 'I want to survive' ... in order to find a mate and to look after my offspring.
2 'I want to be cared for' ... until I'm old enough to find food and to find a mate.
3 'I want to belong' ... in order to find a mate.
4 'I want to procreate' ... to continue the species.
5 'I want to be healthy' ... so that that the species is fit, continues to be so and so that I may have a long life to look after my offspring.
6 'I want to have a long life' ... in order to be able to look after my offspring and to have enough time to achieve other Purposes that will allow me to have a fulfilled life.
7 'I want to have a fulfilled life' (or 'I want to be free') ... in order to use my capabilities to the full in line with the other NFR Purposes.
8 'I want to enjoy my time' ... in order to have a fulfilled life.
9 'I want to be the winner (or others to fail)' ... to stay alive and to procreate with the fittest mate so that the species is fit and continues to be so.

Prenatal

While we are in our mother's womb, our consciousness is already starting to develop and can be affected not only by her health but also from the vibrations that we pick up from outside our mother's body. It has been shown that the fetus can hear during the last trimester of pregnancy and scientists are able to be as precise as to say '30% of the phonetic information is available to the fetus, but intonation is almost perfectly transmitted to the amniotic sac.'[2]

You may have also heard that playing classical music selections to pregnant mothers brings about different responses with the fetus. In one study fetuses were noted to quieten down when Vivaldi's and Mozart's music was played, but kicked and moved violently to Beethoven, Brahms and rock music.[3]

As well as the vibrations from music, I believe the unborn child can pick up the vibrations of what the mother is thinking and feeling.

Generally speaking, if the mother is stressed while she is pregnant, then the baby may be born stressed. It has been identified that babies that were in the womb of a stressed mother could have 'negative behavioural reactions to novel situations, attention regulation, as well as an increase in stress behaviours as infants'.[4] Can you see how close the two consciousnesses are connected and how easily the baby's mind is forming from within the womb?

We should also consider whether the picking up of thoughts can be even more finely tuned than we can currently prove. Some pregnant mothers have thoughts like 'The baby will become my burden once born' or even 'I will become the baby's burden in the future'. What if these thoughts are also picked up by the fetus by way of thought vibrations?

While we wait for advances in neuroscience to confirm these ideas, it can't be denied that what is happening to a mother and fetus during the pregnancy affects the fetus's consciousness.

If you know anything about when your mother was pregnant with you, consider the influence this may have had in how your consciousness was formed. Similarly in developing your character, you can ask questions like, what was the state of mind and environment your character's mother had when she was pregnant? How may this have manifested in your character's thinking?

People in charge (PiCs)

Your parents and/or the people who were in charge of you as you grew up were the strongest influences on your growing consciousness. They affected the way that you have thought throughout your life because they were the people who told you what to do, how to think and how to live.

I know that a large number of us were brought up by people other than our parents – step-parents, grandparents, nannies, foster parents, older siblings, orphanages or even just friends – to keep it simple I will always refer to them as the people in charge (PiCs).

Here are some of the ways in which PiCs had a say in the Formation of our Consciousnesses:

Resonating Consciousness and Mindwaving

Few things are static in nature. Everything vibrates; seasons, moods, hormones, breath, subatomic particles.

As the mother thinks, waves of vibration are Resonating from her brain and being picked up by the baby through what I call Mindwaves. When a baby is born, the connections to the mother are very strong and remain so through childhood and possibly even through to adulthood.

An extreme example of this vibrational connection was reported by a group of Russian scientists in 1970. A mother rabbit was separated from her babies (called kits, short for kittens) and connected to an electronic instrument (EEG) to monitor her brain wave activity. The kits were taken thousands of miles away aboard a submarine and executed one at a time. Precisely at the time each baby was executed, the mother's brainwave activity registered extreme agitation. Because normal radio waves are unable to travel through water from the deep ocean, the scientists concluded that distant, non-verbal communication had occurred between the mother and her offspring.[5]

As a much subtler example, one of my female graduates one day saw that she had the invisible thought that her baby 'was a burden' and her life was 'hard enough without him'. She also noticed she had the Action 'I warn' when she was with the baby. When she became aware of these thoughts and was able to finish them off, then at that exact time her baby, who was at the opposite side of the room at the time, exuded a large smile on his face where he hadn't been smiling before. It seemed that his consciousness was directly affected by his mother's thinking.

This example shows that what the mother is thinking towards the baby *and* towards herself is very important as these thoughts affect the consciousness of the child. I call this *Resonating* consciousness because it is based on the close nine-month connection that the mother and child have had, where the baby's soft and malleable consciousness knows it needs the mother for survival and by default resonates with the mother's consciousness.

Mindwaving encompasses the 'Resonating consciousnesses between mother and pre/new born child' but is more far-reaching.

As the baby grows, its mother and other PiCs continue to unawarely transmit their thoughts to the child through Mindwaves. That is, without any verbal communication or direct eye contact necessary, the child's consciousness like an aerial picks up the thoughts from its PiCs. Research into phenomena like telepathy and extra sensory perception is beginning to show that even adults can Mindwave each other,[6] particularly if there is a strong connection between them.[7] How often have you thought of someone you haven't seen for some months or years and the next day they call you? Or just as you think of someone, the phone rings and guess who it is?

MINDWAVING: The unaware influence on the forming
consciousness by PICs

Considering this may help you see how you may have picked up thoughts from the PiCs in your life and how a similar process will have taken place for the character you are working on.

The Cog metaphor

Imagine that each of your parents' (or important PiCs) consciousnesses is a Cog. Their thoughts and patterns of thoughts are the teeth on the Cog. If they live together harmoniously, then we can say that they have Complementary Thought Patterns.

In this metaphor, this would mean that the Cogs are able to rotate smoothly. Every now and again there's the odd little hitch but basically they fit well with each other (see Figure 5.2).

Next they have a baby (see Figure 5.3).

The baby has a very soft consciousness. It has very few formed thought patterns, mainly the ones that comprise the NFR.

Figure 5.2 The harmonious couple

Figure 5.3 The harmonious couple with child

If you imagine the baby's consciousness as a ball of plasticine ready to be moulded, we add this to the metaphor. The ball sits somewhere on top of the two Cogs (probably more on mummy's than daddy's) and bounces around and around as the Cogs turn. The ball of plasticine never gets dragged between the two Cogs or gets misshapen by their teeth. Instead the parents' Cogs merely influence the Formation of the child's Consciousness with their own, while allowing the child to think for itself.

That is one end of the spectrum.

At the other end of the spectrum is a model which represents the conflict-ridden family. This time mummy thinks that daddy is not nearly as good as her father, and daddy thinks that mummy is not nearly as good as his mother.

When the Cogs try to turn, they jam or they pull away from each other, returning to the Cogs they had with their PiCs (Figure 5.4).

Now *they* have a baby (Figure 5.5).

In this situation the baby's consciousness gets dragged between the parents' Cogs, sometimes even acting as a buffer. The ball of plasticine ends up with deep imprints from the teeth of each Cog as the conflict and stress in the parents' relationship causes wear and tear on the child's consciousness.

In life every family sits somewhere in the spectrum between the two examples above. There is no such thing as a completely harmonious couple nor is there such a thing as a completely conflict-ridden couple either.

Figure 5.4 The conflict-ridden couple

Figure 5.5 The conflict-ridden family

As adults we have negative and positive Cogs with people. You can see negative Cogs working when you are talking to someone and you find yourself getting frustrated or angry with them – this is where their Cog is engaging with yours. The teeth from each of the consciousnesses are jarring with the other. When this happens it is very difficult to retain Awareness because anger (or any other extreme emotion) shrinks your CVT. This is when it is useful to use Going Limp to disengage your Cog; sit out of your thoughts and become aware of what is happening.

Positive Cogs occur when our thinking is complementary to the person that we are with and the teeth of each consciousness interlock very smoothly. The Cogs turn effortlessly, we get on well and time slips away in their company because we are so 'easy' together. Sometimes it is also good to step back from these Cogs as you can get carried away and not always see what you are thinking about.

Why this metaphor is so important is that every time you have a relationship with someone, Cogs are engaged to one degree or another. Scripts are full of relationships, which means that scripts are full of Cogs. Beautiful acting takes place when one character successfully and appropriately engages with the Cogs of the other characters' (as designed by the director).

This is why it is very important that as an actor you start to observe how Cogs work in your own life to be able to apply this understanding to the characters that you create.

Guiding and sharing

PiCs guide their children into having a life when they share with them their knowledge of how things work in the world and how people behave.

When PiCs explain to their child how they have arrived at a certain decision or when they reassure their child that making mistakes is unavoidable and that to acknowledge a mistake is as good as correcting it, then they are giving their child points of reference that will help the child to think, to understand and to grow up to live without fear. What kinds of points of reference were you given as a child? Were they in line with the NFR or far removed from it? What sort of guidance was your character given as a child? How has it manifested in his or her adult thinking and behaviour?

Awareness and Self-Conditioning

As we continue through this chapter, you will see more ways in which we not only have moulded our consciousnesses in childhood but also continue to mould our own consciousnesses throughout our lifetimes. In neuroscience the term 'neuronal plasticity' refers to this ongoing 'rewiring' that takes place in the brain in response to our experiences.[8]

In this section you will find out how Awareness and Self-Conditioning play a big part in how much say we have in that rewiring.

Awareness (if you remember) is defined as the ability to see your own thinking. This phenomenon of seeing your thinking or understanding your thoughts to whatever degree is an ongoing process, one that never stops shaping who you are.

Now consider these definitions:

CONDITIONING: The successful imposition of thinking

---

and

SELF-CONDITIONING: When we successfully impose thoughts upon ourselves

---

You can see – or I hope soon you will see – that this phenomenon also continues throughout our lives.

Why these two phenomena are linked here is because we have no say in the structure of, that is we cannot *re*Form, our consciousness to what we want it to be unless we are aware. If we are aware we can use Self-Conditioning to our benefit, but if we are not aware then Self-Conditioning will happen regardless and thoughts that we may not want will start playing a larger role in our everyday thinking.

Let's first look at how the consciousness has unAwarely Self-Conditioned itself.

Thought-trying-out-process (T-Topping)

T-Topping is the abbreviation for thought-trying-out-process.

When we were children we often put adults' thoughts into our heads and tried them out. It's like it reassured us that when we become adults we will be able to think adult thoughts and belong with adults.

Take an example of a little girl seeing her mother putting on lipstick before she goes out to a party. Her mother could have different thoughts:

- Mummy is thinking that she 'wants the men at the party to find me attractive' so while applying the lipstick she may have the invisible thought 'I want to be desired . . . admired . . . or envied'
  or
- Mummy could instead be thinking that 'even with this lipstick no one will find me attractive' so the invisible thought while putting on the make-up could be 'I want to be frustrated . . . rejected . . . or lonely'.

The little girl will unawarely try out whichever thought the mother has and simply by virtue of T-Topping, the little girl will unawarely programme that same invisible thought that her mother has.

People also T-Top animals.

Have you ever noticed that some people look like their pets? How's that?

I think what possibly happens is that someone has a positive affinity with a particular animal which draws them to be bought as a pet. The owner then spends so much time with the animal that he or she T-Tops the animal's thoughts, which then manifests in their own looks.

T-Topping is also how we decide whether we like someone or not. We T-Top other people's thoughts which either fit us or they don't. If they fit we will probably like them, get on very well and feel secure in their company. If they don't fit then we may dislike them and never know why.

Although this is an unaware process, it is one of the most important tools of the actor.

Your skill as an actor is to make this an *aware* process so that when you create a character you are *awarely T-Topping* the character's thoughts.

To practise, it is useful to awarely do this as you go about your day-to-day life, that is when you are with other people see how you T-Top their thoughts.

Thought-mapping-out-process (T-Mopping)

For convenience we call the thought-mapping-out-process T-Mopping rather than T-Mapping. Using the terms T-Topping and T-Mopping is easier than T-Topping and T-Mapping – as this sentence illustrates. It certainly is when you are giving a two-hour class on the subjects.

'Mapping out' means to walk my thoughts so that I can decide which path I need to take in order for my thoughts to arrive somewhere else. In other words, 'I know what I want, and I decide what I am going to do to achieve it. And if I achieve it, I know what I am going to want next.' As children we begin to think about what life will be like when we are adults and that's when we start mapping out how we are going to achieve our goals.

A good example is when we are taught arithmetic. Do you remember learning long multiplication for the first time? At first you had to map it out very slowly until eventually your brain was able to do it quickly.

The very first time you learnt to tie a ribbon bow or a neck tie or your shoelaces, you had to think about it slowly and with practice you could eventually do it faster and faster. At first you were awarely mapping out what direction the ribbon, tie or shoelace had to go and then eventually you were able to do it without thinking and so it became unaware.

T-Mopping starts as an aware process which becomes unaware as we get older. To become a professional actor, it is important that you can awarely T-Mop so that you can map out the character's thoughts and life. One thing that really helps with T-Mopping is reading maps to navigate around new cities or on country walks – learning to take logical steps from A to B.

Mimicking

When children mimic PiCs by repeating their physical movements, they unawarely pick up the PiC's thinking by default. Let's go back to the example of the little girl watching her mother putting on lipstick. This time, instead of just watching, the little girl picks up another lipstick and copies her mummy trying on the lipstick. As the little girl makes the physical gesture, she picks up her mother's thought, either, 'I want to be desired' or 'I want to be frustrated'.

Mimicking is when we repeat the physical movements of others and unawarely programme the invisible thinking which accompanies this movement. With frequent repetition this Complex (of the physical action and thoughts attached) can become our own.

This also works with Mimicking voices or accents, that is to say the physical inflections in the voice are picked up with their attached thoughts.

You may remember times from your childhood when you mimicked your PiCs. It's worth seeing what thinking you picked up by doing this. When creating your character you will need to consider whether the character that you are playing mimicked his or her PiCs and/or how this thinking has manifested in adulthood.

To reiterate, the difference between T-Topping and Mimicking is that physical movement is involved with Mimicking, whereas with T-Topping it is not.

Texturing

Many of my students found they have an impression of the texture of their thoughts. Some described their thoughts as slippery, or they would say, 'My thoughts elude me', 'My thoughts crush me', 'My thoughts stutter'. People also sometimes have an impression of how their thoughts are held together in their minds, for example like 'water', 'knots', 'matted', 'soapy', 'gritty', 'jumbled'. These observations often reflect a state of mind of an environment that the individual was brought up in.

You may have noticed how some characters in scripts seem to have a texture to their thoughts. For instance Ephraim Cabot in Eugene O'Neill's *Desire Under the Elms* is a very hard character who spent years clearing rocks from his barren land in order to build a farm there. When an actor is playing this character, it could be useful for the actor to contemplate the texture of his character's thinking to be 'rock like'.

At the opposite end of the spectrum, Shipuchin (which translates literally as champagne bubbles) in Chekhov's *The Jubilee* is a light and bubbly character who has a very soft consciousness. Here the actor could contemplate the texture of this character's thoughts as being like champagne bubbles.

Frequent Repetitive Thinking

We have discussed Frequent Repetitive Thinking a number of times: through thinking something over and over again it becomes a Complex. And by now you probably recognize that any thoughts, including those discussed in this chapter, thought over and over again, have developed and formed Complexes in our consciousness.

As we know acting is using Frequent Repetitive Thinking to create Complexes.

But how does one use it?

How many times a day should we think through the character's thoughts?

From experience, once a day would not be enough but twenty times would be too much – that would probably overload your brain.

Three to five times a day should be sufficient not only to create strong Complexes but also for these Complexes to allow your brain spontaneously to create more and more of the character's thoughts as you progress through the rehearsal period.

Finishing-off Thinking

By Finishing-off certain thoughts that we have acquired during the Formation of our Consciousnesses, we as adults can have a say in the reFormation of our consciousness.

Chapter 8 is dedicated to this subject.

Non-Biological

Non-Biological influences include such things as society, language, environments, climate.

You may wonder how climate affects our consciousness. Have you ever been in a country where there is an extreme climate – or one that is extremely different from what you are used to? For example if you went from living in Scotland to an equatorial country then thoughts of the heat would constantly interrupt your thinking, which would become a Complex.

Having a pet as part of your living environment is another example of this. If there is a cat in the house, then every so often you may think 'What is my cat doing?' or 'Oh, isn't my cat cute'. This means a large part of your day-to-day thinking is Complex-ed with thoughts about your pet. Imagine if your character was brought up with Lassie, how much of your thinking would be Complex-ed with thoughts about the dog.

Landscapes affect your consciousness. Think about how you feel after just one day close to the sea (if you are from a city – or vice versa).

Growing up next to mountains has a very different effect on a consciousness compared to growing up next to the sea. Even someone who spent only part of their childhood by the sea and part of it in the mountains would not be influenced the same as a child who had spent their whole childhood in the mountains.

Develop your Awareness of these subtle influences on your thinking. The more that you can bring influences like these to your character's thoughts, the closer to the truth your acting will be.

Social Sway

Let's start this subsection with the question, what does it means to 'have a life'?

It's a phrase used often in society but rarely defined.

To me, it means to use your capabilities to the full and to fulfil your NFR Purposes.

And what does Social Sway have to do with us 'having a life'?

When we were children, we may have had the thought that our PiCs didn't have enough or the right points of reference to teach us how to grow up and have a life.

Do you have any memories or impressions of this?

Consequently we decided to look outside the family to see if we could find some guidance or direction there. We looked towards the people that society said 'have lives'. We saw rich and famous celebrities and powerful politicians. Our brain computed and came up with the thought, 'If I live like them then I will also have a life'.

We never considered, 'What if these people I am looking up to rely on alcohol or drugs to get through their every day, and have no *real* joy in their lives, and what if the politicians are corrupt and without integrity'. If we think these people 'have lives' then, without realizing it, we are picking up the real thinking underneath the façades – the invisible thinking under the visible thinking.

Social Sway can come from all elements of society and not just celebrities and politicians. Have a think about how the following may have influenced your thinking:

- All types of media including television, Internet, magazines
- Electronic games
- Religion
- Economics
- Writers and their characters in fairy tales, novels, plays, films
- Music
- Fashion
- Advertising

I like to use the analogy that the consciousness starts off like a small sailing yacht that sets off on a certain course and a strong side wind comes along from society which can and often does, change the course forever.

> SOCIAL SWAY: The influence of society on the forming
> consciousness

It is fascinating to see the effects of Social Sway on characters that you are playing and it is particularly useful for playing characters from different time periods and cultures to your own. The heroes of society in the period of Elizabethan Britain for example or at the time of the French Revolution would be very different from those in our lifetime.

Language

Languages differ from each other, not only because of the sounds but also because of the impressions that the words give us. The impressions are largely influenced by the culture they come from.

Take the word 'abuse'. It does not exist in certain languages, for instance in Russian there is no such word. The closest word in Russian is probably 'torture'. Phrases like 'hard to get' are also not universal. If these words do not exist in a language, then neither do the impressions.

It's interesting that most languages have just one word for snow but Eskimos have over a hundred, with different labels for the many categories and impressions of snow. This makes sense with snow being of great importance in their daily lives.

Just as the labels that different languages use can have very different effects on the Formation of Consciousnesses, the graphical representation of words must also have an effect. Arabic writing is long and round, some languages have joined-up writing whereas others just use symbols.

The language that we grow up speaking affects our consciousness. Therefore as an actor it is important to think about the language that your character speaks if it is different to your own. The term 'paralanguage' refers to all the non-linguistic accompaniments of speech like pitch, rhythm, speed, stress, sighs. The paralanguage as well as the labels and impressions in different languages manifest very differently and these need to be contemplated. For instance a Latin language would affect the consciousness bearer in a different way to a Scandinavian language.

When working with translations you must also consider the language that your character speaks because it will help you to have the necessary affinities.

Emerging Awareness

We looked at some examples of 'Emerging Awareness' in Chapter 2. To recap – an Emerging Awareness is a collection of the very first thoughts that we have that 'stick'. And because they 'stick' they dictate the patterns of our future thinking.

Not only is it important for us to find our own Emerging Awareness, but also it can be a very useful and enjoyable thing to do for your character too. By looking at the context of the script and the nature of the relationships within it you can design an early memory for your character, so that the patterns of thoughts that resulted from this early memory, occur in the script.

The following example is taken from Gogol's *Marriage*:

Podkolyosin, the central character, is a bachelor who hires a matchmaker to find himself a wife. Visibly he wants to find a wife but his reluctance and indecisiveness clearly seen throughout the play culminate in the final scene where just as he is about to get married, he jumps out of the window and runs away. So invisibly Podkolyosin had no intention of ever getting married or of having sex with a woman. And if we were able to look into his future, it seems clear that he will remain a bachelor and a virgin, for the rest of his life.

The Emerging Awareness I designed for Podkolyosin is that when he was a small boy he overheard his parents making love, particularly his Mother's screams. They were screams of pleasure but he misinterpreted them and thought that his Father was hurting his Mother. Podkolyosin's consciousness then decided to think that men hurt women when they have sex, and because he loved his Mother so much, he invisibly made a decision never to have sex.

Can you see how this Emerging Awareness could give rise to the thoughts: 'Sex is frightening', 'Sex is not for me', 'Men who have sex are vicious', 'Women are not for me'. These thoughts would explain Podkolyosin's Mind Erosion and give the actor clear and tangible pictures to contemplate when creating his character.

Somatic

Soma means body in Latin and here somatic refers to the ways in which our bodies can influence our consciousness for example through hormones, physiological processes, allergies, in short – general health. This can also have an influence on the development of our thinking. We think about our bodies all the time, much more so if there is any ill health. Think about the health of the character you are playing. Be they in constant pain, training for a marathon, sitting in a chair all day – all these thoughts will have an influence on their consciousness.

To conclude

At birth and even before that crucial moment we have a NFR. As we grow and develop we receive many different influences on our consciousness meaning that by the time we reach adulthood we have an Acquired Frame of Reference (AFR).

Acquired Frame of Reference = Natural Frame of Reference + the following major inputs:

- Prenatal
- PiC
- Awareness and Self-Conditioning
- Non-biological
- Emerging Awarenesses
- Somatic

And the myriad of minor or unique inputs to the individual that have not been included here

---

What we think as children makes a significant contribution to the way we are going to live. When we become adults we think we are still making decisions about the direction of our lives, but in reality, by adulthood we are making only miniscule contributions to our life's path because unless we are aware, so much of that path was already securely paved for us in the bedrooms, bathrooms and classrooms of our childhood.

And as it is for you, so it should be for the characters that you play.

SIX

MINDPRINT

A particular thought persisted in, be it good or bad, cannot fail to produce its results on the character and circumstances.

James Allen (1864–1912), philosopher[1]

The mind is made up of thoughts which think themselves irrespective of circumstances. We call these thoughts *important* thoughts. For example if I think, 'People are out to get me', I may when walking down the street think that the people coming towards me are going to attack me, whereas in fact they may just want to ask for directions. Or if I think that, 'Life is a disappointment' then even when I achieve whatever it is I wanted to achieve, I usually find I am not as happy as I had wanted to be.

The mind is also made up of *generalized* thoughts, a term you may now recognize. This process of generalization enables us to grow, it allows us to reapply information again and again without having to relearn it. For example, when children are waiting to cross the road for the first time, they will be told, 'Don't step in front of the approaching car as it will hurt'. This warning may be repeated a few times on successive occasions. Children will generalize the information received about the first few cars they saw as being dangerous and that the cars might hurt them. They will then start to apply this information to all cars, forming a generalized thought, 'Cars are dangerous'.

In human society we generalize in respect of everything. For example, we have generalized thoughts about teachers, bank managers, doctors. These will all have been formed in the same way as children formed their thoughts about cars, that is from our past experiences; what we were told, read or directly experienced. And we take these thoughts, for example,

'Teachers want me to fail', 'Doctors are superior', 'People are selfish' into all situations. With each experience we have, we are slightly reshaping our generalized thoughts which we then take into the next situation. A nice way to visualize this is with the following example.

Every important thought is a little statue and every time you have a thought or experience, you throw a little bit of clay onto the statue, and it spreads itself around and forms part of that statue, changing it slightly. The clay is the generalized thought from the present. These changes are happening all the time. We can say that with every experience, that is, with each Mushroom that we think, the statue is slightly changing.

This brings us to some definitions:

MIND: The thought-creating Complex, that is the totality of important, invisible and uniquely generalized thoughts

MINDPRINT: A verbal embodiment of the elements of the mind, that is of the unaware thought creating totality of important, generalized and invisible thoughts:

- *Important* – because they think themselves irrespective of circumstances
- *Generalized* – because they are summaries of past experiences that are used as points of reference for experiences that are happening or are as yet to happen
- *Invisible* – because we do not see them

Warning

Before we proceed, I would like to give you a little warning. To describe how consciousness works using any other language than that which our individual consciousnesses use is not possible. As Paul will not respond to 'Peter', nor will Jane respond to 'Jill', you will not be given bread if you ask for 'cake', or wine if you ask for 'water'. No element of the consciousness will reply to a name which is not its own. In other words, if you do not use the correct label these elements will not identify themselves for you to see them, see how they manifest and then decide on what action you wish to take on them.

A good example from day-to-day life is when you have a word on the tip of your tongue but you just can't remember it and no matter how many synonyms you come up with, until you remember the precise word you wanted you are not satisfied. So too the precise word must be used when discussing elements of the consciousness.

As we proceed with this chapter (more so than with any previous) you will see that the language of the consciousness in the main is not one people use socially, nor as far as I know, use in their thoughts *all* of the time. You may have already experienced this, when someone you know never swears and then one day is very angry or provoked and lets out a rant which includes words you have never heard them use before.

Where did this come from?

Their consciousness of course.

Therefore if you get easily shocked, offended or hurt by rude words, watch out! The consciousness loves these words. It uses them as labels and I can see no other way to talk to you about consciousness without using them. Here I list the most offensive or rude words that appear – if you are OK with them, please read on. If not close the book and I hope that you have enjoyed what you have learned up until now.

OK, here goes . . .

Fuck
Shit
Whore
Bitch
Bastard
Cunt
Dick
Asshole
Motherfucker

Still there?

Not fallen off your chair?

Good, I shall proceed.

The character's Mindprint

The process of finding a character's and our own Mindprint is the same – by gently asking questions like . . . 'What am I thinking about now?', 'Who do I think I am?', 'What do I think about life?', 'What do I think about people?' and so on.

For us, this helps us to start finding our invisible thoughts and to start to see how we got them and thereby finish them off if they are not conducive to a happy life.

In creating a character we analyse the script (supported as necessary with research and Imagination) to help answer these questions. Once the Mindprint of the character is established, these thoughts can then be programmed to create the consciousness that the actor will think on stage or in front of the camera.

The list that follows are the categories of the Mindprint, followed by the respective abbreviations in brackets. I want you to first see the Mindprint as a totality and then I will proceed to discuss each one in turn providing a definition and where necessary, a discussion and examples. This will provide you with enough knowledge to understand how this works in your own thinking so that you are then able to apply that understanding when you create Mindprints for your characters. The chapter ends with three characters' Mindprints to give you a sense of this tool in practice.

You will notice that most categories of the Mindprint we call 'Events', in that they are intensified thinking in our minds, that is we think them with an intensity which goes beyond normal circumstances. In terms of the order of the Mindprint, the first three are the most important because they form the foundation of the character's consciousness, the remainder are in no significant order until the last two; the Super-Purpose and Germ are found at the end as they generally sum up the totality of the character's Mindprint:

1   Ultimate Communion Event (UC)*
2   Shame Events (ShE)*
3   Sex Events (SxE)
4   Life Events (LE)
5   People Events (PE) (can be broken down into Men Events (ME) and Women Events (WE))
6   (Ghouls and) Ghosts (Gh)
7   Auto Directives (AD)
8   Adjusters (Adj)
9   Mental Statements (MS)
10 Guidelines (GL)
11 Objectives (O)
12 Purposes (P)
13 Self Events (SE)

14   Super-Purpose (SP)*
15   Germ (G)*

* usually only one given to each character

1   Ultimate Communion Event (UC)

> **ULTIMATE COMMUNION EVENT (UC):** Generalized impression of the most secure relationship I can ever be in the stillness of

The UC has a dream or ghost-like texture. Its image is made out of the thoughts and feelings from one's early years when there was a need for security and belonging with someone who provided either care or abuse; this can be through being either loved, rejected, ignored, protected or humiliated. This thought became an idealized impression of security and belonging.

The Ultimate Communion Event seems to be one of the least visible elements of the Mindprint so it may take you sometime to identify yours – interestingly, perhaps paradoxically, it is also the most important element of the Mindprint.

Although what happens in everyday life has an influence on what will happen in the future, it also reflects the pursuit of ultimate belonging and security that the individual believes there to be. The UC is such an integral part of consciousness that achievement of it or in certain cases, return to it, however bizarre and unbelievable, is the most important goal in life.

Most often the UC is with one of the parents. Less frequent is with both parents, other members of the family, more than one member of the family, dead family members, deities like Jesus Christ, Buddha, God or even animals. No element of the Mindprint stands on its own; each is affected by the other elements and influences the other Mindprint Events – none, however, as much as the UC.

People can have more than one UC but when creating a character we provide only one.

Examples

'Closeness with father', 'Being humiliated by my mother', 'In bed with my mother', 'Belonging with my father', 'Close belonging with my pet', 'The smell of my mother', 'Being shouted at by my father'

2 Shame Events (ShE)

SHAME EVENTS (ShE): These thoughts cause me the most
suffering and are ones that I must hide from others and myself.
Thoughts, that I think if seen, will betray the fact that:

- I break the contract with myself to have a life
- I am forced into a contract of not having a life
- I am deprived of the ability of having a life (to not have a life is
  not being able to plan my life or make decisions: decisions are
  made with informed and enough thoroughly cross-referenced
  information in the CVT to make the best decision, without
  background noise)

Although the effect of Shame Events is often easy to detect, the real causes may be quite well hidden. As it was explained in Chapter 5 on the Formation of Consciousness, my mother/father/parents have no life is often the main root of many a ShE.

ShEs have been found to be the major cause of stress and unhappiness in individuals, chiefly as a result of their comparison to the NFR. ShEs prevent us from getting on with our lives as we spend a large proportion of our time covering them up. Importantly they do not allow us to think what we want to think.

Examples

'I am inferior', 'My family is shit', 'My Mother is a whore', 'I am stupid', 'My parents took my life away', 'I can't have a life', 'I have no life', 'I am a woman (for women)', 'I am a woman (for men)' 'I can't think', 'I am shit', 'I am a waste'

3 Sex Events (SxE)

SEX EVENTS (SxE):

- What sex is
- What sex is to me
- The thought that precipitated from my thoughts about sex

Sex Events are an important part of the Mindprint as they form part of the roots of the consciousness (as a part of the NFR), together with ShEs and UC Event. As many people think about sex very often, any important thoughts you may have about sex will have a great effect on your life.

A common SxE is 'Sex is a sin'. A student of mine was brought up in a Catholic family where the subject of sex was never talked about except in connection with sin. She therefore grew up thinking that sex was a sin, that sex was only for sinners and that even to think about sex was a sin. Other thoughts created in this case were 'I mustn't think about sex', 'I mustn't enjoy sex', 'I am a sinner', 'I am a whore'.

Another common SxE is 'Sex is disappointing'. This is the thought that sex is never as good as it should be. This is usually because there is another false point of reference for what good sex should be. One example is the thought 'I am my own best fuck'.

Examples

'Sex is humiliating', '. . . sulking', '. . . perfect union', '. . . a duty', '. . . abuse', '. . . lonely', '. . . belonging', '. . . a game', '. . . a joy', '. . . degrading', '. . . filth', '. . . exciting', '. . . a chore', '. . . not for me', '. . . unattainable', '. . . physical love', '. . . painful', '. . . everything', '. . . holding on', '. . . letting go'

4 Life Events (LE)

LIFE EVENTS (LE):

- What life is
- What I think life is

Important thoughts about life become generalized and are carried into every situation, even when inappropriate.

For one student, his Life Event was, 'Life is a competition': this thought came from the competition he had with his siblings for his parents' attention. The Purposes of wanting to be the winner and of wanting other people to fail, often accompany this thought. If you have this LE the effect on your life can be such that whenever you are working or just being with other people you will think that life is a competition, even when this is inappropriate, inaccurate or destructive – often resulting in much stress and frustration.

If alternatively (although you may have both) you have the LE, 'Life is a waste', it means you must have a point of reference for what it is not to waste time. Everything we think or do in life is measured against the NFR's 'use of time' factor, that is we innately know the value of time. Anything that is not part of an NFR Purpose strengthens this thought.

The LE, 'Life is hard' means that whatever I do, circumstances beyond my control will stop me being able to achieve what I know I could. See my example in Chapter 8 on Finishing-off Thinking.

Examples

'Life is freedom', '. . . not for me', '. . . lonely', '. . . pointless', '. . . short', '. . . long' '. . . a joy', '. . . fascinating', '. . . a duty', '. . . a chore', '. . . depressing', '. . . out there' '. . . a burden', '. . . waste', '. . . passing me by', '. . . suffering'

5 People Events (PE)

Can be broken down into Men Events (ME) and Women Events (WE)

PEOPLE EVENTS (PE): What I think people are

The walking down the street example at the start of this chapter is a good example of how People Events work. A very common PE is, 'People don't care'. This thought is usually formed when as a child, adults do not stop the child from failing or indeed encourage the child to behave or think in a way which is contradictory to the NFR.

As an example, Jenny was caught smoking at school. Her teacher sent a note home to her parents yet did not take any further disciplinary action – leaving that up to the parents. Her parents took no disciplinary action either. This left Jenny with the thought that adults don't care what I do to my health and if people don't care about me, why should I care about my own life or anyone else's. This led to Jenny sulking with her parents, and with the world in general for not caring. It also left her with the thought, 'What's the point in living if no one cares?' As she grew older Jenny took to smoking dope until she smoked every day damaging her health and general state of mind.

Examples

People Events: 'People are bastards', '... stupid', '... selfish', '... boring', '... vicious', '... fascinating', '... cunts', '... unbearable', '... OK', '... hard to get', 'People have lives', '... don't have lives', '... are out to get me', 'People care'

Men Events: 'Men are titillating', '... vicious', '... strong', '... cowards', '... pathetic', '... care', '... thick', '... ungrateful', '... boys', '... belong', 'Men don't care'

Women Events: 'Women are humiliating', '... competition', '... unattainable', '... unpredictable', '... devious', '... caring', '... cunts', '... bitches', '... whores', '... vicious', '... necessary', 'Women care'

6 (Ghouls and) Ghosts (Gh)

GHOSTS (Gh): The word given to the mental impression of a recurring fear that has the Purpose of maintaining an unawarely favoured pattern of thinking

Ghouls are frequent repetition of similar individual thoughts such as 'They don't like me', 'She doesn't like me', 'He doesn't like me'. If not thought through or Finished-off they result in a Ghost such as, 'I can't be liked'.

If as a child I think that my mother does not love me, then this may lead me to think she won't care for me and I won't be able to survive, but I can't think these thoughts and so stop myself from thinking them. Why? Because I have an inclination that if I keep thinking along these lines even more frightening thoughts will come into my head – so I decided to cut them short.

Yes, the thought is cut short.

I leave it unfinished and I confuse myself.

My head knows that there is a fear but I pretend that there isn't so it remains unfinished. This is how I start a Complex of creating Ghouls (unfinished thinking). If we keep creating these and if they have the same name, they get together and all the Ghouls under the same name form a Ghost – I can't be loved, which by now has become a very strong fear. Ghosts are always expressed as 'I can't . . .'

Examples

'I can't have a life', 'I can't be loved', 'I can't succeed', 'I can't be appreciated', 'I can't belong', 'I can't be free', 'I can't think', 'I can't have a family', 'I can't be satisfied', 'I can't be understood'

7 Auto Directives (AD)

AUTO DIRECTIVES (AD): Thoughts that instruct me in what I must or must not do, on the way to achieving my happiness

---

An Auto Directive is a thought that tells me what I must or must not do on the way to achieving my happiness. Regardless of where, when or how they get picked up, if thought often enough they become determining thoughts in our consciousness which we believe to be true.

Examples

I must: 'I must be strong', 'I must make myself stupid', 'I must impress', 'I must cover up', 'I must fail', 'I must confuse myself', 'I must rebel', 'I must atone'

I must not: 'I must not be discovered', 'I must not submit', 'I must not see my thinking', 'I must not fuck', 'I must not go all the way', 'I must not enjoy my life'

8 Adjusters (Adj)

ADJUSTERS (Adj): Thoughts that keep me in my Mind Erosion

Remember the stick man in the ditch? Well, these are thoughts that keep him in the ditch. Adjusters prevent us from seeing other thoughts that we could think, while simultaneously making sure that the ditch gets deeper and deeper.

Examples

'It's not worth it', 'It's all shit anyway', 'It's too late', 'Nobody cares anyway', 'I'll do it later', 'I can't be bothered', 'My mother wouldn't like . . .', 'It's different for me', 'It can't be true', 'It can't be that simple'

9 Mental Statements (MS)

> MENTAL STATEMENTS (MS):
>
> - Thoughts that embody what we think is 'the truth'
> - 'What the truth is; the ideas of life that I "know" to be true'

Mental Statements are often what one's parents or other relations used to say which you have then decided to think. They keep you in your Mind Erosion and keep you living the way you have till now.

Examples

'Happiness is not for me', 'There has to be a way', 'Happiness is fleeting', 'Joy is not for me', 'I'll never make it', 'My life is fucked', 'It's too good to be true', 'Happiness doesn't last', 'Life is not for me', 'Life has past me by', 'There's no logic'

Popular sayings can also become our MS: 'There will be tears before bedtime', 'It takes two to tango', 'Once bitten twice shy', 'The first cut is the deepest', 'Don't count your chickens before they've hatched', 'No pain, no gain', 'If it doesn't kill me, it will make me stronger'.

10 Guidelines (GL)

> GUIDELINES (GL):
>
> - What I need or do not need to do to achieve my happiness
> - Only through achieving certain objectives do I think I can reach my happiness

An example of a Guideline is the thought 'Rich people are happy'. If I have this thought, then once I have achieved being rich, happiness comes as a prize or reward. Let's see this working with another GL. If I have the thought that 'Strong people are admired', then if I achieve being strong, I think being admired comes as a prize or reward, without me doing anything to achieve it.

There are two types of GLs, Forbidding and Encouraging. I might have the thought that successful people are lonely. If I want to be lonely, then this GL would be an encouraging one, that is I would want to become successful so that I can achieve loneliness. If however I wanted to belong, then this GL would be a forbidding one in my head, that is I would not want to become successful as then, according to my thinking, I would become lonely.

Examples

Encouraging GLs: a person with this thought will want to achieve the first part of the GL, so as to achieve the second part of it:

> 'Failures belong', 'Sex-slaves are appreciated', 'Impressive people can't be suspected of having no life', 'People who waste their lives belong', 'Stupid little girls are fuckable', 'Crying people are fuckable'

Forbidding GLs: a person with this thought will not want to achieve the first part of the guideline for fear of achieving the second part:

> 'Successful people are lonely', 'Conscientious people are wankers', 'Rich people are bastards (then if one becomes rich by accident, one will either think one is a bastard, and therefore soon become one, or want to get rid of the money very quickly so as not to be one)'

GLs are sometimes broken down into longer chains of constituent parts because:

- It can help to walk through the thinking from the first part to the second part of the GL
- You may see different elements of the chain at different points in the script
- This can give the actor more pictures to contemplate when creating their character.

For example, the GL 'Abused people take revenge' may be broken into the following chain:

> Abused people suffer → People who suffer have no responsibilities (to have a life) → People who have no responsibilities are helpless → Helpless people are burdens → Burdens can make other people fail → People who make others fail can take revenge.

Here are a couple more examples of these chains:

> People who provoke anger get rejected → People who get rejected are left in peace → People who are left in peace can stay faithful (i.e. belong forever with their PiCs).

> Admired people are envied → Envied people are special → Special people are undiscovered (for thinking they are inferior or for having no lives).

11 Objectives (O)

OBJECTIVES (O):
• What I want to achieve by the time the circumstances have changed
• What I think will make me happy within the circumstances and help me to achieve my Longer-Term Purpose(s)

Stable, overlayable and interruptible pictures and impressions. See discussion of Medium-term Purposes/Objectives in Chapter 4 on Purposes.

Examples

'I want to be desired', and so on: see discussion in Chapter 4, and examples of Purposes in Appendix 1.

12 Purposes (P)

PURPOSES (P): What I want to achieve in the future, that is (far) beyond the circumstances or well after the circumstances have changed
    Or simply,
    What I think will make me happy in the future

Blurred pictures and impressions, when analysed, are found to be made up of clear pictures. (See discussion of Long-term Purposes in Chapter 4.)

Examples

'Happiness is staying faithful', '. . . belonging', '. . . having no life', '. . . taking revenge', '. . . wasting other people's lives', '. . . making others fail'

13 Self Events (SE)

SELF EVENTS (SE)

- What I am
- What I think I am
- I am the result of Conditioning and Self-Conditioning

Whatever we are is the result of our thoughts, and since we all think what we want to think for the unaware mind, we define Self Events as being, 'What I think I am', and for the aware mind, we define SE as being 'I am what I wanted to be', that is all the thoughts I have had about myself up until now. For example, if I choose to think I am inferior, after thinking it enough times I will eventually be inferior: this will be the result I wanted to achieve from choosing to think this thought.

Below are some of the thoughts which students have had about themselves and an explanation of how they acquired these thoughts.

'I am shit': When people think they have no life, that they are inferior, have failed, that they are deprived of happiness, of course they think, 'Why should others have happiness?' This is how the Purposes of wanting others to suffer, fail and take revenge are programmed. We start thinking these thoughts, but every time we do, our NFR knows that this is not right and we end up with the thought, 'I am shit'.

What is the effect of this thought on people's lives? For most this is a ShE because wanting others to fail is socially unacceptable. It is likely that those we want to fail the most are our friends and family, because the thought of them having a life while we fail is unbearable. Therefore people invariably try to cover this thought up and want to be seen as liberal, kind-hearted, warm, generous, caring and so on, and often choose professions which will assist with this cover.

Examples

'I am stupid', '. . . a victim', '. . . unloved', '. . . abused' '. . . a man' (for women), '. . . a woman' (for men), '. . . filth', '. . . numb', '. . . vicious', '. . . devious', '. . . a waste', '. . . a sex-slave', '. . . a clown', '. . . desperate', '. . . immature', '. . . a little boy', '. . . a little girl', '. . . a stupid cunt', '. . . inferior', '. . . an evil genius', '. . . Jesus', '. . . my mother's keeper', '. . . God', '. . . guilty', '. . . lonely', '. . . a failure', '. . . a dick', '. . . victim of circumstances', '. . . abandoned', '. . . an asshole', '. . . trash', '. . . a killjoy', '. . . OK', '. . . capable', 'I have no life'

14 Super-Purpose (SP)

> SUPER-PURPOSE (SP): My main Purpose in life

To find the Super-Purpose for a character, you need to answer the question, 'What is his or her main Purpose in life?' Another way of approaching this is to imagine the character being close to his or her death: 'What thoughts does the character want to have at the end of their life?'. These thoughts should give you a clear idea of what the character's SP has been throughout their life.

15 Germ (G)

GERM (G): My main Self Event

As you may remember, we all have many SEs, as do the characters. Therefore to find the Germ of a character, you need to ask yourself, 'Which is the most powerful of the SEs in the character's consciousness?' and 'Which appears to get activated the most?' The G often appears more visible than the other SEs and may 'obviously' leap out at you when you think about the character.

It is important that the G and the SP are reflected in the script, that is don't select them based on information that we don't see acted out. It is also very important that the SP and G sit together logically. For example if the SP is 'Happiness is always having a fulfilled life' then the G can't be 'I'm deprived'. A better G here would be 'I'm OK' or 'I'm capable'. The SP 'Happiness is always having a lonely life' would work better with 'I'm deprived' and will create a totality of the character's thinking.

The SP and G are very important elements for you to find for your character as they are the anchors of the character's consciousness, and all the other elements of the Mindprint need to fit logically with them.

Some examples of Mindprints

Here are some example Mindprints of characters you may know.

Masha

From *Three Sisters* by Anton Chekhov
UC – In bed with Daddy (with despair of wasted life)
ShE – I am my father's
SxE – Sex is frustrating
LE – Life is frustrating (to the extent that I am ready to blow), disappointing, a waste, long (because very few Events in life)
PE – People don't care, are disappointing
    ME – Men are disappointing, weak, stupid, don't fuck, are titillating
    WE – Women belong, are stupid cunts, are competition
Gh – I can't have a life, I can't be happy
AD – I must be strange (so I can't be suspected of not having a life), I must sulk

Adj – One day we will all be dead anyway (it's all just trivia)

MS – Sex is not for me

GL – Frustrated women have no responsibilities. Women who have no responsibilities make people suffer. Married women can't be suspected of belonging with their father. Sisters belong. People who don't know how to think belong. Women who have no lives have no responsibilities

O – I want to . . . be frustrated, strange, disappointed, I want to be a burden, provoke interest, I want to be needed

P – Happiness is . . . being centre of attention, suffering, being a burden, wanting to be needed

SE – I am a sulking little girl, I am frustrated, abandoned, stupid (I'm wasting my life here; I am intelligent, but I'm fucking my life up)

SP – Happiness is always being disappointed

G – I am deprived

Orsino

From *Twelfth Night* by William Shakespeare

UC – In bed with my mother

ShE – I am a woman, man (My mother is a man)

SxE – Sex is dirty

LE – Life is confusing, a waste, lonely, boring, frustrating, not for me, soft, suffering

PE – People are confusing, inferior, superior, have lives, refined

    ME – Men are women, confusing, filthy

    WE – Women are hard to get, clean, frightening, superior, confusing, inferior

Gh – I can't have a life

AD – I mustn't see my thinking

Adj – It's all pointless anyway

MS – Sex is not for me

GL – Lonely people are special. Special people are special to themselves. People who are special to themselves have wasted lives

O – I want to . . . belong, have it over and done with, suffer, be appreciated, be frustrated, be confused, be special to myself

P – Happiness is . . . belonging, having a lonely life (in Events), being powerful, humiliated, superior (in Events), having no responsibility, being secure

SE – I am stupid, thick, confused, lonely, special, a woman, shit

SP – Happiness is dying having survived

G – I am filth

Teach

From *American Buffalo* by David Mamet

UC – Alone in my room listening to parents fucking

ShE – I am a piece of shit

SxE – Frightening, unbearable

LE – Life is . . . shit, lonely, unfair, humiliating, unobtainable, hard, vicious, frustrating, frightening, complicated

PE – People . . . don't care, have lives, vicious, make me fail, superior, fakes, cunts, stupid

ME – Secure, competition

WE – Frightening, whores, unattainable, humiliating

Gh – I can't have a life, I can't belong, I can't think, I can't be a man

AD – I must be frustrated, I must lose myself

Adj – It's all fucked up anyway

MS – It's kick ass or kiss ass

GL – Stressed people can't think, rejected people are secure, burdens are rejected / have no responsibilities / make others fail, people who lose themselves don't suffer, aggressive people are impressive / left in peace / can't be suspected of being lost

O – I want to . . . impress, exciting life, rejected, stupid, lose myself, frustrated

P – Happiness is . . . being humiliated, failing, having no life, no responsibilities, hard life

SE – Loser, rejected, stupid cunt, lonely, coward, pathetic, abused, confused, deprived, fuck-not

SP – Happiness is always being a burden

G – I am lost

SEVEN

ACTIONS

I have always thought the actions of men the best interpreters of their thoughts.

John Locke (1632–1704), Philosopher[1]

What is the medium of an Artist? How do they get their audience to see what they want them to see?

Writers use words as their medium; their choice of words put the pictures from their heads into the heads of their readers.

A musician uses sounds and silences.

A painter uses shapes and colours.

An actor's medium is the Actions they use; pictures from the designed Mindprint of the character are conveyed to the minds of the audience via the Actions used in the context of the character's life.

It has to be made clear that we are not talking about physical actions but mental Actions. Physical Actions come only as a result of mental Actions; if you stroke a dog it is because you have the mental Action, 'I care' or 'I enjoy'.

In John Locke's quote, he is most likely referring to physical Actions but I believe it is mental Actions that are the best interpreters of thoughts. Actions are more important than words. Words are just words, whereas Actions are the truth behind the words.

When a character says, 'I love you', it can mean many different things depending on the Action behind it. When a lover is feeling uncertain or insecure in a relationship, the words 'I love you' may come with the Action, 'I reassure'. In a different scenario, if one partner is controlling, they may say these words to 'provoke guilt' in order to manipulate the other. Or if one of the lovers knows they are about to be dumped, the words 'I love you' may be said with the Action, 'I plead'.

Are you getting a sense of what Actions are?

Simply put, you might regret or despair when something bad happens, and perhaps enjoy or take pride when something good happens. Or to put it another way, you have an Action, 'I regret' or 'I despair' when something bad happens, and an Action 'I enjoy' or 'I take pride' when something good happens.

At some point in our very distant past, language didn't exist but we still had to attack, love, warn, encourage etc. For millions of years there were no words; Actions were the only way to communicate. Even now that we have words, Actions are still the main way we communicate. When someone is unhappy we can tell without them having to say so.

We can tell that we can't trust someone even though they say we can.

Someone apologizes and we know they don't mean it, no matter how they express it.

What does it mean to know someone well?

It is to know what someone is going to do in hypothetical circumstances.

How do we understand this?

By their Actions.

Why not behaviour?

Because two people can physically behave the same way or use the same words and get different reActions.

For example, two people tell the same joke; one with the Action 'I entertain' and the other 'I doubt' or even 'I humiliate myself'.

Can you see that what you think about somebody depends largely on the Actions they use? This means that what the audience thinks about your character will depend on the Actions that your character uses.

What dictates the Actions we have?

Why have an Action if it isn't to achieve something? What would be the point?

Everything we do in life is to achieve Purposes; nothing more evidently than our use of Actions. If I want to be admired I would probably have the Action, 'I impress' or if I want to superior I'm likely to have the Action 'I condescend'.

This brings us to the simple definition:

ACTION: What I do to achieve my Purpose

Where,

ACTIONS: The relationship between oneself and the object of
Attention

Actions are therefore expressed as 'I' followed by a verb. For example,
'I regret', 'I guide', 'I demand obedience', 'I jump for joy', 'I encourage',
'I pity myself', 'I gloat', 'I panic', 'I lose myself', 'I impress', 'I revel', 'I long
for', 'I dread'.

Qualities of Actions

Actions have a direction in space

Let's imagine I am talking to you now, but I am thinking about having
left the gas lit on the cooker this morning after having made my breakfast.
So our conversation carries on and my mind is going to my kitchen, or
possibly my apartment being on fire. As a result everything that I am
talking to you about is nonsensical because the pictures in my mind do
not match up with what we are talking about. Instead they are directed
elsewhere – my Actions are directed to a different space.

Actions have a direction in time

Notice with the above example that not only would my Actions have been
directed to a different space, but also if I was talking to you while retracing
my moves after I had finished cooking, to see if I could remember switch-
ing the gas off, then my Actions are being directed to the past – to a
different time.

A simple exercise is to think about your next meal.

Think about looking forward to your next meal.

. . .

. . .

You have just held the Action 'I look forward' and it was directed
towards the future.

Now think about telling off your partner yesterday and with hindsight
realizing you were in the wrong.

. . .

. . .

You have just held the Action, 'I regret' and it was directed towards the past.

Think about the following and see what you notice:

- Your first day at school
- Your cousin's farm in Ireland
- A recently discovered planet

Actions have varying degrees of strength

Think about your Action as you are reading this book.

It's probably a gentle 'I contemplate'.

Now imagine being mugged and what the intensity of your Action 'I panic' would be like.

. . .

. . .

The strength of the Action relates to the thinking effort and physical manifestation (moving your eyes and turning a page, compared to physically defending yourself and screaming for help) that we put in to carrying out our Actions. This in turn relates to the obstacle we have in our heads; a read page compared to a six-foot tall, threatening mugger.

The strength of an Action tells you a lot about the thinking behind it.

The stronger the Action, the stronger the thought(s).

Basic and Main Actions

In life we can have many different Actions in any given space of time; these are called Basic Actions. Let's say you're told you can't do something, you might have a Basic Action, 'I regret' but then straightaway think of an alternative which comes with 'I enjoy' and then 'I take pride'.

In Act Two of David Mamet's *American Buffalo*, Teach says 'Shhh' because he thinks Bobby can be overheard telling him some information. In that short space of time (literally the time taken to say 'Shhh') Don has three Basic Actions:

- 'I stop' (because he's too loud)
- 'I apologize' (for having to shut him up)
- 'I encourage' (for him to continue)

Notice, there are easily three different Basic Actions in less than three seconds.

We also have Actions which last for longer periods called Main Actions; these are there to achieve our Objectives. For instance, if you were talking to your bank manager looking for a loan, your Main Action might be, 'I do my best'. If however you were talking about something they did wrong, your Main Action might be 'I complain'.

This Main Action would be held for as long as you held your Objective and would change as soon as your Objective did. Within this period of time you would have many Basic Actions. For example, when looking for a loan you might at one point 'impress' or another time 'ingratiate' but always in the context of the Main Action.

If this is true in life, then it must be true for characters.

Devices

You must at some time have said 'Yes' when you meant 'No' and vice versa.

Why is this?

Consider this story:

Many years ago John and Harry knew each other well and then by coincidence they recently meet at a seminar and have the opportunity to spend some time together. At the end of the seminar they are about to part company and Harry says, 'We should catch up again some time' and John answers 'Yes'.

Although John said, 'Yes', he thought they no longer had anything in common and wasn't sure he would enjoy Harry's company that much. So John said, 'Yes' but really he knew he wasn't going to meet up with Harry again.

I'm guessing a similar experience has happened to you at some time.

If so, like John you will have used a Device.

Devices are used to cover up our Actions. John's Action was really 'I reject' but he covered it up with the Device, 'I look forward'.

We do this because we want people to think that we have different thoughts from those which we have, often because of social etiquette or to ingratiate ourselves.

If an Action is what I do (or mean), then a Device is what I want people to think I do (or mean):

DEVICES: What I want others to think I do

Where Actions have varying strengths, Devices have varying transparencies, which alter how well you can see through them.

You may have experienced the situation where two people are talking about something that's very personal to one of them and as they are chatting a third person joins the conversation. The first two don't want to share the subject of their conversation with the third, but at the same time want to be polite. The third person thinks they are welcome whereas in fact there is a lot going on behind opaque Devices.

Figure 7.1 illustrates (1) an Action, (2) a Device, (3) and (4) a Device covering an Action with varying success. In (3) the Device is very opaque; you can hardly see the Action at all. Whereas in (4) the Device is much more transparent, and you can still clearly see the Action.

In the example with John, he would have wanted to avoid an uncomfortable moment but also did not want Harry to call him up. He might therefore not only have made his Device opaque so that Harry felt OK at

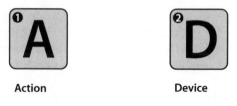

Action   Device

A near perfect Device   A see through Device

Figure 7.1 Device transparency

Device   **Magnified Device**

Figure 7.2 Magnified Device – sarcasm

the time, but also have made it transparent enough for there to be background noise which would have put Harry off calling him up.

Back to the two people chatting when the third person joins them. On occasions like this the people trying to cover up can go too far and their behaviour seems illogical or over the top, leaving the third person uncomfortable and confused. In these situations we can say their Devices are magnified.

There are also situations where one magnifies the Device deliberately.

> Laura has a new-born baby and her best friend Mia calls her up. After greeting each other, Mia asks, 'So how did you sleep last night?'
> Laura replies, 'Like a dream'.

If Laura is telling Mia exactly how it was, because her husband was able to attend to the baby all night, then her Action would have been a straightforward 'I share' or 'I belong'.

If in fact Laura was feeding the baby, changing nappies and unable to get back to sleep, this response would have probably been sarcastic. She would have expressed it in a slightly over-the-top way using the magnified Device, 'I enjoy' – as in Figure 7.2. Her Action underneath would depend on their relationship and could have been, 'I suffer' or 'I provoke sympathy' or even, 'I provoke guilt'.

Main Actions and acting

As we've seen, we can have several different Basic Actions in a short space of time. When we analyse a script, deciding upon each one would be a long process and not always expedient for the average rehearsal time (although this work can be done after the play has opened). Therefore in rehearsals we work with Main Actions.

When you read a scene you get an impression of the Basic Actions used in the scene and with a little consideration, these Basic Actions can be summarized as one Main Action. For instance in a scene character X, a teacher, might want a child to realize they had done something wrong and uses the Action 'I tell off' but also at times the Action 'I reassure' (that everything will be OK) and perhaps at times 'I find out' (that they've understood). The main Action for character X in this scene could be, 'I seek reassurance' (that they've understood they can't do that again). Can you see if you hold the Action 'I seek reassurance' in this context it allows for the other Basic Actions to be there, giving rise to both aggressive and caring Actions.

One of the advantages with using a Main Action is that it not only allows the actor to have a simple point of reference for the scene but also gives them freedom to bring in Basic Actions as they see fit.

Acting and the state of mind

Acting can be said to be a series of thoughts held by the actor over the course of the play. Therefore in any rehearsal probably the most common question an actor will ask is, 'What am I thinking here?'

It seems we all hold particular states of mind for varying periods of time. For example, a young man out on the town on a Saturday night will have a constant state of mind for most of the evening, probably changing only once he's had a successful sexual encounter or realized his wallet has been stolen.

How do we define a state of mind?

This is where the OPAE (pronounced as the individual letters 'O', 'P', 'A', 'E'), which stands for Objective, Purpose, Action and Event, is a fundamental tool. It establishes the state of mind of a character in any given Episode.

Episodes, in a similar way to Stanislavski's 'Units' or 'Bits', are periods of time when the character's state of mind remains the same.[2] Episodes can last many pages or be as short as one line. A change in episodes will depend on whether the character's thinking changes in any way. This can happen at any time but most occur when one or more characters enter or exit (changing the balance of relationships).

EPISODES: Discrete units of time within a script where all the characters' Objectives, Purposes, Main Actions and Events stay the same

A change in Episode usually happens when a character exits or enters or when something is said or done which changes at least one of the characters' thinking

In any Episode, an Event will have taken place which will have caused a character's state of mind (their Main Event).

Where,

MAIN EVENT: What intensifies my thinking in particular circumstances

This Main Event will direct what they want to achieve (Objective and Purpose) for which they must have a way of achieving it (Action). These four elements pin down the state of mind of a character for a given period of time (Figure 7.3).

Objective	what the character wants to achieve in the context
Purpose	their Long-term Purpose
Action	their Main Action, i.e. what they do to achieve their purpose
Event	their Main Event

Think of the analogy of a piece of paper floating unpredictably in the air. The paper is a character's state of mind and you as the actor (with the director) are responsible for allowing the audience to see what is on that piece of paper. If the acting of a character has no design and is just floating

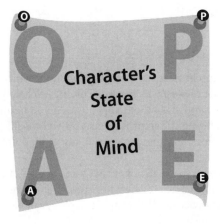

Figure 7.3 Pinning down the actor's state of mind

around there is no enjoyment for the audience, they become bored or dissatisfied.

Imagine the O, P, A and E as four corner pins that establish the design, that is 'pin down' the state of mind of a character in any given Episode. Then each Episode adds to the totality and therefore the beauty of the script. To get you used to what these look like here are the OPAEs of the three characters in *American Buffalo* in the Episode referred to earlier: Don's OPAE:

O: I want to be stupid
P: Happiness is always failing
A: I lose myself
E: Our belonging (Don and Bobby)

Teach's OPAE:

O: I want to suffer
P: Happiness is always being deprived
A: I revel
E: People have lives

Bobby's OPAE:

O: I want to be lucky
P: Happiness is surviving
A: I jump in
E: Coming down (from his last hit)

List of Actions

Appendix 2 contains a comprehensive list of over 200 Actions which in my experience are those that are most widely used. This list will help you start identifying Actions that you and other people use. As you become more accustomed to recognizing different Actions you will be able to identify the appropriate Action for your character at any given point in the script.

The more you refer to the list, you will notice that some of the Actions can be grouped with others which share characteristics. The Actions, 'I brush off', 'I attack', 'I stand my ground', 'I whip', 'I slap' . . . can be seen as different degrees of the same Actions.

Similarly, 'I retreat', 'I shrink' and 'I run away'.

Or, 'I pass time', 'I bide my time' and 'I kill time'.

It is the difference in each of these Action's Tempo-rhythms (which we will come to) which warrants them having their own place on the list.

In your spare time go through the list and visualize (in Active Imagination) the pictures and impressions which accompany each Action, to get a greater understanding of them. For example, with the Action, 'I stand my ground', I see myself in Active Imagination standing in front of a patch of ground, which is mine. I am expecting to be pushed back into it and am prepared to withstand the push, not to attack or hit out, but to endure and resist.

When you go through this process, check that the images you are working with are as clean as possible and not influenced from thoughts from your own personal life.

Working on the list of Actions, to which you will probably be able to add many more, is developing the acting technique to perfection. With time you will notice a fascinating and very enjoyable experience – by naming an Action you will quickly activate it in your mind, for example you will say 'I shrink' and almost immediately a quick flash of the picture 'I shrink' is activated.

This is enough to be considering for now.

I will explain in detail how OPAEs are programmed in Chapter 14.

EIGHT

FINISHING-OFF THINKING

> Patterns of consciousness are always known by pure awareness, their ultimate unchanging witness
>
> Patañjali (exact dates unknown; fourth century BCE or sixth century CE), compiler of the Yoga Sutras[1]

If you have been reading the chapters consecutively, you will already have come across the term 'Unfinished Thinking'. Perhaps you have been able to build up an impression of what it means. It shrinks your CVT (Chapter 2), keeps you in the Dissipation of an Event and leaves you with mental 'background noise' (Chapter 3).

Let's start with the definition and an example to detail the impression you already have.

UNFINISHED THINKING: Thoughts interrupted by fear

What does this mean?
Let's see with an example.

Lucy, a student of mine, told me that as a child she would often go to her mother and say, 'Mummy, can I . . .?' and before she got any further with her question, her mother would say, 'Oh, for Christ's sake, not now Lucy! Can't you see I'm busy?' Lucy saw that her mother wasn't that busy and immediately thought, 'My mother doesn't love me', 'Women don't care', 'I can't be loved' and 'I'm worthless'. Simultaneously with thinking these thoughts, she felt fear. These thoughts were very frightening and unbearable to think, especially for a child.

Why?

Because innately little Lucy knew that she needed her parents (or guardians) to bring her up and show her how to live. The fear was that if this is what Mummy is doing to me at the early age of three or four, then I will never be able to grow up knowing how to live. This was such a frightening thought that she decided not to think about it, so she forced herself to stop thinking it and decided to lose herself in thinking or doing something else.

The trouble is when you lose yourself from a thought, it doesn't disappear, it stays in your head, unfinished. Floating around, it becomes a Ghoul which then becomes a Ghost – remember from Chapter 6 on Mindprint?

GHOST: The word given to the mental impression of a recurring fear that has the Purpose of maintaining an unawarely favoured pattern of thinking

---

The thing is that this was not an isolated incident for Lucy, her mother would often react this way. And so did her father – in a similar way. The result?

(1a) Not only do her thoughts 'My mother/father doesn't love me', 'Men/women don't care', 'I can't be loved' and 'I'm worthless' get thought more and more, creating a Mind Erosion for these thoughts.

(1b) But also she has created a Complex of creating thoughts that are interrupted by fear – she has a Mind Erosion of creating Unfinished Thinking.

The result of (1a) is that Lucy grows up with, 'My mother doesn't love me' or 'I am worthless' taking up a large proportion of her thinking capacity. This is background noise in her head which prevents her from thinking thoughts that would help her live a happy and fulfilled life. Her CVT is shrunk.

How this manifested can be seen in a simple example from Lucy's adult life. Lucy once interviewed for a number of jobs over a period of weeks, jobs that Lucy was more than adequately qualified for. She didn't get any of them and at the time couldn't understand why. Looking back she could see that throughout her preparation for each interview and during the interviews themselves she was thinking, 'I am worthless'.

The background noise took over.

In terms of acting this means that when she needs to play a character who has a Mind Erosion of, 'Being admired', she has great difficulty. It's difficult to hold the thoughts of 'Being admired' while you think 'I am worthless'.

Try it.

Now to (1b):

Lucy now has a Mind Erosion of creating Unfinished Thoughts. She is used to interrupting thoughts with fear before they get thought through to the end.

Let's take a step back. Little Lucy went to ask Mummy a question, Mummy angrily replied, Lucy got scared of the implications of her thoughts and lost herself from these thoughts. Lucy's mother didn't explain why she reacted the way she had, nor did little Lucy know how to find out why her mother had. All she came away with was being fearfully stuck at thinking, 'I am worthless'. With that curtailed thought came a distortion in how she saw reality. Rather than thinking, I am who 'I' am, 'I' had now become worthless. The more this happened, the more the components of the Mushroom capsule precipitated in to the respective piles of thoughts, and Lucy started to change the way she saw herself and the world based on her Unfinished Thinking.

Distorted.

You see the more Unfinished Thoughts we have, the more fear we have and the more fear we have, the more rigid our consciousnesses are with this distorted vision. With time not only is it much harder to think any other thoughts, but also we are seeing the world not as it is, but as we are. To summarize the words of the Roman philosopher Marcus Aurelius, 'A man's life is what his thoughts make of it'.[2]

This is why we have this chapter on Finishing-off Thinking (abbreviated to Foffting) to provide you with tools to find your Unfinished Thoughts and finish them off, to help you become more aware and increase the agility of your consciousness.

ACTING (quality): The quality of acting is in inverse proportion to unfinished thinking

Meaning that the more Finished-off Thoughts you have, the less fear you have and the greater your ability to think the thoughts of your character without background noise interrupting you.

FINISHING-OFF THINKING: Taking thoughts beyond the point where they were interrupted by fear

---

Questions for Finishing-off Thinking

Every Unfinished Thought is like a brass spring in a clock.

If we have a lot of Unfinished Thoughts, we have a head full of these things and you cannot separate them.

Next I am going to show you how to take out an Unfinished Thought and with your finger, unroll it so that you can see all of it and finish it off. If you take your finger off one end of the coil, which you may do, it will roll up again. So you unroll it again and then when you take off your finger it rolls up again, but this time that bit looser than it ever has been – and so you carry on this process until the wire is rolled out and stays that way when you take your finger away (Figure 8.1).

Below are some questions and further tools which will help you to identify Unfinished Thoughts and finish them off.

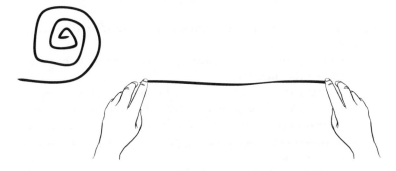

Figure 8.1 The brass coil of Finishing-off Thinking

Finishing-off Thinking Questions

The following questions help to identify and Finish-off Unfinished Thinking:

1 What am I thinking about now? What is bothering me?
2 What other thoughts are in my head at the same time?
3 Why are they there together at the same time?

  • What is the relationship between them? If they are together, they are part of the same Complex
  • What are the Mushrooms and larger Mindprints of these thoughts? How were they formed?
  • What are the other thoughts if these are the visible ones?

4 What am I avoiding thinking about? Which physical tensions do I have with these thoughts?
5 What pay-off am I expecting by thinking these thoughts?
6 How have these thoughts affected my life until now?
7 What made me see my thoughts?
8 How will all these thoughts affect my life if I continue to think them?
9 What is the most cringey or funny explanation for these thoughts?
10 What would be a better explanation?

  • What if my explanation is just a visible thought?

11 What was my real Purpose – what if what I've achieved is what I wanted to achieve?
12 What do I hate or like (for a cover up) most in the visible behaviour of my parents or other people?
13 What general expressions do I remember best? (Examples: Clean as you go; No gain without pain; The grass is always greener on the other side; You made your bed, now lie in it; I can't hear myself think; Don't let the cat out of the bag (keep Shame Event)). Remember these are just expressions.
14 How does this thought link to my Emerging Awareness?
15 What are my fears?
16 What are my most shameful thoughts? (What do I least want people to know about me, i.e. what are my Shame Events?)
17 What Devices do I use to cover up my thoughts?
18 What do I repeatedly think?

19 What will happen if I achieve my Purpose?
   • What will happen if I don't achieve my Purpose?

20 What is so frightening about being free?
21 If I continue doing what I'm doing, what will become of me?
22 What do I use my sulk for? What are the inputs into my sulk?
23 What is the best and the worst that might happen to me through thinking this thought?

Going Limp

In Chapter 3 on Events I loosely defined 'Going Limp' as 'relaxing on a thought'. Now I'd like to give you the precise definition and explain how I came to it so that you can fully understand how it works.

> GOING LIMP: Allowing the thought to be there without repressing it.
> Where allowing yourself to be possessed by the thought, without struggling to get rid of it, will leave enough free thinking to watch it in action (seeing is undoing)

One evening in 1993 I was watching a play and at one point during the performance there was an actor on stage singing. While he was singing I realized there was something in his sound that made me want to think about him and I knew if I put some effort into thinking about his thoughts, I would know what he was thinking. But for some reason I didn't want to.

During the interval this Event was still on my mind. And then the penny dropped. Have you ever noticed when some aspect about someone else sticks in your head and you can't understand why and then you realise that that very thing is something you have in common with them?

During that interval I realized the actor had the thought, 'Life is hard' and the reason it stuck in my head was because I had the same thought. And for the first time I saw it was one of the most important thoughts in my head. I then sighed. Straightaway I noticed it was the same sigh that all my family had . . . which seemed to reflect the thought 'Life is hard'.

Later that evening, arriving home, I remembered being back in the Soviet Union and regularly hearing on the radio that the future comprised a twenty years' struggle and then everything would settle. Life will be hard but then everything will be OK. This was another input into this important thought that was in my head.

Then my mind for some reason went through all the fairy tales that I knew. They were all about life being hard and then everything coming good in the end. These were more inputs into my 'Life is hard'. Soviet imagery of tough muscular fighters and ardent workers had also added to my impression that 'Life is hard'. Over the years without me noticing it I had gone from casually walking the 'Life is hard' path to ending up in a very deep 'Life is hard' ditch. All the above inputs had strengthened this thought, which had now become so important to me. When I saw the actor that evening, a brass coil had popped into my hand and there I was rolling it out to see what it comprised of.

The second evening after the performance, I looked at my face in the bathroom mirror and I could see manifestations of this thought. My face looked heavy-set and of course my beard added to this (two weeks later I shaved off my beard of twenty years). I saw that my face was heavy with the thought 'Life is hard'. But what was I supposed to do with this thought? It felt like there was nothing I could do. At the same time the thought was so heavy that it felt as though I was on the floor being kicked, but still there was nothing I could do. All I could do was wait and see what was going to happen. That was my first feeling of what Going Limp was; the impression of lying still on that floor and not putting up any resistance whatsoever. Only then did the stress begin to fade. The following day I noticed there was a huge void in my head. I had taken out 'Life is hard' and there was nothing to fill it – so much of my thinking did it take up. I remember my students telling me about this void when they had Finished-off Thinking.

Another image that I have since found helpful with Going Limp came to me when I went for a walk on a hot day and wanted to go for a dip in a river. But at the point where I wanted to enter the water, there was an old door very slowly floating past, meaning that before I could get in, I had to wait. There was no need to get stressed, frustrated or annoyed, just to calmly allow the current to move the door in its own time past the point where I wanted to get into the water. Again this was Going Limp. This image is far removed from the image above of lying on a floor being kicked, to one of 'Life is a joy', and every now and then when anything unpleasant comes into my life, if I know if there is nothing I can do, all I do is wait for it to pass.

How do we use 'Going Limp'?

When I know I have a thought that is not good for me, I know I need to Go Limp. For example I know when I have the Purpose, 'I want to be frustrated' or I can see that Purpose coming, I know I have to Go Limp.

In preparation, before a situation that I know will make me feel frustrated, I bring up the impression of 'I want to be frustrated' and that's when I Go Limp. This way I do not have to deal with it within the circumstances – which would be too late because then I am already in the ditch. By having prepared beforehand, once I am in the situation, Going Limp is much easier.

Condescending rejection

This tool goes hand in hand with Going Limp.

To condescendingly reject a thought is to follow an unwanted thought with a visible thought, such as, 'I can see you are a thought in my head but I don't want you'.

You can literally speak the words in your head. This allows you to sit out of the ditch of that Mind Erosion, see what you really think and therefore weaken the unwanted thought (Figure 8.2).

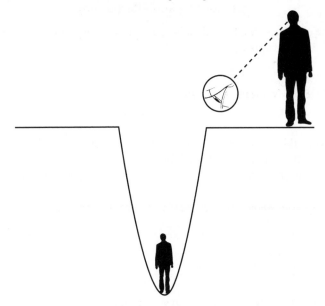

Figure 8.2 Sitting out of the ditch

To keep yourself out of ditches every so often, ask yourself, 'What am I thinking about now?' and see what thoughts you catch yourself thinking.

I want to want . . .

Let's say you want to stop buying a chocolate bar every day as you travel home from class, which you have been doing for the last few months. If you look towards the end of the day with the uncertainty of whether or not you will be able to walk past the confectioners without going in, by the time you get to the confectioners you will be suffering, your head may be in some turmoil and to relieve yourself from these feelings, you go in and buy a bar of chocolate.

However, if mid-morning you think about the confectioners and think, 'When I get to the confectioners, I want to want to keep walking straight past'. And if again an hour later you think the same thought, 'I want now to want to keep walking past . . .'. Then, when you get to the confectioners, your brain will say, 'It's time to keep walking past'. This is an important stage in Finishing-off Thinking.

Foreburning and Afterburning

In the above tool we have already touched on an aspect of Foreburning to Finish-off Thinking:

FOREBURN: Aware Anticipation

When this Event happens within certain circumstances I know I have a certain thought that is not good for me. To overcome this, when I arrive into these circumstances I should Go Limp or choose to do something else.

What you will also find useful is to Afterburn after the Event:

AFTERBURN: Aware Dissipation

Here you see what happened to your thoughts.
Did I walk past the confectioners? What helped me? Did I have clear

pictures when I Foreburned. Or did I go into the shop after all? What was it that allowed my thoughts to run away with me?

You retrace the train of thought.

Further tools for Finishing-off Thinking

1 What would I think if I were to see others thinking my thoughts? This is a good question to ask yourself to help you see what you think about having the thoughts you have.
2 Doing Mushrooms for your thoughts and behaviour helps to Finish-off Thinking. Students often find that after doing a Mushroom and analysing the OPAEs, there is a quietness in their head where there was once noise.
3 Taking thoughts to the extreme, for example what will happen, in twenty years' time if I keep thinking as I think now?
4 If I were to die tomorrow, would I regret having this thought? If the answer is 'Yes', it needs Finishing-off.
5 Make decisions. Unless you make decisions, you don't know what you think.
6 Put yourself into the position of no return. Make yourself do what you've decided is right. Don't leave things unresolved.
7 I did my best and then whatever happens happens.
8 Every hopeless situation has at least two solutions.
9 We'll cross the bridge when we reach it – ensure that you don't interpret this as 'I'll lose myself until it hits me on the head', but as in 'I'll sort out things that need to be sorted out first'.
10 There never was a time that something wasn't afterwards.
11 Tomorrow, today will be yesterday – this also helps to get out of the 'now' box.
12 Whenever you trip over and fall, do not get up until you pick up something, that is learn from your mistakes.
13 After doing a good deed, don't expect gratitude or you'll suffer from ingratitude (I want to be appreciated).
14 The fear of seeing the thought is always worse than the thought itself.
15 Aware watching is undoing.
16 If your past is still important to you, it means you haven't Finished-off Thinking certain thoughts or memories.

As you Fofft you will have to be very honest with yourself and acknowledge that this is an ongoing process but understand that wherever you are in that process is where you need to be at that time. You won't be able to run before you can walk, yet the more you walk the easier you will find it and before you know it you will be running without even noticing the change.

By regularly Foffting you will acquire the freedom and ease to deal with any situation, not only in your personal life but also in your professional life as an actor.

Getting 'there' (in any field of excellence) does sometimes involve upset, frustration or confusion but as long as you consider every step as part of a process which is always adding the quality of your life, there is never a reason to give up on what you want and where you want to go.

Here is a metaphor to reassure and remind you that the process is worth it.

People who have Unfinished Thinking live in houses like the one in Figure 8.3(a). Their reality is what they think it is, rather than what it is. They really think and believe that (for example), 'Life is hard', they are 'lonely', that 'Women don't care', 'Men are competition', 'People are out to get them'.

When you start Finishing-off your thinking, you start putting the house the right way up. Life becomes what it is. Every day is different, bringing new experiences. You are who you are and can be whoever you want to be. People are people and they are all different. Coming to terms with this change in how you view the world can be disorientating. You are going from living in a house that looked like Figure 8.3(a) to one that looks like Figure 8.3(b) and they are very different.

Suddenly the door is at the front of the house (where it should be) but you've never had it there and are not used to it. You may want to go back to your original house because that's all you know, because that's what your Mind Erosion is comfortable with. But remember that in the same

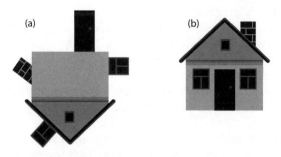

Figure 8.3 Which house is your reality?

way that when you move to a new apartment or house, it takes time for the new place to feel like home. Likewise you need to give yourself time to adjust to your new way of seeing the world.

You will soon see that as the brass coil gets looser each time, you Finish-off more thinking, the more your new house will start looking attractive the right way up. You'll also start to notice that everything works better.

The more Finishing-off Thinking you do, the more you will notice space in your head to think the thoughts that you want, to hold your Attention on what you are doing, to think your character's thoughts without background noise and the easier you will find it to use your Imagination, be spontaneous and remain inspired.

We are now ready to expand the earlier definition of Awareness:

AWARENESS:

- The ability to see one's own thinking
- The ability to replace Purposes at will (impossible unless the thinking is seen first)
- The ability to Finish-off all the thinking one thinks one should

---

And move on to the next chapter . . .

NINE

TEMPO-RHYTHM

Ut imago est animi voltus sic indices oculi
(The face is a picture of the mind as the eyes are its interpreter)
Cicero (106–43 BC), philosopher[1]

Stanislavski discussed Tempo-rhythm in terms of the relationship between 'inner Tempo-rhythm'; feelings and experiences and 'outer Tempo-rhythm'; physical action and speech.[2] He described Tempo-rhythm as a 'two-edged sword . . . helpful and harmful in equal measures' as a consequence a warning to any training actor that Tempo-rhythm cannot be a reliable tool.[3]

> Choose Tempo-rhythm properly and feelings and experiences arise naturally. But if the Tempo-rhythm is wrong, inappropriate feelings and experiences will arise in precisely the same way . . . and you won't be able to put things right until you have replaced the wrong Tempo-rhythm.[4]

After reading this do you, like me, have the impression that Tempo-rhythm is like walking a tightrope? Maybe I'll get it right and stay on the rope . . . But I may also get it wrong and fall off. Either way the fear of getting it wrong would override any good acting I would hope to achieve.

Early on in my teaching career I knew the subject needed to be revisited in terms of what I was finding out about thinking, in particular that feelings, experiences, speech and actions are *all* manifestations of thoughts. Let me show you how Tempo-rhythm works.

> A student once told me a story of a casting he went to. On arrival he asked the receptionist where he should wait. She gave him a choice of, 'Up here'

(a small empty lobby with a couple of chairs) or 'Downstairs in the waiting area'. He chose to stay where he was, even though she had indicated there was a designated waiting area downstairs.

He had his audition and must have done a good job as he got the part.

Later, after his audition, he went to the restroom, which was in the downstairs waiting area. He found it to be a somewhat dark and oppressive area, full of auditioning actors sweating over their scripts – not the best place to be before a casting. On reflection he thought that it was good he had stayed upstairs and that it had helped him get the job.

What had made him stay upstairs?

Luck?

In life we often use a normally unaware 'sense' to make decisions about people and situations.

Have you ever found yourself thinking or saying any of the following:

> 'I don't know but something about the tone of his voice made me think . . .'
>
> 'He said yes, but . . .'
>
> 'She was laughing and said she enjoyed it but for some reason I didn't believe her.'

When I discussed the casting further with my student, it seems that what he picked up from the receptionist was that personally, she wouldn't have wanted to wait in the waiting area. In other words, somehow he picked up her pictures.

How do we pick up other people's pictures?

What is the mechanism?

Have a go at these short exercises. Take some time to imagine yourself in each of these circumstances in turn:

- Sitting in a garden on a summer's day
- Standing on a hot, packed underground train
- Standing by a river bank about to go white water rafting

With each you probably noticed that the speed of the impressions was different, either faster or slower. Most would say that the third was faster than the first. This speed of thinking is called a Tempo. Tempo doesn't necessarily have anything to do with any physical movement (at the start of a rollercoaster ride, the movement is slow but your thinking is already very fast). It is just the speed of mental pictures.

Every situation in life has a speed or Tempo. We don't normally notice it as such, we just get an impression, which we may describe in other terms (exciting, calming, boring). It's only upon closer examination that we recognize a Tempo.

This understanding of Tempo is what alerts us when something isn't right. It's what tells us when something doesn't quite fit the context; when people are lying or when circumstances have changed. Your friend says something but their words don't match the impressions you're getting. You walk into a bank and something is wrong, you can't put your finger on it but it's not right . . . you've just walked into the middle of a robbery.

How are we picking this up? Because we (unawarely) already understand the Tempo of usual and regular situations that happen many times in our lives – we are used to them. Then, when the impression of this particular situation doesn't match, it sticks out.

There are various definitions of Tempo which together help to form a clearer idea of what it is:

TEMPO:

- Speed of thinking
- The speed with which I accept new thoughts into my consciousness
- The speed with which thoughts evolve from my consciousness
- The speed with which I view pictures in front of my mind's eye
- The speed of synthesizing thoughts
- The effort of holding still pictures

Take some time to see how these work in your own mind.

How do we detect Tempo in other people?

When we notice someone is in a mood, it is their Tempo we are detecting. What alerts us is the manifestations of the speed of their thinking. It might be their movement, posture, tone of voice, speed of speaking, gestures etc. These may range in subtlety from almost imperceptible to something drum-bangingly obvious, perhaps picked up only unawarely. These manifestations we call Rhythm:

RHYTHM: The perceivable manifestation of a Tempo

As there is rarely, if ever, a Tempo without a manifestation, we use both words together – Tempo-rhythm. These two things, the speed of someone's pictures along with the perceivable manifestations of those pictures is the way we understand or gauge all of life's situations.

Going back to the example, what was it that made my student make his decision to stay upstairs? When he thought about it later, he could see that the receptionist's pictures of the downstairs area were unpleasant. He had picked this up through her Tempo-rhythm while she was talking.

In life there are three components to understanding what someone is saying:

- Context
- Pictures
- Tempo-rhythm

If we know two of these elements we will understand the third. My student knew the context, a waiting area at a casting suite. He perceived the receptionist's Tempo-rhythm and so he got her pictures – a dark, unpleasant place.

It is not only situations and people that have Tempo-rhythm, everything in life does; paintings, music, colours, objects, words, smells, sounds, tastes . . . everything!

It isn't that an object inherently has a Tempo-rhythm, it is us who give it the Tempo-rhythm. We give it its Tempo-rhythm through our affinities with that object. For instance a knife has a Tempo-rhythm which is different from a chair. And a butter knife has a different Tempo-rhythm from a cut-throat razor.

Clapping custard

Try this exercise.

Imagine a spoonful of custard in front of your eyes which you are just about to eat.

Imagine what it looks and smells like.

Imagine its taste, sweetness, consistency and temperature.

Now hold the Purpose of wanting to eat the custard . . .

. . . and clap the Tempo-rhythm of this custard.

You know the context, eating custard, you have the pictures and so you can clap the Tempo-rhythm.

When I do this exercise in class, I ask the students to describe each other's custard, which, as long as the student who is clapping is holding the pictures clearly, they invariably can. The clearer the student's thinking, the easier it is to see their pictures.

Therefore if the audience knows the context and the Tempo-rhythm, they will get the pictures, and if they get the pictures, they will enjoy the play. If they don't pick up the pictures, they won't enjoy the play. This is why it is important to understand that if the actor's thinking is about the audience, the press reviews, dinner, his or her personal life . . . as opposed to the character's thinking, this will override the performance, interfere with the context and therefore the pictures that the audience pick up are unclear.

On stage or on set, the clapping you just did for your custard to convey pictures (if you were able to hold the picture) is instead conveyed through your voice and movement.

Make a list of about thirty different objects, emotions, and relationships. Fifteen should be in front of your eyes, meaning actual objects you can see or hear and fifteen should be imaginary. Spend ten seconds clapping each.

Something to look out for is that you don't clap a sound that comes from the object but the object itself. If you are clapping a tape recorder, clap the tempo that the picture of the tape recorder gives you, as opposed to the speed at which you think the tape recorder winds the tape.

There is no right or wrong speed to your clapping. It will be influenced by your own consciousness, your particular thoughts towards an object. However on stage, your Tempo-rhythm will be more appropriate if your pictures are within the context of the script and your character's Purposes.

This is sometimes easier said than done. What I often see in class is that students have a thought from their own lives that they can't stop thinking. What happens is that the student creates a parallel train of thought. The result is that when the student claps a Tempo-rhythm, the other students cannot see any pictures because no one is sure what they are clapping. In acting of course this isn't good. A director may ask you to hold two thoughts at the same time but the student cannot because the background noise from these other, 'own life' thoughts are already there. Do you remember in Chapter 3 on Events, we talked about Unfinished Thoughts creating background noise? That is what is happening here. When we can deal with these Unfinished Thoughts then we can focus our Attention on what we want to focus our Attention on.

Before we go on to Part Two let's have a quick chat about eyes.

Eyes, falling in love and Tempo-rhythm

For years we look into the eyes of our nearest and dearest and yet when it comes to describing their eyes, we realize that it is impossible . . . except in very general terms.

Why so?

Why also is it so important for us to see the eyes of the person we are talking to?

Because we don't look at eyes, but through them.

Why else would we forget the detail of something that we are so focused on?

We look through the eyes into the brain to see the thinking.

Whatever the person is saying, it is the thinking behind the words that we are looking for. Yes, we hear the words, but we look for the meaning of the words – the pictures and the Tempo-rhythm of the brain. Again notice Tempo-rhythm is a way of seeing people's thinking.

In terms of love or falling in love, this takes place when two people's Tempo-rhythms fit. We have discussed in this chapter that Tempo-rhythms can be picked up simply by the way someone holds a pen or their little finger. When you are attracted to someone and you see the way they move, talk, smile, you are unawarely picking up on the physical manifestations of their thinking. You then think, 'that person thinks what I need for my life to take place'.

Boom!

That's it.

In other words, falling in love is having sex with Mind Erosions and not with bodies.

And with that priceless knowledge we are ready to look at the Qualities of an Actor.

PART TWO

Qualities of an Actor

TEN

IMAGINATION

I am enough of an artist to draw freely upon my Imagination. Imagination is more important than knowledge. Knowledge is limited. Imagination encircles the world.

Albert Einstein (1879–1955), theoretical physicist[1]

When we were children we believed in the Tooth Fairy, or Santa Claus, or other wonderful characters from our cultures.

We accepted their existence without question (granted there were perhaps one or two, just to check our parents weren't making it up) and with ease we then found a place in our view of the world for this magical being.

Then we grew up.

And our perception of the world became logical and pragmatic.

With increasing frequency and speed, we tested the logic of Events and relationships leading us to accept or reject them . . . based on our own criteria.

Based on our Purposes and our Super-Purposes.

From the point of view of Imagination, becoming an artist is to go back to having a child's Imagination. Back to a time when our unhelpful Purposes didn't run our lives as strongly as they do now – depending on our Awareness.

This is why *The Science of Acting* puts so much emphasis on seeing your thinking and of Finishing-off your thinking, so that the noise that is getting in the way of your Imagination can be put to rest.

As an actor, the less noise you have, the more you can recreate a child's Imagination of being able to awarely see and create pictures for your character and keep creating them until new logic is established, and weave this into your character's life.

The more aware you become, the less effort you will need to put into creating pictures which conform to Purposes which will no longer be important in your life.

If using your Imagination is new to you (or to be more accurate, so long forgotten), when you first become aware of your pictures you will see them only in black and white; with practice you will find they will become colourful and more vivid.

Time for a definition.

The word 'Imagination' is probably used more often than any other term in acting tutorials and rehearsals. Adequate examples are usually provided by tutors or directors.

The best definition I came across was, 'Imagination is thinking in pictures'.

It is so clear that it's pretty impossible to beat.

So I just tweaked it:

IMAGINATION: Thinking in pictures and impressions

PICTURE: A totality of distinguishable shapes

IMPRESSION: A totality of mental and physical sensations

For example, think about your kitchen, that's a picture. Think about what you had for your lunch, again a picture.

Think about being hungry, that's an impression. Think about being on a fairground ride, that's also an impression.

Creating a character

Imagination is one of the main tools for creating a character.

And as you now know, to create a consciousness for the character we have to use our own consciousness as a model. The objection I usually get at this point is that in our lives our consciousness took so many years to create, and we have only four weeks to prepare for our parts, to learn the lines, and so on.

Let's see if it is really so impossible.

A character's past

At the end of this sentence, put down this book and think about your life from the time that you can first remember up until now and then come back to the book.

. . .

. . .

How long did that take?

Most students complete the exercise in about three minutes.

What you did is contemplate your past life in pictures in about three minutes.

This means that to know you have created your character's past, you will need about three minutes worth of pictures. But because you are conscientious and want a stable character you create fifteen to thirty minutes of pictures of your character's past.

You may have noticed that the pictures were of varying importance, relating to the significance of the Events. These can be considered as different sizes of photographs in a photo album where some photos take up a whole page, some half, some a quarter, with others as small as a postage stamp (see Figure 10.1).

From the first week of rehearsal, you can think about these pictures and refresh them every rehearsal day. In order to get into the habit of creating a past life of the character, you need to get into the habit of looking at your own past life, noticing which Events in your own past were important enough to be a photo.

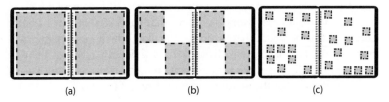

        (a)   (b)   (c)

Figure 10.1 The photo album

A character's day lived

At the end of this sentence put down the book and this time think about the Events of today in chronological order and then come back to the book – taking as long as you need.

. . .

. . .

How long this will have taken depends on what time of day it is, but on average it takes twenty seconds to think through each hour of the day. Notice that it takes a disproportionate amount of time to think through the pictures of your day compared to your entire past.

And this is how we think.

The pictures of your day are fresher and as a result are much more detailed, seem more important and take longer to contemplate. Yesterday's thoughts are of little importance, unless you had a big Event, like breaking your leg.

So when it comes to your performance, you need to know the past life of the character and the day of the character up until the moment when they come on stage or in front of the camera – where you live (the building, the decor, the neighbours, the colours, the smells), waking up (to an alarm?), which side of the bed you sleep on, what sort of bedding, who you spoke to.

A character's day ahead

At the end of this sentence put down the book, this time to think of all the things you are going to do from now until the time when you go to sleep tonight.

. . .

. . .

Notice that we have very clear pictures and impressions of the rest of the day. Similarly we need to create the pictures of the character's day ahead. You would then work out from what you know of the character (daily routine or what is happening in the play) which pictures they will have for the rest of that day. Even if the day doesn't turn out the way that they expect (any Unexpected Event could happen), you still have a general idea of what the pictures are for the rest of the day.

A character's future

One more time.

This time when you put down the book, think about your life from this moment until your death. The Purpose of this exercise is not to create pictures but to see what's there, to see what your Long-term Purposes are.

. . .

. . .

What you should have noticed is that we have an impression of our future. Even if you found that you could see no picture of your future, this probably means that you have no Long-term Purposes, that you don't think you have a future. Another Purpose of this book is to change your pictures of your future, that is to change your Long-term Purposes.

After these exercises, you are already getting an impression of the time (is it as long as you thought?) needed to create your character's past life, the character's day up until you walk on set, the rest of the character's day following this scene and the character's future.

If you have some extra time, and again it won't take that long, you may want to consider dreams. Purposes are things we think we can achieve whereas dreams are things that are quite nice to think, but unattainable. So when you create a character it is useful to ask what the character's dreams are and create those pictures too.

Shrinking pictures

I touched on this subject in Chapter 4, but it is important to revisit here.

You may be thinking, 'OK so it doesn't take as long as I thought, but still that's a hell of lot of pictures to be thinking!'

Thankfully Mother Nature is on your side.

Imagine it is the morning of your fifth birthday party. The Event is so big for you that it is the only thing that you can think about.

The pictures are huge.

Then tomorrow comes . . . and the next day . . .

And with that your pictures of your birthday party began to shrink.

You can't live without shrinking pictures, otherwise we could only ever think about one thing at a time – and we would all still be stuck with the picture of a midwife or doctor delivering us from our mothers!

So in life pictures shrink, to give us the capacity to think new thoughts.

Inevitably when we are creating our character's pictures they will start as large pictures, but as we keep contemplating these pictures, they will, over time, shrink. We have to learn to keep refreshing our character's pictures to the size which we have designed them to be. So that the size of the pictures from the character's past (e.g. of enjoying family summer picnics as a toddler) are relatively proportionate to the pictures of current daily life and any recent big Events.

Together with Sense Data, Actions and Devices should be kept large, as these are what keep the pictures 'alive'.

Different types of Imagination

Thinking in pictures and impressions can be done in a number of ways, some more conducive to good acting than others.

Active and Passive Imagination

Deciding to take a holiday by yourself, you have arrived in Spain.

You have stopped off at your hotel to refresh and are now travelling by bus to the beach for the first time. You're at the penultimate stop before reaching the beach. Think about the following pictures, seeing yourself from the outside:

See yourself on the bus:

See yourself sitting on the bus and the bus is on the right-hand side of the road. See yourself looking out of the window. See yourself thinking it's warm. See yourself thinking it's a nice day. See yourself looking at the trees and the sun. See yourself checking the bag next to you. See yourself seeing the beach. See yourself on the bus as the bus reaches the terminal and the passengers start to get off. See yourself getting up from your seat. See yourself moving down the bus. See yourself stepping onto the pavement. See yourself taking your first steps on the beach. See yourself finding a spot to lie down. See yourself putting your bag onto the sand. See yourself opening the bag taking a towel. See yourself finding a cubicle to change in. See yourself taking your bag and towel and going into a cubicle. See yourself coming out of the cubicle in your swimsuit. See yourself moving down the beach. See yourself putting your bag on the sand. See yourself going into the sea. See yourself swimming in the sea. See yourself covered in water. See yourself coming out of the sea. See the sand stuck to your feet. See yourself walking back to your towel. See yourself sitting on your towel looking down the beach at the ice-cream seller. See yourself opening your bag. See yourself looking in your bag to find your wallet.

Now try it again with you inside of yourself:

You are on the bus. You see your elbow on the window. You feel the sun on your arm. You look out of the window. You see the sun and the trees. You look down the bus. You see the other people on the bus. You look at the seat next to you and see your bag. You feel the bus slow down and approach a bus stop. You feel the bus stop. You stand up and pick up your bag. You move into the aisle and you walk down to the front of the bus. You take the step down from the bus onto the pavement. You take your first steps onto the beach. You feel the sand on our feet. You see a spot, walk toward it and put your bag down. You open your bag and put your towel down. You spot a cubicle to change in. You pick your bag up and your towel. You walk towards the cubicle. You come out of the cubicle and go back onto the beach. You put your bag and towel down and you walk into the sea. You feel the water on your body. You swim in the sea. You taste some salt water as it slips into your mouth. You come out of the sea and you feel the sun's heat drying the water on your body. You feel the sand sticking to your feet. You walk back to your towel. You sit down on your towel. You look down the beach and you see an ice-cream seller. You open your bag. You look in and you see your wallet.

When you are inside of yourself and you can feel the sun, sand and water – all the Sense Data.

This is Active Imagination.

ACTIVE IMAGINATION: Imagining yourself from within, with Sense Data

---

When I asked you to think outside of yourself, you used Passive Imagination; imagining yourself being seen by either others or yourself.

PASSIVE IMAGINATION: Imagining yourself being seen from the outside, by yourself or others

---

When we are creating characters, this has to be done in Active Imagination; by climbing into the body of the character. Most people find Active Imagination more enjoyable because they are using Sense Data. If you found it easier to think in Passive Imagination, this could be because you often see yourself from the outside and think a lot about how you look to other people – because it is important to you what others think about you.

We must always create the character in Active Imagination even if the character thinks in Passive Imagination, that is, it is important to your character what other characters think about them. For example your character is going to a party and thinks about what they look like and whether the other people at the party will be impressed by how they look. This is thinking in Passive Imagination within the context of the play. And this is fine for your character's thinking.

However, if as an actor I am acting on stage and I am thinking about what the audience are thinking about me, then this is the actor's Passive Imagination. I am having thoughts from my life and not the character's, I am seeing myself from the outside and how I appear to the audience.

Passive Imagination usually comes with the Purpose, 'I want to be liked' or '. . . admired' or '. . . secure' with the Long-term Purpose, 'I want to fail'.

When you act you have to have Active Imagination, because this is how we live.

Defining the body

If you are not sure which type of Imagination you are using, or find yourself in Passive Imagination and want to be in Active Imagination, 'defining the body' will help you flip over.

To do this, ask yourself these questions:

- 'If I were in the place of this character, what would I see with my own eyes?'
- 'If I were in the place of this character, what would I hear with my own ears?'
- 'If I were in the place of this character, what would I touch with my own hands?'
- 'If I were in the place of this character, what would I smell with my own nose?'
- 'If I were in the place of this character, what would I taste with my own mouth?'

By defining the body, you climb from outside the character to being inside.

And then you can ask the question, 'What is my Purpose now?' to start thinking the character's thoughts.

When you are in Passive Imagination the same Purpose remains throughout; it is only when you are in Active Imagination that you can change Purposes.

Forced and Free Imagination

Think about what you had for breakfast this morning.

. . .

. . .

Now multiply 14 by 18.

. . .

. . .

Think about the difference between these two thoughts.

Did you find that thinking about the picture of your breakfast was much easier than holding the figures tightly in your head so that you could do the calculation?

Free Imagination describes the thinking about a picture, here no effort is needed.

The majority of us spend most of our time thinking in Free Imagination although circumstances exist which require us to think in Forced Imagination. When we think about objects in Free Imagination the objects are life-sized. If you think about an object, say, your kitchen in Forced Imagination, the picture shrinks and it becomes less real.

FREE IMAGINATION: To see things as they are in size, touch, smell etc. and where they are in reality

---

FORCED IMAGINATION:

- Although visible this Imagination has no Sense Data
- There are always tensions

During the rehearsal period, actors sometimes think that they haven't got the thoughts of the character, and so they may then put thoughts in and hold them there using qualities of Forced Imagination. Remember how it felt to hold the digits and do the multiplication in your head? Not very enjoyable for you or the audience. This is bad acting.

The correct pictures in Free Imagination are quite ephemeral, so it takes experience and reassurance (from a tutor) to get points of reference that these pictures are correct.

I can relate

'I just can't relate to the character.'

This can be a common problem.

Understandably, to be unsure of anything in your profession, to lack the knowledge that will help you deal with each and every happening is unnerving. But what if you knew that you could act any part that you have the opportunity to, and be confident that you could do it well? That would certainly be reassuring and satisfying and it would free up your thinking to enjoy the creative process.

So let's see how we can do this by looking at the problem.

What does 'I can't relate' mean?

First, it might be an inability to understand and therefore to create Purposes (pictures) for the character in question.

Second, it could be an inability to see (in one's mind) the life of the character – his or her past and future, to understand what makes the character see some happenings as Events and others not. To be precise, 'I can't relate . . .' means the actor cannot see the pictures, which match his or her understanding of the character.

Imagine I go home tonight and I have a message from my agent saying that I have an audition for a coveted role in a new play.

I will be auditioning for the part of an Acorn.

Great news!

But an Acorn?

How can I relate to an Acorn?

Where do I start?

The first thing I do is start thinking about the Acorn in Passive Imagination.

Where do I want to see the Acorn?

The script tells me I am hanging on a tree.

And that's where I have to see it, while thinking in Passive Imagination.

And what does an Acorn do?

Nothing, it just hangs there.

My next step is to think as an Acorn if an Acorn could think. I put human thinking into the Acorn's head. Without human thinking we don't have art, because no matter who or what the character is in the play, be it an octopus, an alien, a cup of coffee, a grey dot, the letter 'Q' – it is the thinking attached which is the art.

OK, so I am hanging in the tree and that's all I do, but if it is the thinking that is the art, I start with one of the most important thoughts – my Super-Purpose.

So what's the Super-Purpose of an Acorn?

I guess, to become an oak tree.

How do I programme this? I think in pictures about this Purpose.

Let's say I'm currently hanging on a tree that is part of a forest on the top of a hill. I am on the edge of the forest and I can see the valley below: the valley looks beautiful and I think I would like to grow into an oak tree in that valley.

I know that to be in Passive Imagination will not give me any more thoughts so I have to get into Active Imagination, which I do first of all by defining my body. I, as an actor, have a human body, but to be an Acorn I have to put my human body inside an Acorn's body. I imagine a hat on my head and a stalk coming out of my hat and I already have a better impression of being an Acorn. I have days and nights, I feel the weather, I have a brain and I share my mother tree with my brothers and sisters (these things I couldn't see in Passive Imagination – that's why Active Imagination is so important).

Next I think about my thoughts and start with my most important thought, my Super-Purpose of becoming an oak tree.

Where did I get this impression of my Super-Purpose?

I have to know from somewhere.

My mother talks to me through the rustling of the leaves, so whenever there is a slight wind the leaves move in such a way as to tell me how to live and she tells me the ground in the valley is perfectly fertile for me to spread my roots. And she is happy knowing she would still be able to keep an eye on me. Animals live with their parents to learn from their parents, so that's how I, as an Acorn, learn.

Because of my Super-Purpose to become an oak tree, I know I am going to have to fall so as to get my own life. As falling is an important thought for me, I have to workout how high up I am from the ground. Probably 200 times the height of myself? This may be a pretty frightening thought for a human, but not for an Acorn who knows that he will just bounce off the ground.

And what do I do all day?

I can't go anywhere to drink or eat, I just spend all my time hanging from this branch with my brother. We bask in the sun, swing in the wind, sing in the rain, play 'I spy', predict the weather, listen to the birds, to Mum. We also joke about who is going to fall first. We don't talk about not being together again, that's too sad, so we talk about where we are going to be trees; which birds we'll shelter and which are too noisy.

Now I think about obstacles to achieving my Super-Purpose.

The squirrel!

If I am the size of an Acorn, then when a squirrel's mouth opens, it is huge and all I see is pink flesh and very sharp teeth. This is too much fear to live with every day, so to avoid being a neurotic Acorn I place myself at the end of a very thin branch, one that's too weak to hold a squirrel.

If when I get the part and the director says, 'You have to think that a squirrel could eat you because at the end of the play a squirrel does eat you' (did I mention it was a tragedy?), then I would reconsider this and think about how I would change my circumstances, that is place myself within easy access of a squirrel. As it is, I am more secure where I am positioned now; from here I can see a squirrel running around eating my brothers and sisters. I think this thought with the Action, 'I gloat', because it is not me that's getting eaten and I'm very secure, safe and special with my closest brother knowing that we have much better chances of becoming trees.

There you go.

I just related to an Acorn and it was very simple and enjoyable.

By asking questions and using my Imagination I came up with more and more pictures.

You could also go through the exercises at the start of this chapter to design the Acorn's past up until now, day up until now, day ahead and life ahead to build up even more pictures.

And the beauty of acting is that there is no hard work to it, simply the enjoyment of using your childlike Imagination to create pictures . . . of using your Imagination 'to encircle the world'.[2]

'I' and the character

A character as we know is a totality of thoughts.

If 'I' am playing Hamlet 'I' therefore create and think Hamlet's thoughts (I create his thoughts from the context of the play).

It is my thoughts that create Hamlet.

'I' never cease to exist.

When I am on stage it is my thoughts that have created the character.

People in acting often talk about the character and 'I' as if they are separate things but because it is my thoughts that have created the character, 'I' carry on. 'I' never stop.

For instance, I'm playing Hamlet in a production which has only evening performances. It is early afternoon and while at home I tidy my flat, do some cooking, vacuuming etc. At about 5 o'clock, as I prepare to head to the theatre, I start thinking Hamlet's thoughts. On the journey I start thinking more of Hamlet's thoughts and less of my own. This carries on up until I am on stage, thinking the thoughts in the order that I decided to think them; thinking enough thoughts to be that character. At the end of the play I return back to my own thoughts.

As part of his 'Method' Lee Strasberg would say, 'Given the circumstances of the play how would [actors] behave, react or feel if they were in the character's situation?'.[3] In *The Science of Acting* this does not make sense because if I were the character I would not need to ask this question, I would know.

I would not need to think, 'I am Hamlet, the Prince of Denmark', I just need to have Hamlet's thoughts. What makes me the Prince of Denmark is the fact that I have the thoughts of the Prince of Denmark. I have the memories of growing up in the palace with pictures of Denmark; the Events that took place in the different rooms, the views from the windows, my bed in my bedroom, where and how I wash, the brush and comb I use to tidy my hair, a wardrobe with my clothes.

What then should I think?

Here Stanislavski's 'Magic "If"' helps us, which he described as 'a spur to a dormant imagination'.[4] When you start a question with, 'If it/I were . . .' it is difficult not to be in Active Imagination. The question, 'If I were in these circumstances with this Purpose, what would I think?' can always be used to springboard your Imagination.

To talk about a separate I and the character is to make two separate boxes. This does not work. The character is not separate from me; it is me with the thoughts of the character.

As you use this process, you will notice that you will go to your first rehearsal with fifty pictures and at the end of the rehearsal you will have ninety pictures. You will go home and create more pictures, then giving you one hundred and fifty pictures. After the next rehearsal you have two hundred and fifty pictures. There will come a point when you have so many pictures, your brain will be satisfied that the character is created.

After this point no matter how long the run of the play is, the number of pictures will grow by themselves, provided that you enjoy your life (and keep it on the back burner).

You won't have to work; your brain will do it for you.

ELEVEN

ATTENTION

> If I have ever made any valuable discoveries, it has been owing more
> to patient attention, than to any other talent.
>   Isaac Newton (1642–1727), mathematician and physicist[1]

'You first need exercises which will help you to take your mind off things
you shouldn't be looking at or thinking about and, second, exercises so
you can concentrate inwardly on the things the role needs'.[2] What
Stanislavski is talking about here is Attention or what he sometimes refers
to as concentration. The Circles of Attention that Stanislavski provided
his readers with to help them, work like imaginary static ripples emanat-
ing from the actor in increasing circumferences encompassing him or
herself, other objects, characters, and ultimately the whole stage.

We'll come back to Stanislavski.

I'll start by saying that to act a character well, I have to keep my
Attention on the character's thoughts that I have decided to think.

Leading us nicely to the question, 'What is Attention?' In 1890 the psychologist and philosopher William James (1842–1910) defined Attention
as 'possession by the mind'.[3]

Sound good?

Let's test it.

Think about a cup of coffee.

. . .

. . .

It probably seems that your mind is in possession of it, that it is all that
your mind is focused on. This would agree with James' definition and yes,
your Attention is on it.

But, as you have noticed with everything that you have read so far, that your mind is in 'possession' of many other thoughts at the same time. Think of all the invisible ones.

If this is the case, is it accurate to say that your Attention is on all of them as well as the cup of coffee?

No.

Therefore James' definition doesn't work for us.

Let's find out for ourselves what's going on.

At the end of this short sentence think about a cup of coffee and then read on.

. . .

. . .

OK. So was your Attention on the cup of coffee?

Yes.

How do you know?

Most probably because you saw a cup of coffee with your mind's eye. It was visible.

The thought was in your CVT.

So Attention can be simply defined as:

> ATTENTION: The ability to hold thoughts in the Chamber of Visible Thinking

But we aren't considering both the visible and invisible thoughts.

Back to Stanislavski.

What he created with the Circles of Attention are physical boundaries for thinking, a way for the focal point to become totally absorbing.

So what he was saying is that 'Attention is thinking within a discrete area'.

Let's see if we can use this definition:

You are sitting there reading this book.

You seemingly have your Attention on what you are reading, but are thinking about a cup of coffee you forgot to bring in from the kitchen.

So what is your Attention on?

It's definitely not absorbed in this book.

Can you see that Stanislavski's definition is too generalized for us to work with because he is talking about visible thinking and doesn't consider invisible thinking. In fairness, though, he did admit that 'Questions about the subconscious are not intellectually my business'.[4]

In my search for a definition for Attention that actors could use, I knew that it had to account for both visible and invisible thinking and this is what I concluded:

ATTENTION (FOR ACTING): The ability to hold the designed thinking of the character

---

We have our starting point.

Now let us see how Attention works in our everyday lives and in the life of an actor.

Different types of Attention

Inner and Outer Attention

Pick up an item, any small item like a teaspoon, a pen or some keys . . .
. . . and think about that item.

. . .

. . .

Now put the item away, somewhere out of sight and come back to the book.

Done it?

Now think about the item again.

. . .

. . .

Notice the difference between those two experiences.

With the item in front of you, your Attention was activated by your senses; what you saw, felt and possibly (in the case of the bunch of keys) heard. This was Outer Attention.

OUTER ATTENTION: Attention activated by the senses

When the item was out of sight and you had to think about it, you experienced Inner Attention – Attention activated by your mind.

INNER ATTENTION: Attention activated by the mind itself (i.e. the mind is not stimulated by the senses)

If you eat an orange, that is Outer Attention.
If you think about an orange, that is Inner Attention.
Listen to the sounds outside.

. . .

. . .

When listening to these sounds your thinking was being activated via your senses, i.e. your ears. This is another example of Outer Attention.
Now think about a glacier.

. . .

. . .

Now your thinking is solely activated by the mind. Meaning you have a Purpose, to think about a glacier and this Purpose brought in the picture and impression of a glacier. This is another example of Inner Attention.

Voluntary and Involuntary Attention

Let's use our shoelace tying example, because it works so well. Think of tying a shoelace for the first time. This would have involved putting your Attention on the step-by-step procedure. This was Voluntary Attention – you had to put your Attention on what you were doing to find answers to one question after another: Where does this lace go? Where does it loop? Is my loop long enough? Where do I move my finger to?

VOLUNTARY ATTENTION: Activating visible Purposes

Now having successfully tied your laces many times, a strong Complex has been formed of tying your shoelaces and you no longer need to put your Attention on it.
Nevertheless something takes place in your mind each time you tie your shoelaces.
Imagine a baseball player in the World Series is called up to bat – he looks down and sees his laces are undone; he reaches down and ties his laces.
What is his Attention on?

The shoelaces?

No way!

But yet some part of his thinking ties those laces. This is Involuntary Attention. Or thinking activated by unaware Purposes.

We still have the same thoughts that we programmed as a child but we don't think them visibly any more.

INVOLUNTARY ATTENTION: Activating invisible Purposes

Test it out for yourself next time you tie your laces. Do you decide what you are thinking about or do you just think it?

An example of Involuntary Attention which you may have experienced many times is reading a book, getting to the bottom of a page and not being able to remember what you have just read. Not a word.

Why is this?

This is because your Attention wasn't on what you were reading. Involuntarily your Attention was on something else. You had Involuntary Attention.

The Dot of Attention

The Purpose of this exercise is to find out how to hold your Attention on any object, either in Inner or Outer Attention and see how you can change this object of Attention from Voluntary to Involuntary.

At the end of this sentence focus on The Grey Dot (the object of Attention) in Figure 11.1 and when you think that your Attention has been on the dot for a short while continue reading.

How did it go?

Was your Attention on the dot?

Figure 11.1 The Grey Dot

Are you certain?

Can we be certain that our Attention is on anything?

A good way is to ask questions about it and see the answers pop up.

When we are asking questions and finding answers, we know we are thinking about our object of Attention and therefore we have our Attention on it.

With The Grey Dot you could have asked questions like: Is it light grey or dark grey? What is the texture of the dot? What size is it? What coin is it closest to in size?

Have another go. At the end of this sentence put your Attention on The Same Grey Dot in Figure 11.2, this time ask yourself some questions and see what happens.

And how was that? Did your mind focus more quickly and/or easily?

Were you more certain that your Attention was on the dot than the first time you did the exercise?

This is what we want to achieve – a confidence that our Attention will be where we want it to be.

Once we understand how to focus Attention on one little dot, we can apply the same technique on anything the director wants us to, or we want to put our Attention on.

This time at the end of this sentence look away from this book, stare at the floor or close your eyes and think about The Grey Dot, then come back to the book.

. . .

. . .

Did it pop up clearly?

How much effort was needed to bring the picture in and to keep it there?

Shouldn't have been much (if it was difficult, look at The Same Grey Dot again, using more Voluntary Attention, asking more questions and then repeat this last exercise again).

Figure 11.2 The Same Grey Dot

Here you held The Grey Dot using Involuntary Attention.

Notice how simply by asking questions you were able to hold Voluntary Attention.

Then when you thought about the object a couple of times with Voluntary Attention, it stuck in your head and had changed from Voluntary to Involuntary Attention.

Notice how simple it was.

Again to Frequent Repetitive Thinking and . . . what the hell, let's use the shoelaces again. The first time you learned to tie your shoelaces, you had your Voluntary Attention on each step of the process. You had to activate visible Purposes of where you wanted the laces to go with each step. This was a process that you repeated often, which formed a Complex with Frequent Repetitive Thinking. In due course the thinking you used to tie your laces went from being visible to invisible. Tying your shoelaces became a process where invisible Purposes were activated instead of visible ones, your Attention went from Voluntary to Involuntary. Ultimately this gave you space to think about things which had become more important than thinking about tying shoelaces.

With time and Frequent Repetitive Thinking, Attention moves from being Voluntary to Involuntary.

If you can do this with The Grey Dot and tying your shoelaces, then you can do it with the thoughts of a character.

This innate process allows us to continue learning while retaining knowledge. Understanding this process is absolutely essential to acting well, so I am going to repeat it. By thinking something often, the thoughts will form a strong Complex that in time your brain will move from the visible into the invisible part of your consciousness.

This is nature working.

This is truth.

The exact same process comes into play when creating a character's consciousness; you follow the same procedure, only this time using the character's thoughts.

Attention and creating a character

First you (and when possible, your director) decide what the invisible thoughts of the character should be. These include Character Line, Mindprint, Relationships, and OPAEs. In rehearsal, you then put your Attention on these designed invisible thoughts. You visibly think the designed thoughts in Active Imagination (using all your senses) and with Frequent Repetitive Thinking, these designed thoughts form a Complex and gradually over time will move into your invisible thinking (as in the shoelaces example) and you no longer need to have your Attention on them.

These thoughts will then be *programmed* or *loaded* so that when you come to the performance, you will have the Involuntary Attention of the character and the space to have the visible thinking of the character.
You will be acting just as we live.

We will deal with this more thoroughly in Chapter 14 when we work on a short play, but for now, here is an example of programming a particular character's thoughts when modelling a scene.

You decide that in Sam Shepard's *True West* your character Lee has very vicious thoughts towards his brother Austin at a particular point early on in the play (as a hint of the violence to come). Perhaps while they are talking Lee could 'chop up' some apples from a fruit bowl and although visibly Lee might be thinking this or that, his Involuntary Attention is on hurting his brother. At home the actor contemplates the pictures (punching, strangling, stabbing – whatever you decide, go for it! – there are no prizes for half-heartedness), and then in rehearsals he holds these pictures while he (very slowly at first – if your director doesn't rehearse this way, the slow work will have to be done at home) chops the apples. This is then done every time the scene is rehearsed; the actor voluntarily holds the vicious thoughts while acting out the scene (I would expect any actor, let alone a good one, to also rehearse at home). Then by Frequent Repetitive Thinking these thoughts will simply be there without the actor having to visibly 'hold them' while on stage.

Turning Voluntary Attention into Involuntary Attention by Frequent Repetitive Thinking takes time and this is what the rehearsal period is for.

The actor's/character's thoughts

Take a look at Figure 11.3. This illustrates how at the beginning of the rehearsal period you will be thinking many more actor's thoughts than those of the character. It will be with your 'actor's thinking' that you will be thinking about the character.

See how in Figure 11.4 Frequent Repetitive Thinking over time moves your Attention from thinking actor's thoughts about the character, to thinking the character's thoughts.

Compare the process to learning to cook an elaborate dish. As you become more and more used to *The Science of Acting*, your Complex of acting will become stronger and less Voluntary Attention will be needed for you to do your job. Rather than constantly referring back to the recipe,

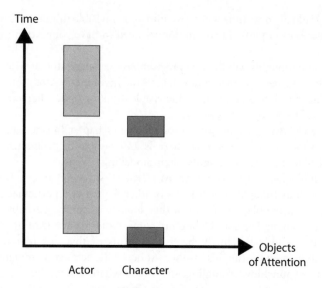

Figure 11.3 The first day of the rehearsal period

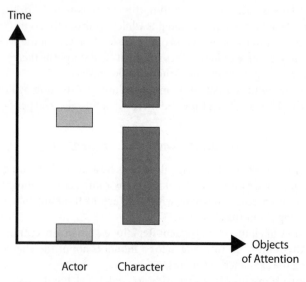

Figure 11.4 The end of the rehearsal period

you will eventually find your hand reaching for the next ingredient – and you had forgotten to take the recipe book off the shelf.

Just as with any learning you must remember there are no short cuts. You didn't tie your laces like a World Series baseball player even after the tenth time you practised, and you still need a peek at the recipe book to complete cooking that dish for the fifth time. To act well and to be proud of what you create, you must programme the thoughts of the character methodically and conscientiously for every performance to be beautiful.

The Actor's Awareness

I often get asked whether when you have successfully programmed all the character's thoughts and are easily losing yourself in those thoughts, do you completely lose yourself to the point that you 'become' the character?

No.

This should never happen and frankly unless you have some mental illness it never will. There will always be some Awareness.

You can't hallucinate away the audience or film crew, you can't ever 'forget' you were born and lived all of your life's experiences. You will always be you plus the character. You will always have a percentage of your thoughts on what you are doing. This is called the Actor's Awareness.

The Actor's Awareness runs alongside everything else, it is part of your professionalism; it is how you managed to help your colleague who dried up, or how you improvised your way round a missing prop.

I teach my students to always Afterburn all their performances, pieces and exercises.

This relies on the part of the Actor's Awareness and the Purpose to remember how it went so it can be improved for next time (as opposed to asking yourself 'How's it going?' during a performance which would bring you out of context).

How does the Actor's Awareness work during a performance?

To be completely lost in the character is impossible; there will always be distractions from outside the context of the play.

Let's say you are on set and someone in the audience coughs loudly. What happens next?

Pavlov helps us answer this question.

To recap, Pavlov noticed that after a period of feeding meat to dogs while ringing a bell, he could eventually ring the bell and the dogs would salivate in expectation of food appearing. A Complex had been created in the dogs' minds with the sound of the bell and food.

Once this Complex was formed Pavlov went on to notice something else. He noticed that if he rang the bell, causing the dogs to salivate, and then stopped ringing the bell – removing the signal of food – the dogs would continue to salivate for three to five seconds. That is to say that the Complex continues to be active for a short period beyond the point at which the stimulus was removed.

How does this relate to the loud cough?

The cough will have taken the Actor's Awareness away from the context of the play.

If the actor can bring their Attention back to the character's thoughts within three to five seconds then the audience will not notice any change in thinking because the actor's thinking will still be in the context of the play, because the Complex of the character's thoughts will still work for three to five seconds. There will have been no interruption.

Creative Attention

Creative Attention is the main type of Attention that the actor uses during the rehearsal process. It is the Attention you place on something for the performance which isn't as you know it in real (the actor's) life.

At the simplest level it is calling your colleague actor 'Dad' within the context of the script, when in fact he is just another actor called Tim.

Or if you are asked to look out to the audience where the director has designed a view.

Or when you need to work with computer generated images.

This is where you use Creative Attention.

CREATIVE ATTENTION: To overlay objects of Outer Attention with objects of Inner Attention

---

In other words to overlay what you can physically see, with imaginary pictures of what you want to see; or to paraphrase again, to have the many pictures and impressions of what your character sees within the context of the script at the forefront of your mind, with what you can physically see not affecting your Attention.

It is very beautiful to watch an actor looking out into the audience when their pictures are in context, in stark contrast to the cringing you feel when you see an actor uncomfortably looking out to the audience, but trying not to.

So what do you do?

Let's say the stage director says to you, 'Here is a window', showing you a space on the set, which if it were a window you would look out and see a brick wall offstage. He then tells you that when you deliver the line, 'Oh, what a beautiful garden', you need to be looking out of this window.

What you will know by now is that if you deliver the line thinking about the brick wall, the audience will get confused because you will be saying the words but the pictures will not match. You therefore need to create a garden in your head, and you will need to create it many times so that eventually the garden is like a photograph in your head.

To create the garden you first have to design it with Sense Data. When you start, no Sense Data will exist, so you simply start to think about the parameters of the garden . . . the placement of the tree and the flowers . . . you then bring in their colours . . . their textures, smells . . . the sparrow that comes in every morning . . . the height of the grass at this time of year etc. Eventually you will have created a garden that you will see every time you see the brick wall.

The acting profession is about creating these pictures . . . hundreds of these pictures.

The first day after your initial design of the garden you are back in rehearsal and you walk towards the 'window' and say the line 'Oh, what a beautiful garden'. When you say the line, you will notice that some of the programmed thoughts come in.

Probably not all, but some.

The second time you notice there are more. Eventually with Frequent Repetitive Thinking about the garden, when you say the line and look at the brick wall you will see the brick wall but your Attention will be on the garden you created, and your thinking will remain in context. If you see the garden, then the audience will have an impression of it and your acting will be very enjoyable to watch.

The Five Ws

There are occasions when an actor does not have time or enough notice to contemplate and rehearse, e.g. castings, workshops. For instance you turn up at a casting and they hand you the script and you have ten minutes to prepare. There are five questions you can ask yourself which help to create some character's thoughts, and to help ensure that your Voluntary Attention is where you want it to be. These are called the Five Ws.

The questions are:

1 What is my Purpose? To include all seven qualities of a Purpose.
2 What is my Action? What do I do to achieve my Purpose?
3 What is my Event? Upon what Event is my thinking intensified?
4 Where am I? The context – how did you get to it, where did you come from?
5 When am I? The time, day of the week, month, season, year?

Dracula is a character we all know and although it is unlikely you would get to a casting like this without notice, it serves as an example of how to use the Five Ws. Let's say the scene you are going to read is the one where you bite Lucy for the first time in the ruins of the abbey.

Here are the five questions again with some possible pictures.

What is my Purpose?

'I want her to fail' (i.e. be unable to resist me). This Purpose should have pictures of biting her as well as affinities to taking her life away, being lost as one of the undead.

What is my Action?

'I titillate', 'I fill her head with sexual thoughts until she is helpless with desire'.

What is my Event?

My thirst – my dry mouth with an impression of her soft neck and the warm blood within it.

Where am I?

Pictures of when I was on board the ship, running onshore as a dog, sleeping in the grave of the sailor and luring Lucy to the abbey high on the cliffs, the sound of the sea below, the temperature of the air, the soft ground beneath my feet.

When am I?

After midnight, summer, 1890s.

As you read the above did you have pictures and impressions in the context? If you did then you would simply need to think these through a bit more and you would have some context for your casting.

TWELVE

FREE BODY

The mental and physical peculiarities or defects of men and women
are the result of heredity or acquired habit.

Frederick Matthias Alexander (1869–1955),
founder of the Alexander Technique[1]

Let's start this topic with an exercise.

If you are not already on one, move to sit on a straight-backed chair,
like one at a desk or at a dining table.

Done?

OK, now while sitting here, think about the taste of a banana . . .

. . . now think about the feel of leather . . .

. . . multiply 17 by 17 . . .

. . . and see if you can remember the tune, 'The Yellow Submarine'.

Next, while sitting on the chair, put this book in your lap, or if you are
sitting in front of a table, place it on the table.

Ready?

Now carry on . . .

Drop your hands and take hold of either side of your seat and using all
your strength, pull up, and also push your feet down into the floor. While
doing this think of the tune, 'The Yellow Submarine' . . .

. . . now think of the taste of an orange . . .

. . . multiply seven by nine . . .

. . . and now think of the feel of silk.

Can you see the difference?

You couldn't recall from your memory or hold your attention on
things as easily when you were tense as when you were relaxed.

Stanislavski uses similar exercises in *An Actor's Work* to also show 'how muscular tension impedes our thinking',[2] because if you are tense you can't think and if you can't think you can't act.

Are you beginning to see why a tension-free body is so important for the actor?

Let's look at the different types of tensions so that you can more easily identify them in yourself.

Natural and Acquired Tensions

If we replace the words 'peculiarities or defects', with the word 'tensions' in Alexander's opening to this chapter, he clearly distinguishes for us the two different types of Tensions that exist.

There are Natural Tensions, which allow us to function at a physiological optimum; to stand up, to walk and run, to breathe – based on 'heredity' – and there are Acquired Tensions – based on 'habit'.

Natural Tensions should be pretty straightforward, but what do I mean by Acquired Tensions?

You may notice that after doing some work you have to relax to get rid of the tensions as there was a build-up of tension – whether the work was digging, sitting at a computer typing or even carrying heavy shopping.

This also indicates how quickly and easily we acquire tensions. We could say that in a way our bodies are predisposed to acquire tensions.

The ease with which we acquire tensions tells us about our adaptability to circumstance – many yoga books tell us a flexible body reflects a flexible mind.

Our development from apes to human beings indicates there is also an evolutionary Purpose to us acquiring tensions. Imagine an ape running around on all fours, swinging from vines and tree branches. Then one day the ape stands up, and manages to stay standing for a little while, and then the ape comes back down to all fours. After this experience there will be some tensions left in the ape's body. Over thousands of years these tensions build up, allowing me and you to be the two-legged, standing animals that we are.

How does this work today?

I remember while I was at college attending a conference where one of the main speakers was a very attractive man who, whenever he spoke, always tilted his head to one side. By the end of the conference, all of the women who attended the conference had fallen in love with him. What was most interesting was that I also remember by the end of the week, more than half the men who attended the conference held their heads tilted to one side. This illustrates how mimicking and copying are ways we acquire tensions.

Have you noticed how people mimic and copy the way famous actors, musicians, models, family members and friends walk, stand, talk . . .?

Awarely and Unawarely Acquired Tensions

Toddlers learning to walk start to develop different tensions to those they were born with; a time when they didn't have the Purpose of wanting to walk. So tension is a manifestation of our thoughts – it is a result of our thinking.

Learning to walk is an Aware Tension. It is the result of the visible thought of 'wanting to get from one place to another'. But if you take some time to think about it you will see there are some tensions you know you have but you don't know why you have them. These are tensions that you have Acquired Unawarely. In other words, these are the physical manifestation of invisible thoughts.

Often we unawarely create tensions when there are obstacles to our Purposes. You know sometimes when you are standing up, you notice your kneecaps move up towards your thighs? This may mean that you have obstacles to the Purpose, 'I want to feel secure', meaning that you are bracing yourself in anticipation of an unpleasant Event. Maybe for you, your knees don't come up, but your shoulders hunch, or a particular crease forms on your forehead?

Another example is when you smile when someone has said something to you that makes you cringe. You are smiling to cover up the fact that you are cringing because you want to be liked and whatever this person has just said is an obstacle to the Purpose, 'I want to be liked'. This is a tension.

Face Reading in Chinese medicine dates back thousands of years and was originally used to diagnose illness. In her book on the subject, Lillian Bridges mentions how her mother tries to identify the thoughts behind wrinkles that she doesn't like on her face by putting tape over the wrinkle and leaving it. Then whenever the tape pulls, she stops and questions herself.[3] Her mother wants to identify the thinking that day-to-day she doesn't know she has. I'm not suggesting you do the same, but remember the Model of Awareness? I would like to encourage you to notice more of your invisible thinking, in this chapter in particular by recognizing your tensions.

Many bodywork specialists and complementary medicine practitioners will tell you that Tensions can lead to disease. For example if you work at a computer all day or you carry a bag on one shoulder all the time, you may not realize that tensions are accumulating and muscles are developing knots. If ignored, these knots go on to affect nerves, which in turn affect joints and organs.

Once you have tension in your inner organs or muscles, you have become susceptible to disease. This is why relaxation is very important because it gets rid of all tensions. And the more you practise relaxing, the more you create a point of reference for a relaxed body. One of the reasons why yoga and relaxation is timetabled every day at my school is that with regular practice it becomes much easier to notice yourself acquiring tensions and so much easier to relieve them.

Tensions and the character

Psychophysical Unity is a principle originated by the founder of the Alexander Technique. Alexander observed that his postural habits were so strong that he would have to 'repattern his mind in order to change these habits'. Psychophysical unity became the cornerstone of his work',[4] and the basis Alexander Technique practitioners use to bring about changes in their clients. As the term implies, Alexander had made the link between our physical beings and our mental processes.

If you consider that every mental process is reflected or expressed somehow within the physical body, can you see how for example body postures, gait and the position of relaxed hands all indicate aspects of the Mindprint of a character? This is because all of these Tensions are physical manifestations of Purposes.

Let's see how this works with hands. Take a look at someone else or yourself when their or your hands are relaxed and not doing anything.

See what you notice.

The following are common patterns:

- Hands that are part curled, in particular the last two fingers, usually is a manifestation of the Purpose, 'I want to be special'
- A little finger sticking out can mean, 'I want to be admired' or '. . . held in awe'
- A closed fist often means, 'I want to be right'
- Thumbs turned into the fist is a manifestation of 'I want to feel good' or 'I want to be secure'

Try working backwards and put your hands into the above positions and see if the thought I have associated with that position pops into your head? Or is it something else?

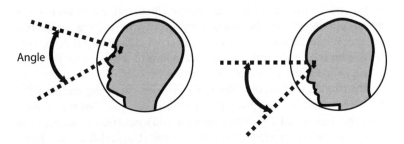

Figure 12.1 The Angle between the line of vision and the axis of the head is a Complex

Now have a look also at the angle between your line of vision and the axis of your head (see Figure 12.1). This is a also a Complex – a very important one because it

- determines the angle at which we get used to seeing the world
- is a reflection of some elements of consciousness. See if you are always looking down on the world . . . or up?

By now you have understood that all of us have particular tensions, as do all characters; ways of walking, holding a pen, and standing. Some people walk with round shoulders; others have very straight, stiff backs. After looking at your hands and head, take a look at your face, your posture. Do you know what you look like when you walk? You will see that your body is manifesting many of your visible and invisible thoughts.

Can you see therefore that tensions are Complexed with thoughts? That your Acquired Tensions are Complexed with your thoughts?

What is important to understand is that if actors have a lot of Acquired Tensions, when they act they will have the same Acquired Tensions, which are a manifestation of the actor's Mindprint, not the character's. This means the acting won't be in context and so will not be as good as it could be. The actor needs to learn how to recognize and relieve tensions. Once the body is free from Acquired Tensions, it is possible to create, manifest and maintain the physical tensions in accordance with the Mindprint of the character.

As well as yoga, students at ASAD also practise relaxation on a daily basis. In brief, this involves lying on your back with your feet about eighteen inches apart and arms slightly to the side with palms facing the ceiling. You then focus your Attention on each major muscle in the body, in turn, relaxing them one by one. Then you do the same with the internal organs one by one. At the end of the process, your body is completely relaxed. While it is not possible or practical to maintain this state for very long, both relaxation and yoga provide points of reference for the body as to what it means to be free from tensions.

Stanislavski was aware of the role of tensions in acting and how the actor's tensions affected good acting. Stanislavski said that if you put a baby on a pillow and then lift the baby off, you would notice that the baby completely relaxes and the imprint of the baby's body is left on the pillow. Similarly if a cat is lying on sand and then gets up, the imprint of the cat's body is left on the sand. However, he said that if a man lies on sand, when he gets up only the back and shoulders are imprinted, this means that there are tensions there.[5] The baby and the cat are both four-limbed animals, both with very different shapes to their spines, so I don't think the same theory can be applied to a two-legged man.

At around the same time, in the early 1900s, when Alexander was working in Australia, he noticed that when he was tired his voice would change and this would depend on his posture. This led to his idea of Strings, based on the idea that a string comes out of the top of your head (from the same place where there once was a hole when we were born) and is threaded through the whole of your spine.[6] In order to keep our body in the correct position, imagine the thread is pulled slightly upwards; in so doing your body will use only its Natural Tensions. For example, when I need to bend I simply imagine a flat platform on my head with the string being gently pulled in a perpendicular fashion. I find this technique much more useful for my human students who have moved on from crawling.

Now that you have a good understanding of how to have an agile mind and body, do you have everything you need to become a great actor?

What about the *je ne sais quoi*? The unknown 'gift' that will propel you to stardom.

What a waste to have come this far to be told that you don't have what it takes.

This is why before we work on a script, there's an important question that needs to be answered . . .

THIRTEEN

TALENT

Never stop searching, and cherish the form which discloses the inner content.

Yevgeny Vakhtangov (1883–1922), Director[1]

'Am I Talented?'

What a disconcerting question.

If someone says that I am, does it mean that I am?

Where is the tangible proof that this is true?

Some people were, are and will be called Talented by some, but called ordinary by others. Often it is the case that the 'most promising student' or a 'tutor's favourite' sadly never 'makes it'.

Can one be truly Talented at anything?

Is an artist's Talent of higher quality than that of a teacher ... or a structural engineer? What qualification does one have to have in order to be decreed Talented? Shouldn't it be God who has the final say?

If a student of acting or painting is asked to leave their course, is it because of their irreversible mediocrity or the opinion of the tutor?

If one critic does not like a style of acting, painting or music where another critic does, who is right?

Maybe neither.

A frightening thought is that an opinion from a consciousness, the quality of which is unknown to us, can, due to its position of power, elevate fakes to fame or sentence the 'Talented' to a life of suffering.

Is there an objective guide for Talent or is it based only on opinion? Who can we say is Talented?

Madonna?

Mozart?

Damien Hirst?

Leonardo da Vinci?

Leonardo DiCaprio?

Do we say that Madonna is Talented backed up only by the fact that so many people also say it? And are they saying it for exactly the same reason?

Salieri was a much more popular composer during Mozart's time, but is now better known as his nemesis. How many of the painters of the Salon de Paris are now known and enjoyed, compared to the then unpopular Impressionists? It seems that time honours Talent and weeds out the purely fashionable. If a hundred years pass and they are still popular, then can we say with some certainty they were Talented?

Gasp of realization . . .

Does that mean I will have to wait a hundred years to know whether I am – and then barely be able to enjoy it, if at all?

The first person in my life who defined Talent was Maria Knebel, my professor of acting and stage directing. She said, 'Talent is the ability to ask oneself questions'.

This sounded strange because I could not understand how it could be measured, not for the actor, puppeteer, painter *or* scientist – although it seemed somewhat clearer for a scientist than an artist.

The definition also seemed incomplete because it did not say anything about finding answers to the 'questions'.

Perhaps she took that for granted.

It took well over two decades for me also to realize that questions can be asked differently; there are questions which come in words like 'What shall I say to impress?' and questions of a very different quality, those that come in pictures and impressions like 'What shall I have for lunch?'

Noticing that Mozart didn't ask himself in words, 'What note comes next?' nor Einstein ask, 'What will be my next discovery?', I came to discover that the more the questions were asked in pictures and impressions, the greater the Talent of the person asking them.

But is it possible to ask the wrong questions in pictures and impressions?

This is where I believe ego comes (interferingly) into the equation. I believe that Mendel would never have discovered genetics had he asked himself what his fellow monks at the monastery thought about him and his work, nor would Newton have discovered the laws of motion if he'd been concerned what his colleagues at the Royal Society had thought. This brings us to another quality of Talent; the less one thinks about being appreciated, respected, remembered or admired, the greater one's Talent.

In other words the degree of Talent is in reverse proportion to the use of Egotistic Purposes. With Egotistic Purposes comes fear and fear shrinks one's thinking capacity.

We now have a definition that we can start with:

> TALENT: The ability to ask oneself questions in pictures and impressions, unadulterated by Egotistical Purposes

If you want to be the most Talented or to stand out for your Talent, you need to keep on asking questions until you come up with something either unique or more interesting or of a better quality than anyone else.

Talent does not entertain the fear of 'not being right' or needing 'to be impressive'. There is no forcing. Simply questions and answers.

But we are not finished there. Let me introduce you to a further consideration.

Have you noticed how often you have reached an understanding about an Event long after it has passed? Leading you to then think, 'Why didn't I notice that at the time?' 'It seems to be so clear now.' 'Isn't hindsight an interesting thing?'

Another example of a similar process can be observed when we are trying to remember a forgotten word. It takes time to recall the word and often it's only a while later that it is suddenly remembered.

These phenomena imply there is a well-hidden 'gadget' in our mind. This gadget performs processes much more often than we realize. We do not know the workings of this process but we do realize its importance.

When you say, 'I'm going to sleep on it', this indicates your appreciation of this gadget's processing system. Neuroscientist Matthew Walker recognizes this 'sleeping on it' phenomenon, 'Sleep seems to stimulate your mind to make non-obvious connections . . . connecting ideas, events and memories that wouldn't normally fit together'.[2]

We can now list all that we know about what this gadget outputs. It provides us with:

- clear understanding of a past Event – in hindsight
- sudden recollection of information
- clarification of circumstances with time – sleep on it

This list can be summarized as the *synthesizing* properties of the brain. The brain's ability to 'work' on information without our Awareness. Yes, without our Awareness. What is so interesting is that despite our inability to control it (as it works unawarely) this is a reliable process which is working all the time.

Even and particularly while we sleep!

We can now extend our definition:

TALENT: The Intensity of synthesizing thoughts unadulterated by Egotistical Purposes

---

In Daniel H. Pink's book *A Whole New Mind*, he refers to the finding that 'in general the left hemisphere [of the brain] participates in the *analysis* of information ... [and] the right hemisphere is *specialized* for synthesis', going on to conclude that 'analysis and synthesis are perhaps the two most fundamental ways of interpreting information'.[3]

I would agree that analysis – asking questions, and synthesis – the processing performed by our gadget are fundamental ways of interpreting information, but would add that in terms of Talent and ensuring that one's Talent is ever growing, one needs not only to acknowledge this Purpose, but also to feed it on a regular basis.

I now want to refer you back to the questions I brought up in the Preface. Questions you may have had when you started this book:

'*Does this mean that once you have finished reading this book you will know what to do to act better than you do now?*

Yes.

Will you become a better actor?

Yes.

Will you become more talented?

Yes.

Will you be able to act really well?

No.'

And then I went on to tell you that to act well you would need to practise.

It is with practice that you will increasingly build on or feed your Talent. By asking more and more questions in pictures and impressions without Egotistical Purposes, and allowing the synthesis of the thoughts that come up, you will go from being Talented to more Talented and from more Talented to the most Talented.

One minute!
Back to the first of the four questions.
You haven't finished reading the book yet!

So far we have looked at the elements, patterns, formation, classifications and Finishing-off of thinking. And we have brought this knowledge about consciousness firmly into the actor's context with discussions on Imagination, Attention, Free Body and Talent.

Now it is time for all the pieces to come together and for you to learn the Ten Steps to creating a character as we go through the process of Working on a Script.

PART THREE

Working on a Script

FOURTEEN

THE TEN STEPS

And finally to the Ten Steps.

The Ten Steps is a clear structure for actors or directors to follow from first read through to first performance (and even beyond, as actors continue to refine their work). It provides a path for the rehearsal process to follow which allows the cast to explore the play in depth and develop a clear, precise and entertaining production while ensuring that the cast are kept on track.

Added to all that you have learnt up until now, by the end of this chapter you will know how to:

- Analyse a play, a character and their relationship to other characters
- Design a consciousness that will fit as perfectly as possible within this framework
- Programme this consciousness into an actor's consciousness so that it can be activated on request and take over (well, almost) the running of the actor's consciousness

You may think that what follows is a lot of work to fit into the rehearsal period. I would however encourage you to do as many of the Steps as you have time for, particularly Steps 1 to 9. Step 10 involves greater detail, working at the level of Basic Actions and Basic Events; you may decide that you are happier taking that 'final Step' once you have mastered what precedes it. I leave that up to you.

As an overview the Ten Steps are as follows:

Beginning of analysis

1 Plot
2 Facts and Happenings
3 Germ of the script

Character's analysis and Actor's contemplation

4 Mindprint
5 Character Line
6 Relationships
7 Events and Happenings
8 Episodes and their OPAEs

Standing Up

9 Programming
10 Affinities, Basic Actions, Basic Events and their Modelling

For you to get as clear an understanding of the Ten Steps as possible, *A Marriage Proposal* by Anton Chekhov follows this chapter for us to use as a working example. Although this is a short play, it won't be possible to include the entire analysis that would take place during a typical rehearsal period, instead (starting with Step 2) I will limit my examples and focus on one instead of all three characters. I will always, where possible, use the most beneficial example for you to understand how each Step works.

Be reassured that in line with the Purpose of this book, I will provide you with enough knowledge for you to be able to start implementing the Ten Steps yourself, and in time you may find that all you need is the table in Appendix 3 as a useful to-hand guide.

When you are ready – that is, when you have had time to read the play and consider it without interruption – do so and then return to this point.

Beginning of analysis (Steps 1–3)

Step 1 Plot

Before we do anything else, we need to establish the Plot because this is the foundation for all the analysis to come. Above all with this Step it is important that our personal feelings (and you will certainly see them creep in) are not allowed to influence the process. For instance, I might believe that Macbeth's decisions are made to please his wife, who I might think he finds overbearing, but this may be because I have an overbearing wife or had an overbearing mother.

Even if the entire cast agree that Macduff kills Macbeth in revenge for the murder of his family, that would still be an *interpretation*, which at this Step should be kept out. All we are interested in is the objective Plot. For *Macbeth* this could be: Macbeth, a Scottish warlord, in agreement with his wife, kills his king and is later given the crown. After Macbeth becomes king, Lady Macbeth appears to go mad. The family of another warlord (Macduff) are killed on Macbeth's orders. Macduff fights Macbeth and kills him.

When discussing the Plot the cast should think through all the Events and Happenings and decide whether these are reflected in the main characters' thinking. If they are, they are included, if not, they are omitted. For example, in a script a maid may be going out with her fiancé one evening but as this is merely the writer's device to facilitate action, it is not important enough to be included in the Plot.

> PLOT: The description of the main Events and Happenings of the play *only*, described in simple terms without any interpretation

Now to the Plot of *A Marriage Proposal*. What happens here?

A man turns up at a neighbour's estate. He asks for the estate owner's daughter's hand in marriage. They argue. She accepts. They continue arguing.

Anything else?

Well, we could add something about Lomov's illness but we don't know if it's genuine. Knowing that we have to stick to the circumstances without adding interpretation, we leave this point out.

The Marriage Proposal Plot

A Russian landowner visits his neighbour's estate to ask for his daughter's hand in marriage. They all agree to the proposal after having had two heated arguments.

Step 2 Facts and Happenings

FACTS: Events and Happenings that have taken place beyond doubt

---

Hamlet kills Polonius (albeit through a curtain).

Fact. We see it happen.

Facts are also things which happen offstage or in the past, but these need to be confirmed by independent witnesses. We do not see Ophelia die but more than one person says that she has. They go unchallenged, therefore this is also a Fact.

If a character says something which is never confirmed, can we be sure that they're not lying, exaggerating or assuming? Again, one character's words cannot be relied on as Fact; instead because it is blurred, it is termed a Blurred Fact. With the Plot of *Macbeth*, I said Lady Macbeth 'appears' to go mad. Her madness is probably a Fact, but just how mad is a matter of interpretation. This is an example of a Blurred Fact, where,

---

BLURRED FACTS: Facts within a script that cannot be relied on

---

I will come back to what we do with these.

In life we often make assumptions without first seeing whether the Facts justify the assumption. We believe what our Mind Erosions have us believe. This is why for actors it is so fundamental to increase their Awareness – it allows them to interpret situations more objectively and sift through misunderstandings with greater ease.

By establishing the Facts at this stage in the process we not only bring to the surface any faulty logic within the script but also we save ourselves from big headaches further down the line. In *How the Other Half Loves*, for example, Alan Ayckbourn uses a comic device where Mary leaves Teresa's house and very quickly enters another house where earlier Teresa took a bus to make the same journey. This may have been intended as a theatrical joke but the cast should still try to make logic of it. Characters must live in a world that is logical. It doesn't have to be naturalistic but it must make sense, otherwise actors can't hold it in their thoughts. This doesn't mean there can't be any manner of styles (musicals are worlds where people sing all the time!). Even in the most beautifully written plays there can be circumstances which don't make sense and when this happens we need to 'truthify' it. By truthify I mean to make sense of the circumstances. We need to create a way that they can exist.

To solve the problem in the Ayckbourn play, we decided that the two houses had gardens that were close but the front doors were on different streets and Teresa took a bus on the earlier visit because she initially intended to travel further than she did. Creating this logic means that the audience doesn't get distracted or frustrated with something that doesn't make sense, nor do the actors have to periodically lose themselves from the 'holes' in the script during the performance.

The Marriage Proposal Facts

Lomov wears evening dress
Lomov is 35
Lomov owns an estate; he inherited it from his aunt and uncle
Natalia is 25
Natalia has been working
Her workmen have been harvesting hay
Lomov's father is dead
Lomov and Natalia have known each other since childhood
Their estates border each other

To illustrate how easy it is to make assumptions in the list above, I have included something that isn't a Fact.

Did you spot it?

Lomov's father's death is not a Fact.

All that we know is that Tschubukov says of him, 'And your dear father was a gambler', giving us the impression that he is dead but this is never explicitly said. I could look at the original Russian text to see if anything was lost in translation, but for the purpose of this exercise let's assume this script is all we have.

Clarifying Blurred Facts

In every script there will be plenty of useful details which the writer will not have included. These can include time of year, time of day, professions, and the character's ages and daily lives, that is who does what, where, when, how etc. In the absence of these details we need to work them out by looking at what other Facts within the script lead us to, or what is implied by the script. Age is a good example. If you have the ages of some family members you can usually work out others.

What can help us decide on an age for Tschubukov?

We know Natalia is 25, so he's at least 45.

We also know that Tschubukov says to Lomov that he is twice his age.

Although this last clue cannot be relied on, it seems reasonable to suggest he's getting on a bit. If Tschubukov was over 70, he might have said 'I'm more than twice your age', i.e. he is more likely to exaggerate while arguing (which they are when he says this). So Tschubukov is between 45 and 70. If he were 30 when Natalia was born he'd only be 55 now, which would make this exaggeration over the top. If instead he were 35 (Lomov's age now) when he had Natalia, he'd now be 60 which is more realistic. And if we add a couple more years, then he can 'feel' more like twice Lomov's age. So let's say **Tschubukov is 62** (this also helps explain why Natalia seems to be an only child, i.e. they might have been trying many years before she was born).

The impressions we gain from what characters are saying can also lead us to calculated guesses ('by the way he talks about his job it seems to me that he is a manual worker'). On occasion there are no Facts, implications from the script or impressions to help us find the information we need. When this happens we simply use our Imagination to think what would best suit the context of the play by *creating* pictures of Happenings and Circumstances that are implied by the context of the script.

Many Facts are clarified when we reach Character Line, however there are some that should be done now as they influence the remainder of the analysis. With *A Marriage Proposal*, time of day, the year and time of year are all Facts that we should clarify at this point.

Now to finding out the time of day. This is pretty simple.

Natalia offers Lomov something to eat but he replies that he's had lunch. If it were well past lunch time, she would more likely have offered him a drink rather than food, so being just after lunch but not much, let's go for **2pm**.

How do we set the year if it is not said?

If a playwright has written a play and says it is set in the 'present', what 'present' does he mean? Ours or his?

He means the present when he wrote the play as these are the pictures he had while writing. There is usually a lag time between a play being completed and the first performance, with the play being published soon after. A reasonable lag time is about a year so here we choose the present to be the year before it was published, which in this case was 1889, so we **set it in 1888**.

The clues which help us identify the time of year are the Facts that they are harvesting hay and that it rained yesterday: these point toward **late summer**.

Step 3 Germ of the script

GERM OF THE SCRIPT: A summary of the cast's thinking of what
they think the play is about

Every script has a Germ which is used as the main point of reference for
the analysis. A playwright does not write with a Germ in mind but every
play will have one because the writer's Mind Erosion will have influenced
his or her work (Beckett, Williams, O'Neill each had 'themes' which per-
vade all their work).

The Germ comes from impressions the cast have after reading the play.
For example, after reading Alan Ayckbourn's *Absent Friends* one has the
impression that 'everyone is losing themselves in trivia', or with Brian
Friel's *Dancing at Lughnasa* there is an impression that they 'don't know
what to do to improve their lives'. Germs often come in the form of a
Guideline but can be any element of the Mindprint. For example in
Absent Friends the Germ is 'People who lose themselves in trivia belong'
and for *Dancing at Lughnasa* it is 'Women confused by not being able to
find a path to a different life'.

When considering the Germ, think of it as a bird's eye view of all of the
script's impressions. Here's how to do it. After reading a script, simply sit
and relax and think about the play, its characters, their relationships, their
Purposes and so on. Impressions will come up and eventually words will
suggest themselves.

When you first do this it may take a while, perhaps hours, but with
practice you will become faster. If at first you have any difficulty, it is
useful to take a break and come back to it later or to read the play again.

The Germ should be reflected in the thinking of all main characters,
that is they must share this thinking to some degree. The Germ is then
used as a yardstick for the analysis. Every decision about Character Lines,
Mindprints, Relationships, OPAEs, in fact the entire design of the play
must be in line with the Germ.

An example of when an element of a production doesn't fit the script's
Germ is sometimes seen when a popular television actor from a long-
running soap opera is cast in a play; the actor has a Mind Erosion which
won't or can't adapt (isn't agile enough) to suit the play, resulting in productions which although commercially viable, are often artistically poor.

Ask yourself what impressions come to mind when you think about *A
Marriage Proposal*. Do the following come up:

- Stubbornness?
- Stupidity?
- Obstinacy?
- Infuriation?
- Pettiness?

All this negativity and two heated arguments between people who seem to like each enough to consider marriage!

To argue about something (the land) they are nevertheless prepared to give way when two people's happiness is at stake suggests that having an argument is more important to them than anything else.

Therefore they must like arguing.

Once you establish that they like to argue and the arguing is important (think how much of the play it comprises) you are getting close to the Germ.

Is this the first time they have been involved in a row with each other?

Remember it is during the rows that Tschubukov and Natalia accept Lomov's proposal.

If it were the first time they had had such a row, it would surely be too big an Event to overlook. They clearly like each other.

Lomov wants to marry Natalia. Natalia is very upset when she thinks she may have messed up his proposal, Tschubukov is very warm towards Lomov and even after two heated arguments he still brings the couple together.

In fact it's not that they like each other despite their argumentative nature, it's that their argumentative nature means they 'belong' more, i.e. they are like minded. We could therefore say the Germ is probably something like **Argumentative people belong.**

Now that the Germ is set (though never in stone – one should always be prepared to change one's mind) we can use it as a guide for the rest of the analysis. In particular the Germ can help back up and clarify a very important Blurred Fact:

Who owns the meadows?

Can you see that we should never really know who owns the meadows? Even the actors should not know.

The Germ has identified that 'Arguing to belong' overrides the importance of 'Who owns the meadows'.

If the audience were to think that either party is right, then the script's Germ collapses.

If they believe that Lomov owns the meadows, then the play becomes about two people bullying a neighbour.

If we believe that Natalia and her father own the meadows, then they think the play is about this twit Lomov screwing up.

Maybe these characters don't always argue like this? Well, if this play shows us an exception to their normal behaviour then we are stuffed and analysis would be pointless. We have to assume that their behaviour is part of their Mind Erosions. That is why so much of this book has been showing you how Mind Erosions rule our lives, so that you can see how they rule the lives of our characters.

Character's analysis and actor's contemplation (Steps 4–8)

Step 4 Mindprint

As with Character Lines and Relationships, all of the Mindprint elements need to be contemplated and cross-referred to pictures from the character's life.

If our character has the People Event, 'People don't care', we need to contemplate experiences which led to or strengthened this thought. If this were my character, I could imagine as a child being taken swimming, where in the sweet shop afterwards my uncle buys only his children snacks and nothing for me, or a time when I invited a school friend to stay over and they let me down at the last minute with a lame excuse. To reiterate, this type of contemplation needs to be done for each Mindprint element.

As you may recall the important elements of the Mindprint are the Super-Purpose and Germ of the character. The Super-Purpose is the Purpose that underlies and therefore manifests itself most in the character's thinking and the Germ of a character is the main Self Event, for example, 'I'm Lonely', '. . . Stupid', '. . . Superior'.

When looking for Super-Purpose and Germ, we look for not only the most accurate ones that we can find but also ones which will best suit the character, that is, which Super-Purpose and Germ unite as many of the character's affinities as possible.

For instance we might decide that Hamlet's Super-Purpose is 'Happiness is always suffering' and then decide the Germ is 'I'm frustrated' (because he thinks he can't do anything about taking revenge). The problem with this choice of SP and G is that the impressions of the two are very similar, that is, frustration comes with a lot of suffering. They don't encompass enough affinities. So we look for other aspects of his thinking to add.

Let's look at some other options. If we keep Hamlet's Super-Purpose as 'Happiness is always suffering', what other Germs could we choose?

'I'm a coward' (he takes so long before taking revenge) or 'I'm lost' (doesn't know what to do) or 'angry' (at his uncle's treachery and his mother's betrayal) 'lonely' (not having anyone to turn to).

But which one? And does it matter?

Try this. Bring to mind the impression of 'Happiness is always suffering' and then add an impression of 'I'm a coward', and then do the same with each of the other Germs (above) in turn and see what the difference is.

Can you see how the impressions change? That's why we need to be as precise as possible; because these choices make a difference to our characterization and the audience's enjoyment.

Because the Super-Purpose and Germ are the fundamental elements of an actor's characterization, their contemplation needs more work than the other Mindprint elements.

Natalia's MP

In Chapter 6 on Mindprint I explained each of the individual elements and gave you some examples. Here I would like to give you the reasoning behind my interpretation (and of course yours could be very different – as much as you are different from me) of Natalia's Mindprint.

I'm sure you haven't forgotten the warning I gave you in Chapter 6 on Mindprint, and to remind you that before we get to the Ultimate Communion Event that this is one of the least visible elements of the Mindprint. Given this, when I say that sexual pictures within family members are not visible to the individuals (although they can be), nor would they see them immediately if told what they are, nor indeed would anything happen given an opportunity, I am preparing you for what's to come.

For instance, if I were to say Natalia has a Purpose with her father – **'Happiness is always being fucked'** – it does not mean that she actually wants intercourse. 'Being fucked' are the words which the brain understands and sum up the impressions she has. She has grown up, like many girls, to want to belong with her parents in general and her father in particular (or as has been overly stereotyped of Italian men, their mothers in particular).

As she is attracted to the opposite sex, her consciousness cannot help having thoughts about her father – visible ones being of enjoying his company, admiration, feeling cared for, and the invisible ones of her attraction to him. This pattern is not rare and could explain why we often settle with partners who have many physical as well as mental attributes of our parent of that sex. Indeed there are many academic psychology and popular psychology books on the subject.

So to Natalia's Ultimate Communion (UC).

How do we find a character's UC?

By identifying the impressions they have about the way they live, impressions about their relationships and their Purposes.

My impression of Natalia is that she very much belongs with her father and that many of her Purposes lead to ways of belonging with him.

So Natalia's UC is probably with her father.

But what are the circumstances of the UC?

Remember the definition of the UC is the 'Generalized impression of the most secure relationship I can ever be in the stillness of'.

And what is that normally in life?

Apart from the bond between a mother and child, as adults the closest we ever get is sex between two people who care about each other, and our brains know this. So sex can't help but be an element of the UC – to varying degrees.

So is that it then, sexual closeness with her father?

Yes, but with some affinities.

Within their relationship there is a lot of frustration. She is very frustrated (being a 25-year-old virgin can't be easy), and he gets angry. We have to assume this play-off between the two of them happens very often. And if so it must have an influence on her UC.

Ultimate Communion Event

In bed with Papa (having been ravished after getting him angry – see paragraph above).

Given my preamble to the UC, somewhere in Natalia's consciousness this thinking causes her shame because her faithfulness to her father does not allow any other men to take his prized position in her consciousness. She knows that she supports him even when he is wrong, she argues a point even though she knows it is stupid because she thinks he would do the same. Yet at the same time as all this she knows that it is not right to have sexual thoughts about him. It is this shame (the fear that she may see these thoughts) that keeps the Ultimate Communion Event so invisible. Even so, the shame is there.

Shame Event

'I'm a fatherfucker'.

Natalia believes sex will happen one day and is excited by the prospect but she has no clear pictures of it; it's something of a dream, therefore.

Sex Event

'Sex is exciting', 'Sex is a dream'.

Life Event

'Life is belonging' – with father, workers, house staff, friends.
'Life is lonely' – she needs a man in her life.
'Life is hard' – have you ever met a Russian without this thought?

People Event

'People have lives' – people get on with each other much better than she does.

She may have a thought that if men were really men they would just take her in their arms and !"!**? But they don't. They just chat and play cards and chat some more and time passes and nothing happens!

Men Event

'Men are titillating', 'Men are frustrating'.

Women Event

'Women are competition' – for men's attention.

Auto Directives

'I must lose myself . . . in work, rows etc.'.

Ghosts

'I can't be free' – to choose my own life.

Adjuster

'I have too much work to do' – when offered the opportunity to change her routine.

Mental Statement

'**My life's a duty** . . . to the estate, its workers, my father/family'.

Guidelines

Frustrated women provoke anger.
Argumentative people can lose themselves in anger.
Faithful daughters belong – with daddy.
Hysterical little girls get their own way.

Objectives

'**I want to provoke anger/frustration**', '. . . be important', '. . . be stupid',
'. . . belong'.

Purposes

'**Happiness is being fucked**', '. . . frustrated', '. . . faithful', '. . . belonging', '. . . lost in anger'.

Self Events

'**I'm lonely**', '. . . stupid', '. . . a little girl', '. . . unfucked'.

Super-Purpose

'**Happiness is always belonging**'.

Germ

'**I'm a hysterical little girl**'.

Having gone through all of Natalia's Mindprint, does the UC make more
sense? Or are you still on the floor?

As a rule we *all* have thoughts like this to some degree (the word
'motherfucker' didn't arrive by accident). It is because we don't know that
others also have these thoughts that we repress them. I'd say 90 per cent
of the students I have taught have been able to see these thoughts and,
having done so, now laugh at them rather than cringe, squirm or suffer.
Remember these are just thoughts, not Purposes, aspirations or inten-
tions.

Step 5 Character Line

CHARACTER LINE: A chronologically arranged sequence of Events from the character's life, as perceived by the character, i.e. in Active Imagination

In other words the Character Line is all the character's experiences up to the beginning of the script: first memories, school days, adolescence, working life, personal life and so on. Many pictures will be from daily life because these pictures and impressions provide a critical basis for the actor to build their character. Consider how much daily life comprises your life and how much it has influenced who you are. Consider how the daily life of a peasant is different from that of a princess or that of a politician or that of a steel worker. (Here's a good place to look back at the Creating a Character section in Chapter 10 on Imagination).

Bear in mind, when you come to establish the character's Mindprint, you must cross-refer it to important Events in the Character Line. For example, your character might have the People Event, 'People care', backed up by Character Line experiences which could include Events like a teacher staying behind after school to help you with classwork, or your first employer making an extra place for you as an apprentice when all the places were filled that year. Contemplation and cross-referral of this kind must be done for every period of the character's life.

Let's look at Lomov: what do we know about him?

He inherited the estate from his aunt and uncle and has known Natalia since childhood; this seems to suggest that he was often on the estate. There is no mention of his mother and Tschubukov says his father was a gambler (this can't be relied on as it was said during a heated argument but can be used to support analysis based on Facts).

Following on from this I would propose **Lomov's mother died in childbirth and his paternal uncle and aunt raised him as their own. Perhaps his father took to drinking and gambling after the death of his wife?** This less-than-perfect start to life could explain the lack of confidence that Lomov seems to have. So could the idea that his father didn't visit much and that his aunt or uncle were a little frightening. I'd even say his aunt was a big, frightening woman (Tschubukov says that Lomov's housemaid wears the trousers, so perhaps he's used to having women like this around?) who often argued with her husband. By going through this process we are creating more and more inputs into his current thinking.

Add to this some more obvious Events for a man of his class and you have the basis for the rest of his Character Line, i.e. **His father's infrequent visits, his aunt's overbearing style of care, her volatile relationship with his uncle, time spent with Natalia over the years, social gatherings, some private tuition, gymnasium, university, some awkward (perhaps failed) attempts at courtship, return to the estate to help with its running, slowly taking over as his aunt and uncle got older.** Note, all decisions about a Character Line are logically taken from the context of the play.

Once the Character Line is established, you need to spend time imagining each part of his life. For example, take the private tuition mentioned above; this means imagining the room where he studied, books and teaching aids, his teacher or teachers, if they were strict, how were they, etc. Very useful aids are photographs either from books, or from an increasingly useful source, the Internet. Find a picture of a small schoolroom and then imagine yourself in it. At first you will get a good impression of being there, as though you are standing in the spot where the photo was taken; notice how much Sense Data you get just by looking at the photo. Once you have done that for a little while, imagine yourself in the entire room with all the walls and furniture around you. Then add your teacher (from another photo of someone from that period) and away you go!

This process is surprisingly easy and quick as we do it naturally all the time. If a friend says, 'You know that café on the corner', you immediately get a picture of it as though you are there.

Step 6 Relationships

It can be said that a script is about the relationships between characters, but this is often the main thing that is missing when I see plays performed. Actors I see have no doubt discussed their character's relationships, but is discussion enough?

I once saw a play where two characters had aggressive Actions towards each other and because it was out of context of the play, I thought this was due to a poor analysis. Only later did I find out from another cast member that the two actors 'didn't get on'. In other words because they didn't know how to act their characters' relationships, they were left with the relationship they had with each other as actors.

To create relationships between characters, you need to know what they invisibly think about each other:

The invisible thoughts will be elements of Mindprint which are activated when they think of that person, e.g. 'Entertaining people belong',

'Depressed people are a burden', 'Abusive people are secure', 'I envy', 'I long for', 'Men belong', 'Women are competition' etc. These elements are what you invisibly believe your relationship is and you will need to contemplate pictures which have led to this relationship.

Let's say your character, Jane, has the invisible thought, 'Depressed people are a burden' whenever she thinks about her friend Sally. To do this you would create some memories that have led you (Jane) to having this thought about Sally. For example, you could have the pictures of an evening when after a hard day at work, all you wanted to do was relax on the couch, but Sally kept calling you to talk about her problems. You could also create the memory of bumping into Sally in the street when you're in a hurry and having to be polite while she tells you about her 'uncommitted' boyfriend.

No relationship within the script can be overlooked. We must consider the relationships between each character whether they appear or not. As we see in *Waiting for Godot*, Estragon has a relationship with Godot which gets activated every time he mentions or hears Godot's name.

The only exceptions are relationships which begin during the play, that is people who haven't yet met.

> RELATIONSHIPS: Pictures one has about another and the generalized thoughts that the relationship is based on

---

Let's look at Tschubukov and what he thinks about his daughter.

He must first have some belonging thoughts about her, 'Faithful daughters are secure', 'Family belong'.

What else?

Does he wish she were married?

Does it bother him that she isn't settled and his years are numbered? Probably.

Does he think that she kicks up a fuss because of her own frustrations? That she gets a bit hysterical? Would he rather not have these stresses?

One element of their relationship could be, 'Unmarried women are a burden'.

We know he gets very frustrated with Natalia at the end of the play, we get the impression that he feels worn out by her, that he doesn't understand her, can't keep up with her moods. So perhaps 'women are exhausting'. You could argue that she isn't always like this, but we do get the impression that Tschubukov doesn't seem to think so.

Step 7 Events and Happenings

> EVENTS AND HAPPENINGS (Step 6 of the Ten Steps):
> Chronologically arranged Events of the script and their influence
> on the main characters' thinking

Some scripts have many Events, some have few, but all are important to
varying degrees. Indeed it could be said that directing is choosing which
Events to highlight in a script. Most Events are because of a Happening,
such as Hamlet's father's death.

Over the course of a script there may be a number of Events, but for
each Main Event of the play the characters will have their own Event. In
A Streetcar Named Desire, Stanley and Stella both have an Event when (the
Happening) Blanche comes to stay. Stanley's Event will be different from
Stella's. Each Event of the play needs to be named, in this case 'Blanche

Table 14.1 Events in *A Marriage Proposal* and the Events triggered in the
          characters

Events of the play	Lomov's Events	Tschubukov's Events	Natalia's Events
Lomov's arrival	My uncertain life	My suspicion	I long for (after she enters)
Lomov asks for Natalia's hand	My uncertain life	About bloody time	
The first argument	People abuse	What cheek	Being provoked
Natalia discovers Lomov's intentions		My confusion	My stupidity
The second argument	Being abused	People are infuriating	Obstinate cunt
Natalia accepts	Being a stupid cunt	Life is unbearable	Being a stupid cunt

comes to stay', and each character's Event needs to be named. Stanley's might be 'Women can't be trusted' and Stella's might be 'Belonging with my Sister'.

Not all Happenings are Events. A prince in a fairy tale who gets gifts all the time might not have an Event when he gets another one, but for a poor woodcutter's son a present would be a big Event.

Occasionally even big Happenings aren't an Event. In Bram Stoker's *Dracula*, Mina's mother is killed by Dracula, but her death is only part of the Event. It is overshadowed by 'the threat of Dracula'.

Often we find that at the beginning of a script there is no clear Event: nothing has happened yet. Nevertheless there would still be an Event, it may simply be an Accumulated Event that the characters live with, such as Tschubukov's Event at the very beginning, (perhaps while dozing in a chair) is **Life is hard**. See Table 14.1 to see how Events in *A Marriage Proposal* trigger personal Events for each of the characters.

By spending time identifying all the major Events, we are getting closer to understanding the state of mind of each character during the different sections of the play. This helps when we later come to the design of the play, in particular the OPAEs.

Step 8 Episodes and their OPAEs

As introduced in Chapter 7 on Actions, a script is broken down into Episodes, periods of time where the characters' thinking stays the same; specifically where all the characters' Objectives, Purposes, Main Actions and Main Events remain the same within that Episode. To remind you, this often happens when a character exits or enters or when something is said or done which changes at least one of the characters' thinking (e.g. 'I'm leaving you').

Once you have decided where an Episode begins and ends, you then need to decide the OPAEs for each of the characters in that Episode. When does the first Episode in *A Marriage Proposal* begin and end?

There would probably be an Episode for the time Tschubukov is alone at the beginning (we'd call this Episode 0). But for the purpose of this exercise, it would be better if we work with an Episode with more than one person in it. The first Episode starts when Lomov enters and starts talking to Tschubukov. To find out where it ends we carry on reading until one or both of them have a different state of mind.

Have a read again now and see when you think that is.

You might think that Tschubukov's thinking changes only once he knows Lomov has come to ask for something, but I would argue that he suspects from the very start. And we know the states of mind have definitely changed when Lomov asks for Natalia's hand. So it starts before the first line and ends after the line, 'I've come to ask for the hand of your daughter Natalia Stepanova'.

We have delineated the Episode, now we design the OPAEs:

Tschubukov's OPAEs

He likes Lomov and is glad to see him but something is up; Lomov is wearing evening dress, he's very nervous, he wants something, but what is it? And how should Tschubukov handle whatever it is without upsetting Lomov?

O I want to orientate myself . . . to what he wants
P Happiness is belonging . . . enjoying his company for years to come
A I search for clues
E People can't be trusted . . . last year it was the thresher, what this time?

Lomov's OPAEs

Lomov knows this is going to be difficult, he is already feeling unwell and it's going to get worse, he's going to get stressed and feel ill, but he also knows he has to do it all the same.

O I want to be accepted . . . as a suitable suitor
P Happiness is being secure . . . if they agree, nothing very unpleasant will happen
A I brace myself . . . for their reaction
E My exciting life (affinities to frightening life) . . . he's shitting himself

Try contemplating Lomov's OPAEs in pictures and/or impressions.

What are the mental pictures?

Starting with the objective, 'I want to be accepted', remember that Lomov doesn't have much self-worth so the best he can hope for by way of being accepted are pictures in his mind of Tschubukov gravely nodding and Natalia at the very least not telling him to leave and perhaps having a 'considering' expression.

Long-term Purposes are usually just impressions. Here, with 'Happiness is being secure', Lomov could have pictures of travelling home feeling relieved that they are at least considering his proposal.

If I say, 'Now brace yourself', what impression came into your head?

One of freezing and waiting? This is more or less the Action, 'I brace myself'.

Now hold that impression in your head for a while so that you get used to it.

An impression of the Event, 'My exciting life' will probably come to you just saying the words; probably an impression that anything could happen as well as an increased heart rate and more intense breathing. You would also need concrete pictures of talking to each of them about marriage as well as people staring at your evening dress. Now gently hold all these thoughts at the same time. This Event would need careful rehearsal; slowly building up the impressions and then gently holding them together, frequently and repetitively.

Now try and hold the O, P, A and E at the same time. Don't force them to be there. If something drops (which is normal) gently bring it back; if things keep dropping, keep bringing them back. After a while they will start to form one impression and if you leave a break and come back to it a couple of times, this impression will get easier and easier to hold.

Standing up (Steps 9 and 10)

Step 9 Programming

It's all very well doing all this work, but if the character is going to exist on stage, it has to be contemplated and Programmed so that the Complexes we have created become stronger and stronger and therefore automatically get activated in performance.

Programming comes in two stages; the first deals with the character's thinking before the play begins and the second stage deals with the character's states of mind throughout the play.

First stage: Programming the Character Line, Relationships and Mindprint

This first stage comes after the actor has contemplated the Character Line, Relationships and Mindprint and by now these three will have started to combine into one impression. The actor then sits in front of the director (assuming this process is with a Science of Acting director, otherwise this work will have to be done outside of rehearsal time) and gently brings their Attention to the pictures and impressions, first of their Character Line. Here the actor slowly talks through the pictures (chronologically) about their life in general terms as though they were telling someone about their past, early childhood, school days, adolescence, adulthood, (obviously) stopping at the age or time where the play starts. All programming is done slowly, the pictures and impressions are held in one's mind's eye and the actor speaks at a much slower speed than normal. This allows the brain to make a solid Complex. If it isn't done this way, the Complex is too weak and the actor's own thoughts will push their way in.

Having covered the Character Line, the actor next works on Relationships, again holding the mental pictures they have of their Relationships and slowly saying out loud a brief sentence or two about their Relationship with each character. Then while the actor holds one particular element of their Relationship they slowly say that element, e.g. family belong ('ffaaamily beeelonngg') doing this until all the elements of all the relationships that have been decided on are covered.

The Mindprint is programmed the same way, starting with the Super-Purpose and Germ, and holding the impressions of these two elements while slowly talking through each of the other elements in turn.

As well as forming Complexes to ensure that they are later activated, the process of Programming gives the actors and director time to ensure that they are on the right track.

If you are thinking this is a lot of stuff to hold in your head, I should say that by this time all the pictures you have contemplated for Character Line, for instance, have started to merge into a single impression. Then, when you get to OPAEs, the Character Line, Relationships and Mindprint will also begin to merge together into one single impression which will be easy to recognize and hold. Our brain does this naturally to allow us to hold more thoughts – see Shrinking Pictures section in Chapter 10 on Imagination, pp. 149–150).

Second stage: Programming of OPAEs

Ask any actor how they end up knowing their lines and they'll say something like, 'I don't know, they just stick. When I pick up the glass I find myself saying the line'. In other words during the rehearsal process, the lines and the movements on stage have formed a Complex and all the actor has to do is turn up. So if the actor wants to have the character's thoughts onstage, they just need to hold those thoughts during rehearsal and they will also stick.

The play is stood up in the normal way but with a few differences. Actors prepare several Episodes in advance (by contemplating the OPAEs and reading the lines slowly while holding the OPAEs) of each day's rehearsal.

The actors start at the first Episode of the script and go through each one, consecutively saying each line very slowly while holding a now single impression of the Character Line, Relationships and Mindprint (those Shrinking Pictures), their SP, Germ and OPAEs (to be able to do this takes practice). None of the actors has the script in their hands; if they forget a line they are prompted. The most important part of this process is holding the character's thoughts. Knowing they will get a prompt means actors can have their full Attention on characterization – forming Complexes.

Each Episode is rehearsed this way. The next day these scenes are then gone over again gradually increasing (until reaching normal) speed with each run through, before starting on the next new Episodes.

Step 10 Affinities, Basic Actions, Basic Events and their Modelling

Affinities

OPAEs cover the state of mind for an Episode but that's not everything that needs to be considered. Each moment will have specific thoughts, impressions and Events that need to be added.

As an example, if a character says to a friend, 'Pass me that tennis racquet', if it's his own racquet, he'll have pictures of where he bought it, when he's used it, maybe it's a special racquet because he won his first tournament with it, etc. These are Affinities he has with the tennis racquet.

In Chapter 1 on Complexes, I introduced Affinities generally as thoughts, other than the main one, that are activated in a Complex of thoughts. For the Ten Steps here is an expanded definition:

AFFINITIES:

- Every activated thought in a Complex other than the main one
- Impressions and sometimes pictures that evolve as a result of thinking about the entity under consideration in Active Imagination

---

Two characters are talking about a bus journey they are considering. One has pictures of an adventure and seeing new things. The other thinks of a hot, sweaty, uncomfortable ride. Each is their Affinities to the subject or entity in question. Affinities are considered because they develop the character and the actor's performance (to say nothing of the enjoyment) as well as strengthening the audience's understanding of the character and the play in general.

When Tschubukov mentions Lomov's evening dress, he has his own Affinities to do with this. **Perhaps he likes dressing up, making an effort on a festive occasion where there's a bit of dancing, some drinks.** Or he might **hate having to wear such 'pompous' clothes, 'I feel like a stuffed shirt, all uncomfortable, much prefer my regular stuff'.** I'll leave the choice of Affinity here up to you.

Basic Actions

Each actor has a Main Action for each Episode but as you may remember, within that Main Action there will be many Basic Actions (see pp. 119–120 in Chapter 7). In general we can say there is a Basic Action for every line of the play. Basic Actions are programmed by holding the Action and then saying it out loud and straightaway saying the line(s) related to it.

In the first few lines Lomov says, 'No, I have no engagement except with you, Stepan Stepanovitch'. What is his Action, bearing in mind he 'wants to be accepted' and 'bracing himself' is his Main Action?

By saying this line Lomov prepares himself for what he has come to say, he hints that something is there to be said and hopes that by provoking interest his request won't be too great a shock, hence the Basic Action **I ease my way in.**

Tschubukov then says, 'But why in evening clothes, my friend? This isn't New Year's!' Tschubukov is suspicious so it is probably – **I test.** But because he wants to belong, he adds a thick Device with the New Year reference – **I joke.**

To Programme this, the Action is held by the actor who then says the line, while holding the Action and then immediately says the Action out loud. If this is done frequently and repetitively, the Action will stick.

Basic Events and their Modelling

We have hundreds of Basic Events every single hour of the day: I open the fridge with a picture of getting a sandwich but when I do the fridge is almost empty; I reach for a pen from the table and it's not there; I bite into an apple and it's delicious. We therefore have many Short-term Purposes and to each one there is a reaction as to whether it was achieved or not, either, 'I enjoy' (because the outcome is or is better than I wanted) or 'I regret' (it's worse than I wanted).

> **BASIC EVENTS:** The result of the comparison between the Purpose and the result that was achieved by the Action activated by this Purpose to achieve itself, and sealed with the mini Action 'I regret' or 'I enjoy'

Although in life we have many Basic Events, with a script we need to choose ones that are important to the Plot. In a scene where a man waits for his in-laws who are arriving to stay (he thinks) for just the weekend, he opens the door and each has a large suitcase in their hands – for him that's a Basic Event. Another could be a young woman working in a shop and a colleague she's in love with smiles at her, a man who has forgotten his wife's birthday is asked what he bought her. Scripts are full of Basic Events like these and the actor needs to design his or her thoughts accordingly.

> **MODELLING:** The physical embodiment of the most important Basic Events in an impressive form which as a result convey the Plot and artistic image of the play

For example the shop assistant who gets a smile can pull her hair over her ears (with the Action, 'I preen'). The man who has forgotten to buy a present could scratch his left eyebrow with his right hand partially obscuring his eyes ('I avoid').

Some Basic Events are more important than others and need careful Modelling to ensure the audience's understanding. In a play about loneliness a woman who lives on a farm on her own during the Second World War is seen sitting at the kitchen table peeling potatoes when a love song comes on the radio. She freezes for a few seconds, then turns to the radio before looking at herself in the mirror, making a half-hearted attempt to fix her hair before turning the radio off and going back to peeling. This may not be clear enough, so instead of using the mirror she could run her finger down a photo of a man in uniform or she could go over to a coat stand and pull the arm of a heavy man's coat over her shoulder and rest her face on the sleeve for a few moments. The Basic Event (prompted by the song) is 'My lonely life' but can you see how the Modelling seals the audience's understanding? As this is an important moment in the play, the actor will need to contemplate specific pictures and impressions for that moment and Programme them in rehearsals.

This last paragraph is clearly verging into the director's arena, a subject far beyond the scope of this book, but included here for completeness.

If it's the case that you will rarely be working with a Science of Acting director, yet want to incorporate this technique into your work, I suggest doing as much (depending on your circumstances) as is possible. For instance if you are doing a two-week rehearsal for a fringe play with a short run, you might have time for only the analysis and Programming of Character Line, Relationships and Mindprint as you'll be doing this work out of formal rehearsal time and the run will no doubt end when your OPAEs are just starting to set.

If another time you have four weeks of rehearsal and an eight-week run, you will be able to do all of it (although again, much will be outside of rehearsal). If you just have a casting, then I'd suggest you simply use the Five Ws (Chapter 11) to give you some context.

Most good directors will give you Modelling or stage direction to do and provide you with reasons for picking up that glass or punching that wall. If you find that they don't, you can refer to Step 10 and work out which pictures of your Basic Event make you do whatever it is you need to do. Even after a thirty-week run of a play, an actor can still contemplate the life of their character by adding more detail or simply more contemplation: you should never stop enjoying your work.

And there we have it.

You have reached the end of the book (apart from the added extras to follow).

So. What next?

If I were you . . . I'd close the book, sit back and contemplate all that you have read.

Have a cup of coffee.

Perhaps make a ham sandwich.

Maybe glance down at your shoes to see whether your laces need tying . . .

Then pick up the book once more, open the front cover and start reading it again.

Yes, again.

Why?

I'll let Schopenhauer explain:

Any book that is at all important ought to be at once read through twice; on a second reading the connection of the different portions of the book will be better understood, and the beginning comprehended only when the end is known; and partly because we are not in the same temper and disposition on both readings. On the second perusal we get a new view of every passage and a different impression of the whole book, which then appears in another light.[1]

I don't doubt you read every word on your first read through. Perhaps often thinking 'Hmm . . . yes . . . I understand. That makes sense. Now I'm ready for the next paragraph . . . page . . . chapter.'

But reading the words, even understanding the concepts in the moment that you read or understand them, isn't enough for this work to be of lasting value to you.

So much of this book is about noticing your thoughts – which are there one second and then gone the next that you may not have noticed many of the thought patterns you were looking out for. Or in fact you may have noticed them – which is great – but perhaps only for a second . . . and then they were gone the next.

To gain lasting value from this book, I will say it again, you need to take the time to test everything and see how it works for you in your everyday life.

And this cannot be done fleetingly!

Not as in 'Ah yes, I saw that . . . now to move on', but to recognize your thoughts and their patterns more and more, for as much of the day, every day.

For example, have you started seeing a main thought and been able to recognize the Complex it is a part of? Do you notice that your affinities with a main thought are based on your consciousness . . . which may be different from someone else's? Your character's? Your kitchen and Cleopatra's kitchen?

Are you noticing the difference between visible thoughts and invisible? Are you becoming more aware of the Mushroom/capsule attached to many of your thoughts, how you precipitate the same thoughts over and over? Did you try creating a Mushroom for one of your own thoughts? Or for a character's?

Have you noticed that your thinking about an Event is unique to your consciousness and will differ from someone else's thoughts about that Event – and therefore your character's thoughts about an Event must likewise be unique to them?

When an Unexpected Event takes place in your life, can you see what you expected to happen, and how if you were to act that Unexpected Event, you simply need to hold the pictures of what you expected to happen?

Are you noticing your Short-, Medium- and Long-term Purposes in different situations? Can you identify these for your character in different

Episodes? Are you noticing what your thoughts of happiness are? Are they based on wearing the Cinema Screen glasses – or are you able to take them off? Does your character wear Cinema Screen glasses?

Can you see how the many inputs that formed your consciousness gave you important thoughts that still have an influence on how you live, making you, 'you'? Isn't it enjoyable to contemplate the same influences on the formation of your character's consciousness – do you find that it makes your character more real, within the context of the script?

Can you see how the elements of your Mindprint are working every day and how they are dictating your reality? Notice the importance of this and the value in understanding your character's Mindprint. Have you thought about writing out your Mindprint? And then doing the same for a character you have played or are about to?

How about the use of Actions (and Devices)? Are you aware of how you use them to achieve your Purposes? Do you notice how others use them? Can you see their qualities in time and space? Do you see the value of understanding your character's Action for each Episode – how together with the Objective, Purpose and Event you can establish the state of mind for the character at that time – giving you a firm point of reference for your acting?

Did you try out the Finishing-off Thinking questions with a thought you wanted to finish off or did you just read them, thinking 'Hmm, yes Kogan . . . very interesting'? Can you see how you can come back to these questions over and over again – and that every time you Finish-off a thought which gives you background noise, you are creating more space in your head to think the thoughts you want, making your consciousness more agile and therefore easier to think your character's thoughts?

Have you practised Going Limp or did it just make for an 'interesting read'?

Did you practise clapping custard?

Really?

Have you started to notice the different Tempo-rhythms of people you meet and objects in your home? What about the difference in your Tempo-rhythm depending on the Event you or others are in? Notice the importance in identifying your character's Tempo-rhythm and how it fits with the people and objects in their life.

Are you beginning to see why it may be worth reading the book again? I'll let Gladwell give you a nudge:

Practice isn't what you do once you're good. It's the thing you do that makes you good.

Malcolm Gladwell[2]

Getting it?

Starting to think I may have a point?

I'll keep going just in case . . .

Imagination. Can you see that this is one of the most important tools in your toolbox? And how it makes acting one of the most enjoyable professions there is. That by understanding the different types of Imagination and how you can switch between the different types as well as how to use Stanislavski's Magic 'If', there is no limit to the scope of characters you can play.

Have you noticed how you use the different types of Attention in your everyday? How it is very simple to hold Voluntary Attention on something – but that at times Involuntary Attention slips in. Would you say that perhaps it slipped in a couple of times when you were reading this book? Wouldn't it be worth reading the book again – just to check you didn't miss anything?

Next, your body. Have you started to notice where and when you hold Acquired Tensions and therefore how our consciousness creates our postures? How this must also apply to our characters?

Do you think you can become a Talented actor or do you think you missed out at birth?

Have you thought about trying out the Ten Steps with say a two or three-page short play? This would start to create a Mind Erosion for the process, so that each time you do it, it would be easier and easier . . .

Just like tying your shoe . . .

Yes, reading through the book again is what I would do if I were you. Think of it as another suggestion that you should test for yourself.

A MARRIAGE PROPOSAL

A Comedy in One Act

by

ANTON TCHEKOFF

English version by

HILMAR BAUKHAGE

and

BARRETT H. CLARK

A Marriage Proposal

PERSONS IN THE PLAY

STEPAN STEPANOVITCH TSCHUBUKOV   *A country farmer*
NATALIA STEPANOVNA   *His daughter (aged 25)*
IVAN VASSILIYITCH LOMOV   *Tschubukov's neighbor*

SCENE: *Reception-room in* TSCHUBUKOV'S *country home, Russia.*
TIME: *The present.*

A Marriage Proposal

SCENE: *The reception room in* TSCHUBUKOV's *home.*
TSCHUBUKOV *discovered as the curtain rises.*
(*Enter* LOMOV, *wearing a dress-suit.*)

TSCHUB. (*Going toward him and greeting him*) Who is this I see? My dear fellow! Ivan Vassiliyitch! I'm so glad to see you! (*Shakes hands*) But this is a surprise! How are you?

LOMOV. Thank you! And how are you?

TSCHUB. Oh, so-so, my friend. Please sit down. It isn't right to forget one's neighbor. But tell me, why all this ceremony? Dress clothes, white gloves and all? Are you on your way to some engagement, my good fellow?

LOMOV. No, I have no engagement except with you, Stepan Stepanovitch.

TSCHUB. But why in evening clothes, my friend? This isn't New Year's!

LOMOV. You see, it's simply this, that – (*Composing himself*) I have come to you, Stepan Stepanovitch, to trouble you with a request. It is not the first time I have had the honor of turning to you for assistance, and you have always, that is – I beg your pardon, I am a bit excited! I'll take a drink of water first, dear Stepan Stepanovitch. (*He drinks*)

TSCHUB. (*Aside*) He's come to borrow money! I won't give him any! (*To* LOMOV) What is it, then, dear Lomov?

LOMOV. You see – dear – Stepanovitch, pardon me, Stepan – Stepan – dearvitch – I mean – I am terribly nervous, as you will be so good as to see – ! What I mean to say – you are the only one who can help me, though I don't deserve it, and – and I have no right whatever to make this request of you.

TSCHUB. Oh, don't beat about the bush, my dear fellow. Tell me!

LOMOV. Immediately – in a moment. Here it is, then: I have come to ask for the hand of your daughter, Natalia Stepanovna.

TSCHUB. (*Joyfully*) Angel! Ivan Vassiliyitch! Say that once again! I didn't quite hear it!

LOMOV. I have the honor to beg – –

TSCHUB. (*Interrupting*) My dear, dear man! I am so happy that everything is so – everything! (*Embraces and kisses him*) I have wanted this to happen for so long. It has been my dearest wish! (*He represses a tear*) And I have always loved you, my dear fellow, as my own son! May God give you His blessings and His grace and – I always wanted it to happen. But why am I standing here like a blockhead? I am completely dumbfounded with pleasure, completely dumbfounded. My whole being – ! I'll call Natalia –

LOMOV. Dear Stepan Stepanovitch, what do you think? May I hope for Natalia Stepanovna's acceptance?

TSCHUB. Really! A fine boy like you – and you think she won't accept on the minute? Love-sick as a cat and all that – ! (*He goes out, right*)

LOMOV. I'm cold. My whole body is trembling as though I was going to take my examination! But the chief thing is to settle matters! If a person meditates too much, or hesitates, or talks about it, waits for an ideal or for true love, he never gets it. Brrr! It's cold! Natalia is an excellent house-keeper, not at all bad-looking, well educated – what more could I ask? I'm so excited my ears are roaring! (*He drinks water*) And not to marry, that won't do! In the first place, I'm thirty-five – a critical age, you might say. In the second place, I must live a well-regulated life. I have a weak heart, continual palpitation, and I am very sensitive and always getting excited. My lips begin to tremble and the pulse in my right temple throbs terribly. But the worst of all is sleep! I hardly lie down and begin to doze before something in my left side begins to pull and tug, and something begins to hammer in my left shoulder – and in my head, too! I jump up like a madman, walk about a little, lie down again, but the moment I fall asleep I have a terrible cramp in the side. And so it is all night long!

(*Enter* NATALIA STEPANOVNA.)

NATALIA. Ah! It's you. Papa said to go in: there was a dealer in there who'd come to buy something. Good afternoon, Ivan Vassiliyitch.

LOMOV. Good day, my dear Natalia Stepanovna.

NATALIA. You must pardon me for wearing my apron and this old dress: we are working to-day. Why haven't you come to see us oftener? You've not been here for so long! Sit down. (*They sit down*) Won't you have something to eat?

LOMOV. Thank you, I have just had lunch.

NATALIA. Smoke, do, there are the matches. Today it is beautiful and only yesterday it rained so hard that the workmen couldn't do a stroke of work. How many bricks have you cut? Think of it! I was so anxious that I had the whole field mowed, and now I'm sorry I did it, because I'm afraid the hay will rot. It would have been better if I had waited. But what on earth is this? You are in evening clothes! The latest cut! Are you on your way to a ball? And you seem to be looking better, too – really. Why are you dressed up so gorgeously?

LOMOV. (*Excited*) You see, my dear Natalia Stepanovna – it's simply this: I have decided to ask you to listen to me – of course it will be a surprise, and indeed you'll be angry, but I – (*aside*) How fearfully cold it is!

NATALIA. What is it? (*A pause*) Well?

LOMOV. I'll try to be brief. My dear Natalia Stepanovna, as you know, for many years, since my childhood, I have had the honor to know your family. My poor aunt and her husband, from whom, as you know, I inherited the estate, always had the greatest respect for your father and your poor mother. The Lomovs and the Tschubukovs have been for decades on the friendliest, indeed the closest, terms with each other, and furthermore my property, as you know, adjoins your own. If you will be so good as to remember, my meadows touch your birch woods.

NATALIA. Pardon the interruption. You said 'my meadows' – but are they yours?

LOMOV. Yes, they belong to me.

NATALIA. What nonsense! The meadows belong to us – not to you!

LOMOV. No, to me! Now, my dear Natalia Stepanovna!

NATALIA. Well, that is certainly news to me. How do they belong to you?

LOMOV. How? I am speaking of the meadows lying between your birch woods and my brick-earth.

NATALIA. Yes, exactly. They belong to us.

LOMOV. No, you are mistaken, my dear Natalia Stepanovna, they belong to me.

NATALIA. Try to remember exactly, Ivan Vassiliyitch. Is it so long ago that you inherited them?

LOMOV. Long ago! As far back as I can remember they have always belonged to us.

NATALIA. But that isn't true! You'll pardon my saying so.

LOMOV. It is all a matter of record, my dear Natalia Stepanovna. It is true that at one time the title to the meadows was disputed, but now everyone knows they belong to me. There is no room for discussion. Be so good as to listen: my aunt's grandmother put these meadows, free from all costs, into the hands of your father's grandfather's peasants for a certain time while they were making bricks for my grandmother. These people used the meadows free of cost for about forty years, living there as they would on their own property. Later, however, when – –

NATALIA. There's not a word of truth in that! My grandfather, and my great-grandfather, too, knew that their estate reached back to the swamp, so that the meadows belong to us. What further discussion can there be? I can't understand it. It is really most annoying.

LOMOV. I'll show you the papers, Natalia Stepanovna.

NATALIA. No, either you are joking, or trying to lead me into a discussion. That's not at all nice! We have owned this property for nearly three hundred years, and now all at once we hear that it doesn't belong to us.

Ivan Vassiliyitch, you will pardon me, but I really can't believe my ears. So far as I am concerned, the meadows are worth very little. In all they don't contain more than five acres and they are worth only a few hundred roubles, say three hundred, but the injustice of the thing is what affects me. Say what you will, I can't bear injustice.

LOMOV. Only listen until I have finished, please! The peasants of your respected father's grandfather, as I have already had the honor to tell you, baked bricks for my grandmother. My aunt's grandmother wished to do them a favor – –

NATALIA. Grandfather! Grandmother! Aunt! I know nothing about them. All I know is that the meadows belong to us, and that ends the matter.

LOMOV. No, they belong to me!

NATALIA. And if you keep on explaining it for two days, and put on five suits of evening clothes, the meadows are still ours, ours, ours! I don't want to take your property, but I refuse to give up what belongs to us!

LOMOV. Natalia Stepanovna, I don't need the meadows, I am only concerned with the principle. If you are agreeable, I beg of you, accept them as a gift from me!

NATALIA. But I can give them to you, because they belong to me! That is very peculiar, Ivan Vassiliyitch! Until now we have considered you as a good neighbor and a good friend; only last year we lent you our threshing machine so that we couldn't thresh until November, and now you treat us like thieves! You offer to give me my own land. Excuse me, but neighbors don't treat each other that way. In my opinion, it's a very low trick – to speak frankly – –

LOMOV. According to you I'm a usurper, then, am I? My dear lady, I have never appropriated other people's property, and I shall permit no one to accuse me of such a thing! (*He goes quickly to the bottle and drinks water*) The meadows are mine!

NATALIA. That's not the truth! They are mine!

LOMOV. Mine!

NATALIA. Eh? I'll prove it to you! This afternoon I'll send my reapers into the meadows.

LOMOV. W – h – a – t?

NATALIA. My reapers will be there to-day!

LOMOV. And I'll chase them off!

NATALIA. If you dare!

LOMOV. The meadows are mine, you understand? Mine!

NATALIA. Really, you needn't scream so! If you want to scream and snort and rage you may do it at home, but here please keep yourself within the limits of common decency.

LOMOV. My dear lady, if it weren't that I were suffering from palpitation of the heart and hammering of the arteries in my temples, I would deal with you very differently! (*In a loud voice*) The meadows belong to me!

NATALIA. Us!

LOMOV. Me!

(*Enter* TSCHUBUKOV, *right.*)

TSCHUB. What's going on here? What is he yelling about?

NATALIA. Papa, please tell this gentleman to whom the meadows belong, to us or to him?

TSCHUB. (*To* LOMOV) My dear fellow, the meadows are ours.

LOMOV. But, merciful heavens, Stepan Stepanovitch, how do you make that out? You at least might be reasonable. My aunt's grandmother gave the use of the meadows free of cost to your grandfather's peasants; the peasants lived on the land for forty years and used it as their own, but later when – –

TSCHUB. Permit me, my dear friend. You forget that your grandmother's peasants never paid, because there had been a lawsuit over the meadows, and everyone knows that the meadows belong to us. You haven't looked at the map.

LOMOV. I'll prove to you that they belong to me!

TSCHUB. Don't try to prove it, my dear fellow.

LOMOV. I will!

TSCHUB. My good fellow, what are you shrieking about? You can't prove anything by yelling, you know. I don't ask for anything that belongs to you, nor do I intend to give up anything of my own. Why should I? If it has gone so far, my dear man, that you really intend to claim the meadows, I'd rather give them to the peasants than you, and I certainly shall!

LOMOV. I can't believe it! By what right can you give away property that doesn't belong to you?

TSCHUB. Really, you must allow me to decide what I am to do with my own land! I'm not accustomed, young man, to have people address me in that tone of voice. I, young man, am twice your age, and I beg you to address me respectfully.

LOMOV. No! No! You think I'm a fool! You're making fun of me! You call my property yours and then expect me to stand quietly by and talk to you like a human being. That isn't the way a good neighbor behaves, Stepan Stepanovitch! You are no neighbor, you're no better than a landgrabber. That's what you are!

TSCHUB. Wh – at? What did he say?

NATALIA. Papa, send the reapers into the meadows this minute!

TSCHUB. (*To* LOMOV) What was that you said, sir?

NATALIA. The meadows belong to us and I won't give them up! I won't give them up! I won't give them up!

LOMOV. We'll see about that! I'll prove in court that they belong to me.

TSCHUB. In court! You may sue in court, sir, if you like! Oh, I know you, you are only waiting to find an excuse to go to law! You're an intriguer, that's what you are! Your whole family were always looking for quarrels. The whole lot!

LOMOV. Kindly refrain from insulting my family. The entire race of Lomov has always been honorable! And never has one been brought to trial for embezzlement, as your dear uncle was!

TSCHUB. And the whole Lomov family were insane!

NATALIA. Every one of them!

TSCHUB. Your grandmother was a dipsomaniac, and the younger aunt, Nastasia Michailovna, ran off with an architect.

LOMOV. And your mother limped. (*He puts his hand over his heart*) Oh, my side pains! My temples are bursting! Lord in Heaven! Water!

TSCHUB. And your dear father was a gambler – and a glutton!

NATALIA. And your aunt was a gossip like few others!

LOMOV. And you are an intriguer. Oh, my heart! And it's an open secret that you cheated at the elections – my eyes are blurred! Where is my hat?

NATALIA. Oh, how low! Liar! Disgusting thing!

LOMOV. Where's the hat – ? My heart! Where shall I go? Where is the door – ? Oh – it seems – as though I were dying! I can't – my legs won't hold me – (*Goes to the door*)

TSCHUB. (*Following him*) May you never darken my door again!

NATALIA. Bring your suit to court! We'll see!

(LOMOV *staggers out, center.*)

TSCHUB. (*Angrily*) The devil!

NATALIA. Such a good-for-nothing! And then they talk about being good neighbors!

TSCHUB. Loafer! Scarecrow! Monster!

NATALIA. A swindler like that takes over a piece of property that doesn't belong to him and then dares to argue about it!

TSCHUB. And to think that this fool dares to make a proposal of marriage!

NATALIA. What? A proposal of marriage?

TSCHUB. Why, yes! He came here to make you a proposal of marriage.

NATALIA. Why didn't you tell me that before?

TSCHUB. That's why he had on his evening clothes! The poor fool!

NATALIA. Proposal for me? Oh! (*Falls into an armchair and groans*) Bring him back! Bring him back!

TSCHUB. Bring whom back?

NATALIA. Faster, faster, I'm sinking! Bring him back! (*She becomes hysterical*)

TSCHUB. What is it? What's wrong with you? (*His hands to his head*) I'm cursed with bad luck! I'll shoot myself! I'll hang myself!

NATALIA. I'm dying! Bring him back!

TSCHUB. Bah! In a minute! Don't bawl! (*He rushes out, center*)

NATALIA. (*Groaning*) What have they done to me? Bring him back! Bring him back!

TSCHUB. (*Comes running in*) He's coming at once! The devil take him! Ugh! Talk to him yourself, I can't.

NATALIA. (*Groaning*) Bring him back!

TSCHUB. He's coming, I tell you! 'Oh, Lord! What a task it is to be the father of a grown daughter!' I'll cut my throat! I really will cut my throat! We've argued with the fellow, insulted him, and now we've thrown him out! – and you did it all, you!

NATALIA. No, you! You haven't any manners, you are brutal! If it weren't for you, he wouldn't have gone!

TSCHUB. Oh, yes, I'm to blame! If I shoot or hang myself, remember *you'll* be to blame. You forced me to it! You! (LOMOV *appears in the doorway*) There, talk to him yourself! (*He goes out*)

LOMOV. Terrible palpitation! – My leg is lamed! My side hurts me – –

NATALIA. Pardon us, we were angry, Ivan Vassiliyitch. I remember now – the meadows really belong to you.

LOMOV. My heart is beating terribly! My meadows – my eyelids tremble – (*They sit down*) We were wrong. It was only the principle of the thing – the property isn't worth much to me, but the principle is worth a great deal.

NATALIA. Exactly, the principle! Let us talk about something else.

LOMOV. Because I have proofs that my aunt's grandmother had, with the peasants of your good father – –

NATALIA. Enough, enough. (*Aside*) I don't know how to begin. (*To* LOMOV) Are you going hunting soon?

LOMOV. Yes, heath-cock shooting, respected Natalia Stepanovna. I expect to begin after the harvest. Oh, did you hear? My dog, Ugadi, you know him – limps!

NATALIA. What a shame! How did that happen?

LOMOV. I don't know. Perhaps it's a dislocation, or maybe he was bitten by some other dog. (*He sighs*) The best dog I ever had – to say nothing of his price! I paid Mironov a hundred and twenty-five roubles for him.

NATALIA. That was too much to pay, Ivan Vassilivitch.

LOMOV. In my opinion it was very cheap. A wonderful dog!

NATALIA. Papa paid eighty-five roubles for his Otkatai, and Otkatai is much better than your Ugadi.

LOMOV. Really? Otkatai is better than Ugadi? What an idea! (*He laughs*) Otkatai better than Ugadi!

NATALIA. Of course he is better. It is true Otkatai is still young; he isn't full-grown yet, but in the pack or on the leash with two or three, there is no better than he, even – –

LOMOV. I really beg your pardon, Natalia Stepanovna, but you quite overlooked the fact that he has a short lower jaw, and a dog with a short lower jaw can't snap.

NATALIA. Short lower jaw? That's the first time I ever heard that!

LOMOV. I assure you, his lower jaw is shorter than the upper.

NATALIA. Have you measured it?

LOMOV. I have measured it. He is good at running, though.

NATALIA. In the first place, our Otkatai is pure-bred, a full-blooded son of Sapragavas and Stameskis, and as for your mongrel, nobody could ever figure out his pedigree; he's old and ugly, and as skinny as an old hag.

LOMOV. Old, certainly! I wouldn't take five of your Otkatais for him! Ugadi is a dog and Otkatai is – it is laughable to argue about it! Dogs like your Otkatai can be found by the dozens at any dog dealer's, a whole poundfull!

NATALIA. Ivan Vassiliyitch, you are very contrary to-day. First our meadows belong to you and then Ugadi is better than Otkatai. I don't like it when a person doesn't say what he really thinks. You know perfectly well that Otkatai is a hundred times better than your silly Ugadi. What makes you keep on saying he isn't?

LOMOV. I can see, Natalia Stepanovna, that you consider me either a blindman or a fool. But at least you may as well admit that Otkatai has a short lower jaw!

NATALIA. It isn't so!

LOMOV. Yes, a short lower jaw!

NATALIA. (*Loudly*) It's not so!

LOMOV. What makes you scream, my dear lady?

NATALIA. What makes you talk such nonsense? It's disgusting! It is high time that Ugadi was shot, and yet you compare him with Otkatai!

LOMOV. Pardon me, but I can't carry on this argument any longer. I have palpitation of the heart!

NATALIA. I have always noticed that the hunters who do the most talking know the least about hunting.

LOMOV. My dear lady, I beg of you to be still. My heart is bursting! (*He shouts*) Be still!

NATALIA. I won't be still until you admit that Otkatai is better!

(*Enter* TSCHUBUKOV.)

TSCHUB. Well, has it begun again?

NATALIA. Papa, say frankly, on your honor, which dog is better: Otkatai or Ugadi?

LOMOV. Stepan Stepanovitch, I beg of you, just answer this: has your dog a short lower jaw or not? Yes or no?

TSCHUB. And what if he has? Is it of such importance? There is no better dog in the whole country.

LOMOV. My Ugadi is better. Tell the truth, now!

TSCHUB. Don't get so excited, my dear fellow! Permit me. Your Ugadi certainly has his good points. He is from a good breed, has a good stride, strong haunches, and so forth. But the dog, if you really want to know it, has two faults; he is old and he has a short lower jaw.

LOMOV. Pardon me, I have palpitation of the heart! – Let us keep to facts – just remember in Maruskins's meadows, my Ugadi kept ear to ear with the Count Rasvachai and your dog.

TSCHUB. He was behind, because the Count struck him with his whip.

LOMOV. Quite right. All the other dogs were on the fox's scent, but Otkatai found it necessary to bite a sheep.

TSCHUB. That isn't so! – I am sensitive about that and beg you to stop this argument. He struck him because everybody looks on a strange dog of good blood with envy. Even you, sir, aren't free from the sin. No sooner do you find a dog better than Ugadi than you begin to – this, that – his, mine – and so forth! I remember distinctly.

LOMOV. I remember something, too!

TSCHUB. (*Mimicking him*) I remember something, too! What do you remember?

LOMOV. Palpitation! My leg is lame – I can't – –

NATALIA. Palpitation! What kind of hunter are you? You ought to stay in the kitchen by the stove and wrestle with the potato peelings, and not go fox-hunting! Palpitation!

TSCHUB. And what kind of hunter are you? A man with your diseases ought to stay at home and not jolt around in the saddle. If you were a hunter – ! But you only ride round in order to find out about other people's dogs, and make trouble for everyone. I am sensitive! Let's drop the subject. Besides, you're no hunter.

LOMOV. And are you a hunter? You only ride around to flatter the Count! – My heart! You intriguer! Swindler!

TSCHUB. And what of it? (*Shouting*) Be still!

LOMOV. Intriguer!

TSCHUB. Baby! Puppy! Walking drug-store!

LOMOV. Old rat! Jesuit! Oh, I know you!

TSCHUB. Be still! Or I'll shoot you – with my worst gun, like a partridge! Fool! Loafer!

LOMOV. Everyone knows that – oh, my heart! – that your poor late wife beat you. My leg – my temples – Heavens – I'm dying – I – –

TSCHUB. And your housekeeper wears the trousers in your house!

LOMOV. Here – here – there – there – my heart has burst! My shoulder is torn apart. Where is my shoulder? I'm dying! (*He falls into a chair*) The doctor! (*Faints*)

TSCHUB. Baby! Half-baked clam! Fool!

NATALIA. Nice sort of hunter you are! You can't even sit on a horse. (*To* TSCHUB) Papa, what's the matter with him? (*She screams*) Ivan Vassiliyitch! He is dead!

LOMOV. I'm ill! I can't breathe! Air!

NATALIA. He is dead! (*She shakes* LOMOV *in the chair*) Ivan Vassiliyitch! What have we done! He is dead! (*She sinks into a chair*) The doctor – doctor! (*She goes into hysterics*)

TSCHUB. Ahh! What is it? What's the matter with you?

NATALIA. (*Groaning*) He's dead! – Dead!

TSCHUB. Who is dead? Who? (*Looking at* LOMOV) Yes, he is dead! Good God! Water! The doctor! (*Holding the glass to* LOMOV.'s *lips*) Drink! No, he won't drink! He's dead! What a terrible situation! Why didn't I shoot myself? Why have I never cut my throat? What am I waiting for now? Only give me a knife! Give me a pistol! (LOMOV *moves*) He's coming to! Drink some water – there!

LOMOV. Sparks! Mists! Where am I?

TSCHUB. Get married! Quick, and then go to the devil! She's willing! (*He joins the hands of* LOMOV *and* NATALIA) She's agreed! Only leave me in peace!

LOMOV. Wh – what? (*Getting up*) Whom?

TSCHUB. She's willing! Well? Kiss each other and – the devil take you both!

NATALIA. (*Groans*) He lives! Yes, yes, I'm willing!

TSCHUB. Kiss each other!

LOMOV. Eh? Whom? (NATALIA *and* LOMOV *kiss*) Very nice – ! Pardon me, but what is this for? Oh, yes, I understand! My heart – sparks – I am happy, Natalia Stepanovna. (*He kisses her hand*) My leg is lame!

NATALIA. I'm happy, too!

TSCHUB. Ahh! A load off my shoulders! Ahh!

NATALIA. And now at least you'll admit that Ugadi is worse than Otkatai!

LOMOV. Better!

NATALIA. Worse!

TSCHUB. Now the domestic joys have begun. – Champagne!

LOMOV. Better!

NATALIA. Worse, worse, worse!

TSCHUB. (*Trying to drown them out*) Champagne, champagne!

CURTAIN

AUTHOR'S AFTERWORD

If I have achieved my Purpose, you should now be confident that you have all the tools you need to become a professional actor; an actor with an agile enough consciousness and body to act any part at any time with any director, in any style, in any venue.

This knowledge alone isn't enough to become a professional actor. To hold not just one foreign thought but a whole, though small, consciousness is not an easy task for a consciousness to do, and yes, this requires time and practice.

In addition you need to develop certain qualities. On top of Attention, Imagination, Awareness and Talent, are the finer qualities of Self-Discipline, Sensitivity and Dedication.

Self-Discipline is a subject that is a favourite with philosophers and psychologists and yet I found no definition adequate for actors among their work. For an actor there is no point talking about Self-Discipline if there is no indication as to how to improve it.

What we call Self-Discipline is the conscious creation of Purposes, that is the ability to create Purposes in pictures and impressions which compel us to Actions. That is, not to follow the Purposes that are in our heads as a result of our lives and which are unaware to most people, but to awarely understand the Purposes that are propelling us and replace them with ones healthy and attractive enough to become the driving force shunting us towards our Super-Purpose.

Sensitivity. In life when we say that someone is sensitive, we mean that 'he or she sees more into a situation than was evident' or that 'they get easily upset'. In my view Sensitivity is the ability to perceive one's own and other people's thoughts. A sensitive person does not show that they have perceived anything, and more often than not they will not react to what they have perceived. In life you will notice that the deeper and the more one can see behind the facets of life, the calmer (not to be mistaken for lazier) that person is – or to rephrase, the calmer someone is the more they notice in others and the more sensitive they are.

What makes them sensitive is their Awareness, their ability to watch their own thoughts. They became this way by noticing their own thoughts in all situations and that's what makes them understand others. Therefore high Sensitivity (a high rate of aware perception) is a result of developed Awareness.

Of all the qualities, however, it is my opinion that the most important for an actor is Dedication.

Dedication to acting as a way of life.

The dictionary tells us that dedication means 'Selfless devotion'. But this tells us nothing about how we can develop our Dedication. If I go to a Thesaurus to find something more suitable, the closest I get to what I want is 'Love'. Most of us have loved something or someone at some time in our lives and acknowledged that that was love. This synonym makes our 'Dedication' picture clearer but it doesn't tell us how to develop it.

So we have to ask the questions: What is 'Love'? How do we know that we Love?

We know that we Love when we frequently think about someone or something.

If we love 'it', we often think about 'it', so by frequent thinking we increase our love . . . our Dedication.

While we cannot make ourselves feel certain feelings, we can with an agile mind easily think when and what we want to think. Therefore if we make ourselves frequently think about acting, we will develop our Dedication to acting. That is not to say we think about our success in acting (fans, reviews, red carpets . . . etc.), it is thinking about acting. Period.

Having arrived at this point in the book it should be clear to you that thinking about acting really means thinking about oneself – therefore it isn't really Dedication to acting that's at the core of *The Science of Acting*, but Dedication to oneself.

FINAL WORD

'A young man asked Socrates how he could get wisdom.

'Come with me,' Socrates replied. He took the lad to a river and shoved his head underwater. He held it there until the boy struggled for air.

Then he let him go.

Once the boy regained his composure, Socrates asked him, 'What did you desire most when your head was underwater?'

'I wanted air', the boy told him.

Socrates nodded slowly.

'When you want wisdom as much as you wanted air when you were immersed in the water,' he said, 'you will receive it.'[1]

Just as the boy desperately wanted air, Sam spent most of his life gasping to understand why people think the way they do and how they can change it to create beautiful characters and live happy, fulfilled lives.

I sincerely hope this book helps you do both.

HK

This book is long overdue and would have been further delayed if it were not for the contributions, help, support and advice from the graduates and students of ASAD, in particular David Bark-Jones, Nick Cawdron, Semeli Economou, Thomas Garvey, Elizabeth Bowe, Nick Piovanelli, Audrey Sheffield, Jennifer Mushumani, Philip Bulcock, Katie Bartrop, Alex Dower, Andrew Byron, William Ribo, Paul Mushmani, Neil Sheffield, Odette Garvey, Elanor Wallis-Scott, Sacha Grimsditch, Teresa Grimsditch, Roger Vilonius, Barbara Hatwell, Sally Cancello and Peter Sunnegren.

Additional thanks and gratitude to Pillai Sambhu, Teresa Irvine Hendrix, Stewart Pearce, Jaap van Etten, George Xanthou (illustrations),

Monica Lowenberg, Lee Hurley, Stuart Creton, Joseph McCauley, Rina Hill, Claudia Auger, Denis Murphy, Yasmene Shah, Tim Hatton, Zoe Coates, Kappy, Steve Walpole, Chris Sherliker, Adam Pierpoint, Steve Willey, Jennifer Rainsford, Suzy Crook, Abel Azdad, Michael Morris, Taisia Pianov, Johnine Stone, Richard Stone, John Matthews, Claudia Cuffey, my Mum and Dad.

Words are not enough.
Thankfully.

APPENDIX 1

LIST OF PURPOSES AND THEIR DEFINITIONS

I want to HAVE A LIFE
I want PiCs to care for me in a way that will make me capable of living my life to the full.

I want to KNOW HOW TO THINK
I want to acquire a consciousness that reflects, rather than constructs/distorts, the outside world, including the thinking of other people. As a result I will be able to make decisions.

I want to be LOVED
I want other people to think about me all the time and give me care, pleasure and security, disregard all my faults and mistakes, and to be prepared to make sacrifices for me, but primarily to accept my Shame Events as their own.
Note: this is for the Unaware Mind.

I want to LOVE
Reverse of the above, with the addition of wanting to suffer for the other party's Shame Events to atone for my own.
Note: this is for the Unaware Mind.

I want to be IN LOVE
I want to love in return for being loved (see above).

I want to be LIKED
I want my Shame Events to pass unnoticed so that I can achieve a high degree of approval and acceptance.

I want to be ADMIRED
I want others to want to become part of my life at the expense of theirs. I want them to envy me and think of me as being a little mysterious.

I want to be HELD IN AWE
I want to be a mystery to others, I want them to think that my position is
unattainable to them, that most of my qualities are inborn or given to me
by God, and that my thinking is imperceptible to them.

I want a DISAPPOINTING LIFE
Happiness is having fucked my life up.

I want to be IMPORTANT
I want people to have fear of me so that they put my interests first, and
live in accordance with my wishes.

I want to be POWERFUL
I want to be unquestionably obeyed. I want others to be so scared of me
that they think that they are, or should become, my slaves.

I want to be ACKNOWLEDGED
I want to be appreciated for my skills by people of equal status with me
because they understand how difficult what I do is.

I want to be CENTRE OF ATTENTION
I want to be the main object of somebody's or everybody's thinking.

I want to be FAMOUS
I want to be known by everyone.

I want to be LUCKY
I want to be favoured by fate.

I want to be RICH
I want to have so much money so as not to know what to do with it.

I want to be HEALTHY
With regard to my body I want to have thoughts of its good health only.

I want to have a LONG LIFE
I want to live for as long as I want.

I want to be BEAUTIFUL
With regard to my beauty I want to have peace of mind and enjoy my
looks, and know that others do so too.

I want to be APPRECIATED
I want people to be grateful to me for my qualities and actions, e.g. hos-
pitality, generosity, suffering, kindness.

I want to be REMEMBERED
I want to become a frequently used memory.

I want to be CHOSEN BY GOD
I want to be special to God for my faith, suffering and sacrifices for Him, and for being his frequent object of attention.

I want to be SPECIAL
I want to be unique for being sensitive, talented, courageous etc.

I want to be RESPECTED
I want others to appreciate my superior position either because of my work or qualities, and as a result, fulfil my wishes without my having to express them.

I want to be ENVIED
I want to be hated for my qualities and/or achievements by people power-less to catch up with me or harm me.

I want to be ACCEPTED
I want to pass the threshold considered from negative or non-existent relationship to a positive one.

I want to be CARED FOR
I want others to solve my problems, make my life easier, more soothing, pleasant, comfortable and secure.

I want to be THE WINNER
I want to be the first to achieve the aims that others have too.

I want to be STRONG
I want to be in complete command of my mind and body.

I want to be FREE
I want to be in command of my own destiny.
I want to think what I want to think.

I want to be PERFECT
I want to take pride when comparing my body and/or my mind with the ideal.

I want to FIND OUT
I want to see the meaning of things behind their appearances or mani-festations.

I want to SURVIVE
I want to stay alive.
I want to get through (a period of) life unscathed.

I want to HELP PEOPLE
I want to make people think for themselves.

I want to MAKE PEOPLE HAPPY
I want to let people achieve their Purposes.
I want to do what I think is best for them (and me), that is I want people to fail.

I want to LOSE MYSELF
I want to avoid thinking painful or shameful thoughts by speeding up my thinking, or by numbing my brain with self-produced and/or introduced drugs, alcohol, food, pain, sound – even that of my own voice, self-punishment, or by making myself think pleasurable thoughts.

I want to DIE
I want to end my suffering. I want to have peace forever.

I want to HAVE PEACE OF MIND
I want to be free from thinking unpleasant thoughts.

I want to HAVE A PEACEFUL LIFE
I want to have no Unexpected or unpleasant Events.

I want to BELONG
I want those with whom I and my Shame Events are safe, to be a part of my life.
I want others to think that they with their Shame Events are secure with me.

I want to DO MY DUTY
I want to do a touch more than needed to complete the task so as to have complete peace of mind.

I want to FEEL SECURE
I want to fail so as to avoid unpleasant happenings in the future.

I want to be SECURE
I want to be reassured that nothing unpleasant is going to happen.

I want to DO MY BEST
I want all my efforts, mental and physical, to be focused on what I am doing.

I want to HAVE A COMFORTABLE LIFE
I want to be able to afford all the material possessions that I want.

I want to HAVE AN EASY LIFE
I want to have as few obstacles as possible and to do things with as few obstacles as possible.

I want to HAVE A FINE LIFE
(To avoid thinking about my Shame Events)
I want to live among refined people and/or refined things, that is selected for being especially different.

I want to HAVE A BEAUTIFUL LIFE
(To avoid thinking about my Shame Events)
I want to draw enjoyment from living among beautiful things, visiting beautiful places, knowing beautiful people.

I want to HAVE A FULFILLED LIFE
I want to live my life so as to be satisfied with the way I used my time towards the fulfilment of an aware Purpose.

I want to ENJOY MY LIFE
I want to be achieving Purposes with finished thinking.

I want to ATONE
I want to be punished enough for my Shame Events to restore my peace of mind.

I want FAIRNESS (JUSTICE)
I want to be given good will for the good will that I gave first.

I want to TAKE REVENGE
I want to enjoy other people's suffering for the suffering I had (and still have) to go through.

I want to RELAX
I want to be free of mental and physical tensions.

I want to be RIGHT
I want to live as I think I should, in accordance with my visible idea of happiness.

I want to ORIENTATE MYSELF
I want to establish as many affinities as possible.

I want to be SUPERIOR
I want to know that I am above others within the qualities I compare.
I want others to know that I am more special and important than they are.

I want to be UNDERSTOOD
I want others to know what I think and feel (even without my telling them).

I want to be ASSURED
I want to know that things are as I thought they were.

I want to SUCCEED
I want to lose myself within well-deserved or well-earned circumstances.
I want to achieve what I have decided to achieve.

I want to be NEEDED
I want others to think that they will be unable to live without me, or that without me they will be unable to think the thoughts they wish they could.

I want to be INTELLIGENT
I want to know that I have knowledge to match that of other people.

I want to IMPRESS
I want others to know that I have achieved (or I can easily achieve) the high goals that I set out to achieve.

I want to UNDERSTAND
I want to create totalities from the bits of information available.

I want to be SPECIAL TO MYSELF
I want to revel or wallow in my very own thoughts and feelings (unfinished thinking with imagined security).

I want to be PROUD OF MYSELF
I want to take pride in succeeding where others (would have) failed.

I want an EXCITING LIFE
I want to have as many (Unexpected) Events as possible.
I want to lose myself in risky pleasures.

I want to FAIL
I don't want to achieve what I can.

I want to be CONFUSED
I do not want to understand what I might understand.
I want to have too many, too few or no points of reference so as not to be able to arrive at any conclusions.

I want to have a state of mind which does not allow me to understand anything.

I want to SUFFER
I want to be in (mental or physical) pain (e.g. I want to have a hard life).

I want to be LOST
I don't want to know anything.
I don't want to know where I am or what I am.

I want to DESPAIR
I want to wallow in my helplessness of knowing I cannot (ever) achieve my Purpose(s).

I want to FEEL GUILTY
I want to suffer (from a gnawing feeling in my chest) because of the knowledge that I have done what I should not have done.

I want to be GUILTY
I want to do something that will make me suffer from the knowledge that I have done what I should not have done.

I want OTHERS TO FAIL
I want to prevent others from achieving what they want and can.

I want to be UNHAPPY
I don't want to enjoy what I can.

I want to be HELPLESS
I want to be unable to do what I am expected (even by myself) to do.

I want to be STUPID
I want to be unable to understand.
I don't want to have clear thoughts.
I don't want to know what I know.
I don't want to know what the people I want to belong with don't know.

I want to be THICK
I want to be unable to see my thoughts.

I want to have a FRIGHTENING LIFE
I want to think that at any moment something terrible is going to happen, or is being prepared to happen.

I want to be REJECTED
I want others to loathe my company.

I want to PLEASE
I want to live the way I think other people want me to.

I want A WASTED LIFE
I want to spend much more time than is expedient on achieving Purposes.

I want to be UNDISCOVERED
I don't want to be found out for what I really am.

I want to be DISCOVERED
I want to be found out by others for what I really am, without my telling them.

I want to be PUNISHED
I want to have pain, physical and/or mental, inflicted on me by others for the wrongs I did.

I want to be INFERIOR
I want to know that I am worse than others.

I want to be LONELY
I want to think that I am not thought of by anyone.
I want to think that there is no one with whom I can share my life.

I want to be DEPRIVED
I want fate or people in a position of power to refuse me what others get with little or no effort.

I want to FORGET
I don't want to remember my past.

I want to be HATED
I want people to loathe me or to want to beat me senseless or to want to kill me.

I want to be DESIRED
I want people to want to ravish me.

I want to be RAVISHED
I want others to gorge on me with insatiable lust.

I want to be HARD TO GET
I want others to use extra time and effort to make me belong with them.

I want to be HUMILIATED
I want others to denigrate me for my worthlessness.
I want others to laugh at my failure.

I want to be SUSPECTED
I want others to think I have knowingly broken or will break a contract.

I want to be MISUNDERSTOOD
I want others to think that I am something else other than what I really am.
I want others to be mistaken about me.

I want to be a MYSTERY TO MYSELF
I don't want to understand myself.

I want to be STRANGE (A FUCK UP)
I want to have unconventional thinking.

I want to be MAD
I want to be unable to control my thoughts or emotions.

I want to be SCHIZOPHRENIC
I want to split my consciousness to the extent that I do not see that my life was/is being taken away from me.

I want to be SEDUCED
I want to be brought to the state where I will be unable, through titillation, to resist the pressure to have sex.

I want to be FUCKED
I want to be penetrated. I want to have sex.

I want to be INFLUENTIAL
I want people to change their lives as a result of them thinking about me, my words and my deeds.

I want to be UGLY
I want to be rejected as soon as I am seen.

I want to be REPULSIVE
I want others to cringe in disgust every time they look at me or think about me.

I want to be MY OWN SHAME
I want to suffer for being uniquely disgusting.

I want to be LOST IN TRIFLES
I want to be preoccupied with trivia.

I want to be FRUSTRATED
I want to be angry for having unnecessary obstacles thrown in my way by fate or by people or even myself.

I want to be TRUSTED
I want others to have complete faith in my integrity.

I want to have NO RESPONSIBILITIES
I want to blame forces outside my control for my deeds, faults and mistakes.

I want to be a BURDEN
I want to drag others down.

I want to be BETRAYED
I want my trust to be abused.

I want to be other PEOPLE'S SHAME
I want others to cringe from being associated with me.

I want to have SHAME EVENTS
I want to cringe when seeing my thoughts.

I want to be SHIT
I want to be the lowest of the low.

I want to be DISAPPOINTED
I want nobody and nothing to live up to my expectations.

I want to be NORMAL
I want to think and believe as I was meant to by nature.

I want to be FATED
I want to be incapable of controlling the events of my life.

I want to PROVOKE SUFFERING
I want to cause others (physical and/or mental) pain.

I want to be LET DOWN
I want to rely on unreliable people or things.

I want to REMEMBER
I want to keep my memories visible.

I want to be TOLD OFF
I want people to make me have to realize my mistakes.

I want to be a VICTIM OF CIRCUMSTANCES
I don't want to be responsible for my life.

I want to FEEL GOOD
I want to enjoy my physical well-being.

I want to be FORCED INTO SHAME
I want to please or blackmail the other party of my ultimate communion.

I want to be LOST IN SHAME
I want to be unworthy of life.

I want to be UNPREDICTABLE
I don't want to know and/or others to know what I am going to think or do next.

I want to PROVOKE ANGER
I want others to feel aggressive negative actions towards me so their CVT shrinks and as a result (a) they are unable to think (b) they do what I want them to do.

I want to be DEVIOUS
I want to use the circumstances to my advantage.

APPENDIX TWO

LIST OF ACTIONS

I accept
I accuse
I acquiesce
I admire
I admit
I agree
I allow
I apologize
I appease
I appreciate
I ask for help/understanding
I assess
I assume
I atone
I attack
I attract attention
I avoid
I back off
I belong
I betray
I bide my time
I blackmail
I blame
I bluff
I boast
I brace myself
I bribe

I brush off
I bully
I care
I care for myself
I challenge
I clutch at straws
I compare
I complain
I condescend
I condescend to myself
I confess
I contemplate
I corner
I cover up
I cringe
I curse
I defend
I demand
I denigrate
I despair
I direct attention
I disagree
I do my best (I want peace of
    mind – I want to be proud
    of myself leads to forcing,
    i.e. I force myself)
I do my duty

I doubt
I draw attention
I dread
I dream
I duck
I ease my way in
I encourage
I enjoy
I entice
I envy
I evade
I explain
I expose
I feed the bait
I find out
I find out about
I fish for flattery
I flatter
I flirt
I force myself
I forgive myself
I fuck myself
I give in
I give leeway
I give up
I gloat
I go limp
I gorge myself
I greet
I grieve
I grovel
I guess
I guide
I hit out
I humble myself
I humour
I hunt
I hush up
I impress
I indulge
I indulge myself

I ingratiate myself
I insist
I instruct
I joke
I jump in
I justify
I keep my fingers crossed
I keep up conversation
I kill
I kill time
I let go
I like
I long for
I look forward
I lose myself
I lure
I make peace
I memorize
I mock
I nudge
I offer help
I order
I orientate myself
I pacify
I paint a picture
I parry
I pass my time
I pass the buck
I persevere
I pity myself
I plead
I please (I want to make people
     happy)
I plot (a mischief)
I postpone
I pounce
I preach
I pre-empt
I preen
I prepare
I prime

I probe
I prod
I promise
I protest
I provoke
    anger/attack/interest/regret/
    remorse/worry
I punish myself
I push
I put down
I put off
I reassure
I recall
I reflect
I regret
I regroup
I rehearse
I reject
I relax
I remember
I remind
I reproach
I rescue
I retreat
I revel
I runaway
I save face
I scold
I scream for help
I search for clues
I search my memory
I seek sympathy
I set the hook
I share
I show interest, care etc.
I shrink

I shrug off
I sneer
I snub
I soothe
I spit
I squirm
I stab (in the back)
I stand my ground
I stop
I stress
I suffer
I sulk
I survive
I suspect
I take a risk
I take my time
I take pride
I take revenge
I taunt
I tease
I tell off
I terminate
I test
I threaten
I torture
I trap
I triumph
I wait
I want to be liked, accepted,
    appreciated
I want to lose myself
I warn
I whip
I wish
I worry

APPENDIX 3

The Ten Steps

---

1 PLOT
The description of the main Events and Happenings of the play *only*, described in simple terms without any interpretation

2 FACTS AND HAPPENINGS
1 Circumstances and Happenings that have taken place beyond doubt
2 True facts that are confirmed by independent witnesses

CLARIFYING BLURRED FACTS:
Creating pictures of Events and offered circumstances that are implied by the context of the play

3 GERM OF THE SCRIPT
Summary of the cast's thinking of what the play is about

4 MINDPRINT
Verbal embodiment of important generalized thinking which make up the character (cross-referred with the Character Line, Relationships and Events that lead to it)

5 CHARACTER LINE
Chronologically arranged sequence of Events from the character's life, as perceived by the character, i.e. in Active Imagination (cross-referred with the Mindprint)

The Ten Steps continued

6 RELATIONSHIPS	Establishing the pictures one character has about another and the generalized thoughts that the relationship is based on (cross-referred with the Mindprint)
7 EVENTS AND HAPPENINGS	(Chronologically arranged) Events and Happenings from the script and how they are reflected in the main characters' thinking
8 EPISODES AND THEIR OPAEs	Breaking down the play into sections in which most, if not all, of the character's Objectives, Purposes, Actions and Events remain the same
9 PROGRAMMING	1 Programming the Character Line, Relationships and Mindprint 2 Programming of OPAEs

10 AFFINITIES, BASIC ACTIONS, BASIC EVENTS AND THEIR MODELLING

AFFINITIES
Establishing impressions and sometimes pictures that evolve as a result of thinking about the entity under consideration

BASIC ACTIONS
Same definition as Main Action (What I do to achieve my Purpose), but covering a much smaller unit of time

BASIC EVENTS
The smallest visible unit of thinking. The result of the comparison between the Purpose and the result achieved by the Basic Action activated by the basic Purpose (Short-term Purpose) and sealed by a mini Action, i.e. I enjoy/I regret

MODELLING
The embodiment of the most important Basic Events in impressive form to convey the Plot and artistic image of the play

GLOSSARY

ACCUMULATED EVENTS: An Event that was unnoticeably created from a series of unimportant thoughts, over a much longer period of time than a sudden Event

ACQUIRED FRAME OF REFERENCE = Natural Frame of Reference + the following major inputs:

- Prenatal
- PiC
- Awareness and Self-Conditioning
- Non-biological
- Emerging Awarenesses
- Somatic

And the myriad of minor or unique inputs to the individual that have not been included here

ACTING (quality): The quality of acting is in inverse proportion to unfinished thinking

ACTING TECHNIQUE: Aware use of usually unaware thinking processes

ACTION: What I do to achieve my Purpose

ACTIONS: The relationship between oneself and the object of Attention

ACTIVE IMAGINATION: Imagining yourself from within, with Sense Data

ADJUSTERS (Adj): Thoughts that keep me in my Mind Erosion

AFFINITIES:
- Every activated thought in a Complex other than the main one
- Impressions and sometimes pictures that evolve as a result of thinking about the entity under consideration in Active Imagination

AFTERBURN: Aware Dissipation

ANTICIPATION:
- Increasing intensity of thinking in imaginary pictures and impressions
- ANTICIPATION = INSPIRATION + FEAR

ART:
- (Aware) Life selected and rearranged, designed to entertain
- (Unaware) A layer of consciousness which is used as a cover for Unfinished Thinking

ATTENTION:
- Possession by the mind
- The ability to hold thoughts in the Chamber of Visible Thinking

ATTENTION (for acting): The ability to hold the designed thinking of the character

AUTO DIRECTIVES (AD): Thoughts that instruct me in what I must or must not do, on the way to achieving my happiness

AWARENESS:
- The ability to see one's own thinking
- The ability to replace Purposes at will (impossible unless the thinking is seen first)
- The ability to Finish-off all the thinking one thinks one should

BASIC EVENT: The result of the comparison between the Purpose and the result that was achieved by the Action activated by this Purpose to achieve itself, and sealed with the mini Action 'I regret' or 'I enjoy'

BLURRED FACTS: Facts within a script that cannot be relied on

CHARACTER: A collection of thoughts (experiences), and results of their interactions

CHARACTER LINE: A chronologically arranged sequence of Events from the character's life, as perceived by the character, i.e. in Active Imagination

CIRCUMSTANCE: Mundane happening, e.g. brushing teeth, shaving

COMPLEX: A circle of thoughts where when one is activated then so are the others to different degrees

CONDITIONING: The successful imposition of thinking

CONSCIOUSNESS: An ever changing totality of thoughts and neuro-biological processes that shape and are shaped by them

CREATIVE ATTENTION: To overlay objects of Outer Attention with objects of Inner Attention

DEVICES: What I want others to think I do

DISSIPATION: Decreasing intensity of thinking in real but interpreted pictures and impressions

EDUCATION: Learning to think for oneself under the guidance of a tutor who provides points of reference, which in turn prompts the restructuring of consciousness based on continuous testing and cross-referencing

EMERGING AWARENESS: The totality of first perceived and most remembered episodes from one's life

EMOTION: The bio-physiological result of a thought

EPISODES: Discrete units of time within a script where all the characters' Objectives, Purposes, Main Actions and Events stay the same
    A change in Episode usually happens when a character exits or enters or when something is said or done which changes at least one of the characters' thinking

EVENT:
• Anything which intensifies our thinking
• Intensified thinking itself

EVENTS AND HAPPENINGS (Step 7 of the Ten Steps): Chronologically arranged Events of the script and their influence on the main characters' thinking

FACTS: Events and Happenings that have taken place beyond doubt

FEAR: The anticipation of failure or suffering (to varying degrees)

FINISHING-OFF THINKING: Taking thoughts beyond the point where they were interrupted by fear

FORCED IMAGINATION:
- Although visible this Imagination has no Sense Data
- There are always tensions

FOREBURN: Aware Anticipation

FREE IMAGINATION: To see things as they are in size, touch, smell etc. and where they are in reality

GERM (G): My main Self Event

GERM OF THE SCRIPT: A summary of the cast's thinking of what they think the play is about

GHOST (Gh): The word given to the mental impression of a recurring fear that has the Purpose of maintaining an unawarely favoured pattern of thinking

GOING LIMP: Allowing the thought to be there without repressing it.
    Where allowing yourself to be possessed by the thought, without struggling to get rid of it, will leave enough free thinking to watch it in action (seeing is undoing)

GUIDELINES (GL):
- What I need or do not need to do to achieve my happiness
- Only through achieving certain objectives do I think I can reach my happiness

HAPPENING: A change in the physical world

HAPPINESS: Achieving Purposes

IMAGINATION: Thinking in pictures and impressions

IMPRESSION: A totality of mental and physical sensations

INNER ATTENTION: Attention activated by the mind itself (i.e. the mind is not stimulated by the senses)

INSPIRATION:
- INSPIRATION = ANTICIPATION – FEAR

INVOLUNTARY ATTENTION: Activating invisible Purposes

KNOWLEDGE: Unfailingly tested information

LIFE EVENTS (LE)
- What life is
- What I think life is

MAIN EVENT: What intensifies my thinking in particular circumstances

MENTAL STATEMENTS (MS):
- Thoughts that embody what we think is 'the truth'
- What the truth is; the ideas of life that I 'know' to be true

MIND: The thought-creating complex, that is the totality of important, invisible and uniquely generalized thoughts

MIND EROSION:
- Unaware thinking, not preceded by orientating process
- Unaware use of formed patterns of thoughts of various qualities, their sequence and desirable processes
- Patterns of thinking followed irrespective of visible circumstances

MINDPRINT: A verbal embodiment of the elements of the mind, that is of the unaware thought creating totality of important, generalized and invisible thoughts:
- Important – because they think themselves irrespective of circum-stances
- Generalized – because they are summaries of past experiences that are used as points of reference for experiences that are happening or are as yet to happen
- Invisible – because we do not see them

MINDQUAKE: A thought which requires much more thinking effort than most other thoughts

MODELLING: The physical embodiment of the most important Basic Events in an impressive form which as a result convey the Plot and artistic image of the play

OBJECTIVES (O):
- What I want to achieve by the time the circumstances have changed
- What I think will make me happy within the circumstances and help me to achieve my Longer-term Purpose(s)

OBSTACLE: Something that needs my effort to overcome it, so that I can achieve my Purpose

OUTER ATTENTION: Attention activated by the senses

PASSIVE IMAGINATION: Imagining yourself being seen from the outside, by yourself or others

PEOPLE EVENTS (PE): What I think people are

PICTURE: A totality of distinguishable shapes

PLOT: The description of the main Events and Happenings of the play *only*, described in simple terms without any interpretation

PURPOSE: What I want to achieve in the future, that is (far) beyond the circumstances or well after the circumstances have changed because I think it will make me happy
  Or simply,
  What I think will make me happy

RELATIONSHIPS: Pictures one has about another and the generalized thoughts that the relationship is based on

RHYTHM: The perceivable manifestation of a Tempo (see Tempo-rhythm)

SELF-CONDITIONING: When we successfully impose thoughts upon ourselves

SELF-DISCIPLINE:
• Conscious creation of Purposes
• The ability to create Purposes in pictures and impressions which compel us to Actions

SELF EVENTS (SE):
• What I am
• What I think I am
• I am the result of Conditioning and Self-Conditioning

SENSATION: Perceivable deviation from the unnoticeable norm

SENSE DATA: The information received through the five senses: hearing, sight, taste, touch and smell

SENSITIVITY: Ability to perceive one's own and other people's thoughts

SEX EVENTS (SxE):
• What sex is
• What sex is to me
• The thought that precipitated from my thoughts about sex

SHAME EVENTS (ShE): These thoughts cause me the most suffering and are ones that I must hide from others and myself. Thoughts, that I think if seen, will betray the fact that:

- I break the contract with myself to have a life
- I am forced into a contract of not having a life
- I am deprived of the ability of having a life (to not have a life is not being able to plan my life or make decisions: decisions are made with informed and enough thoroughly cross-referenced information in the CVT to make the best decision, without background noise)

SOCIAL SWAY: The influence of society on the forming consciousness

SUPER-PURPOSE (SP): My main Purpose in life

TALENT:
- The ability to ask yourself questions in pictures and impressions, unadulterated by Egotistical Purposes
- The Intensity of synthesizing thoughts unadulterated by Egotistical Purposes

TEMPO-RHYTHM:

TEMPO:
- Speed of thinking
- The speed with which I accept new thoughts into my consciousness
- The speed with which thoughts evolve from my consciousness
- The speed with which I view pictures in front of my mind's eye
- The speed of synthesizing thoughts
- The effort of holding still pictures
  Where,
- RHYTHM: The perceivable manifestation of a Tempo

ULTIMATE COMMUNION EVENT (UC): Generalized impression of the most secure relationship I can ever be in the stillness of

UNEXPECTED EVENT:
- An Event without Anticipation or Foreburn
- An Event that happens where another Event was expected

UNFINISHED THINKING: Thoughts interrupted by fear

VOLUNTARY ATTENTION: Activating visible Purposes

NOTES AND BIBLIOGRAPHY

Citations have been provided in full where possible. In cases where original sources were unidentifiable or unavailable, secondary references have been used or reference made to the author's personal notes.

Dedication

1 H. Spencer, *First Principles of a New System of Philosophy*, New York: Appleton, 1888, p. 123.

About this book

1 S. Carnicke, *Stanislavsky in Focus*, Amsterdam: Harwood, 1998, p. 25.
2 E. Berne, *A Layman's Guide to Psychiatry and Psychoanalysis*, London: Penguin, 1969, p. 53.
3 E. Laszlo, *Science and the Akashic Field: An Integral Theory of Everything*, 2nd edn, Rochester, VT: Inner Traditions, 2007, p. 163.
4 K. Stanislavski, *An Actor's Work*, Abingdon: Routledge, 2008, p. 118.
5 Ibid., p. 208.
6 Ibid., p. 118.
7 Ibid., p. 118.
8 Ibid., p. xxiv.
9 A. Einstein, *The World as I See It*, trans. A. Harris, London: Bodley Head, 1934.
10 J. Benedetti, *Stanislavski and the Actor: The Final Acting Lessons, 1935–38*, London: Methuen, 1998, p. vii.
11 Ibid., p. viii.
12 Ibid., p. viii.
13 S. Moore, *The Stanislavski System: The Professional Training of an Actor*, London: Penguin, 1984, p. 6.
14 R. L. Solso, 'Mind sciences and the 21st century', in R. L. Solso (ed.) *Mind and Brain Sciences in the 21st Century*, Cambridge, MA: MIT Press, 1997, p. 312.

Preface

1 R. Descartes, *Discourse on the Method of Rightly Conducting the Reason and Seeking the Truth in the Sciences*, The Harvard Classics, Part IV, New York: P. F. Collier & Son, 1909–1914, p. 3.
2 T. Cole and H. Krich Chinoy, *Actors on Acting: The Theories, Techniques, and Practices of the Great Actors of All Times as Told in their Own Words*, New York: Crown, 1970, p. 585.
3 A. Woolcott, *Mrs. Fiske: Her Views on Actors, Acting, and the Problems of Production*, New York: Century, 1917, p. 79.
4 Ibid., p. 159.
5 K. Stanislavski, *An Actor's Work*, Abingdon: Routledge, 2008, p. 276.
6 Ibid., pp. 98–102.
7 Ibid., p. 124.
8 Ibid., pp. 161, 186.
9 SK's personal notes referring to Stanislavski's 1936 rehearsals of *Tartuffe*.
10 S. Moore, *The Stanislavski System: The Professional Training of an Actor*, London: Penguin, 1984, p. 91.

Acknowledgements

1 Examples of these books include K. Stanislavksi, *Sobranie sochinenij v vos'mi tomakh*, [Collected Works of K. S. Stanislavski], edited by M. N. Kedrov, 8 volumes, Moscow, 1954–1961. V. I. Nemirovich-Danchenko, *Iz proshlogo (Moy 20 vek)* [My Life in Russian Theatre], Moscow: Academia, 1936. V. I. Nemirovich-Danchenko, *Povesti i pesy*, Moscow: Government Press, 1958.

Introduction

1 H. Dukas and B. Hoffman (eds) *Albert Einstein, the Human Side*, Princeton, NJ: Princeton University Press, 1989, p. 38.
2 F. Hirsch, *A Method to their Madness: The History of the Actors Studio*, New York: Da Capo, 1984, p. 143.
3 W. A. C. Darlington, *Through the Fourth Wall*, Manchester, NH: Ayer, 1968, p. 11.
4 B. Russell, *Wisdom of the West*, London: Rathbone, 1959, p. 68.
5 P. Thomson and G. Sacks (eds) *The Cambridge Companion to Brecht*, 2nd edn, Cambridge: Cambridge University Press, 2007, p. 283.
6 Dukas and Hoffman, *Albert Einstein*, p. 38.
7 Thomson and Sacks, *Cambridge Companion to Brecht*, p. 283.

1 Complexes

1 E. Berne, *What Do You Say After You Say Hello?* London: Corgi, 1988, p. 31.
2 Ibid., p. 31.
3 A. Freud, *The Writings of Anna Freud*, International Universities Press Inc. Online. Available http://thecjc.org/pdf/af_biblio.pdf (accessed 21 December 2008).

2 Awareness

1 A. Nin, *The Diary of Anaïs Nin, 1939–1944*, New York: Harcourt, Brace and World, 1969.
2 M. Lewis and J. Brooks-Gunn, 'Toward a theory of social cognition: The development of self', in I. Uzgiris (ed.) *New Directions in Child Development: Social Interaction and Communication during Infancy*, San Francisco, CA: Jossey-Bass, 1979, pp. 1–20.
3 Nin, *The Diary of Anaïs Nin*.

3 Events

1 K. Casey, *A Life of my Own: Meditations on Hope and Acceptance*, Center City, MN: Hazelden, 1993, p. 25.
2 For discussion, see www.ericberne.com/transactional_analysis_description.htm (accessed 16 April 2009).

4 Purposes

1 K. Stanislavski, *An Actor's Work*, Abingdon: Routledge, 2008, p. 39.
2 SK's personal notes.

5 Formation of Consciousness

1 A. Schopenhauer, *The Wisdom of Life and Counsels and Maxims*, trans. T. Bailey Saunders, Digireads.com Publishing, p. 77.
2 D. Querleu, X. Renard, F. Versyp, L. Paris-Delrue and G. Crèpin, 'Fetal hearing', *European Journal of Obstetrics Gynecology and Reproductive Biology*, 28, 1988: 191–212.
3 M. Clements, 'Observations on certain aspects of neonatal behavior in response to auditory stimuli', Paper presented at the Fifth *International Congress of Psychosomatic Obstetrics and Gynecology*, Rome, 1977.
4 M. J. Lazinski, A. K. Shea and M. Steiner, 'Effects of maternal prenatal stress on offspring development: a commentary', Archives of Women's Mental Health 11, 2008: 363–375.
5 S. Ostrander and L. Schroeder, *Psychic Discoveries Behind the Iron Curtain*, Englewood Cliffs, NJ: Prentice Hall, 1970, pp. 132–134.
6 D. Radin, *Entangled Minds: Extrasensory Experiences in a Quantum Reality*, London: Pocket, 2006.
7 E. Laszlo, *Science and the Akashic Field: An Integral Theory of Everything*, 2nd edn, Rochester, VT: Inner Traditions, 2007, p. 150.
8 E. S. Levine and I. B. Black, 'Trophic interactions and neuronal plasticity', in M. S. Gazzaniga (ed.) *The New Cognitive Neurosciences*, 2nd edn, Cambridge, MA: MIT Press, 2000, p. 159.

6 Mindprint

1 J. Allen, 'As a man thinketh', in T. Troward, S. H. Martin and J. Allen, *How to Master Life*, Richmond, VA: Oaklea Press, 2007, p. 130.

7 Actions

1 J. W. Yolton (ed.) *The Locke Reader: Selections from the Works of John Locke: With a General Introduction and Commentary*, Cambridge: Cambridge University Press, 1977, p. 121.
2 C. Stanislavski, *An Actor Prepares*, London: Methuen, 1986, pp. 113 and 137–138.

8 Finishing-off Thinking

1 Patañjali, Yoga Sutra 4.18, in S. Cope, *The Wisdom of Yoga*, New York: Bantam Dell, 2007, p. 291.
2 Marcus Aurelius, *The Thoughts of the Emperor Marcus Aurelius Antoninus*, trans. G. Long, Whitefish, MT: Kessinger, 2004, pp. 1–3.

9 Tempo-rhythm

1 M. T. Cicero and J. E. Sandys (eds) *M. Tulli Ciceronis Ad M. Brutum Orator: A Revised Text*, Cambridge: Cambridge University Press, 1885, p. 69.
2 K. Stanislavski, *An Actor's Work*, Abingdon: Routledge, 2008, Chapter 21.
3 Ibid., p. 469.
4 Ibid., p. 469.

10 Imagination

1 G. S. Viereck, 'What life means to Einstein: An interview', *Saturday Evening Post*, 26 October 1929.
2 Ibid.
3 K. Hollinger, *The Actress: Hollywood Acting and the Female Star*, London: Routledge, 2006, p. 12.
4 K. Stanislavski, *An Actor's Work*, Abingdon: Routledge, 2008, p. 53.

11 Attention

1 T. Edwards, *A Dictionary of Thoughts*, Read Books, 2007, p. 120.
2 K. Stanislavski, *An Actor's Work*, Abingdon: Routledge, 2008, p. 108.
3 W. James, *The Principles of Psychology*, New York: Henry Holt, 1890, pp. 403–404.
4 Stanislavski, *An Actor's Work*, p. 208.

12 Free body

1 F. M. Alexander, *Articles and Lectures*, London: Mouritz, 1995, p. 62.
2 K. Stanislavski, *An Actor's Work*, Abingdon: Routledge, 2008, p. 121.
3 L. Bridges, *Face Reading in Chinese Medicine*, Edinburgh: Churchill Livingstone, 2003, p. 12.
4 F. Simpson, *The Lucid Body: A Guide for the Physical Actor*, New York: Allworth, 2009, p. 18.
5 Stanislavski, *An Actor's Work*, p. 124.
6 D. Kerr, *Mind, Body and Spirit*, Huddersfield, UK: Jeremy Mills, 2006, p. 61.

13 Talent

1 S. Moore, *The Stanislavski System: The Professional Training of an Actor: Digested from the Teachings of Konstantin S. Stanislavski*, New York: Viking Press, 1965, p. 100.
2 K. Wighton, Waiting for that life changing idea? Just sleep on it. The London Times Online. Available www.timesonline.co.uk/tol/life_and_style/health/article5206704. ece (accessed 21 March 2009).
3 D. H. Pink, *A Whole New Mind: Why Right-Brainers will Rule the Future*, London: Marshall Cavendish, 2008, p. 22.

14 The Ten Steps

1 Quotation taken from A. Lang, *The Pleasures of Literature and the Solace of Books*, Charleston, SC: BiblioBazaar, 2008, p. 113.
2 M. Gladwell, *Outliers: The Story of Success*, New York: Little, Brown, 2008, p. 42.

Final word

1 Quotation taken from J. Murphy, *The Power of your Subconscious Mind*, New York: Reward, 2000, p. 214.

INDEX

Page references in **bold** refer to figures, references in *italic* refer to tables.